THE
GREATEST
GLASS
HOUSE

THE RAINFORESTS RECREATED

ROYAL BOTANIC GARDENS, KEW

THE GREATEST GLASS HOUSE

THE RAINFORESTS RECREATED

SUE MINTER

with contributions from
CHRIS JONES, PETER MORRIS and PETER RIDDINGTON

London: HMSO

© The Board of Trustees of the Royal Botanic Gardens, Kew, 1990.
First published 1990

British Library Cataloguing in Publication Data

A CIP catalogue record for this book is available from the British Library

Design: HMSO Graphic Design, Guy Myles Warren

HMSO publications are available from:

HMSO Publications Centre
(Mail and telephone orders only)
PO Box 276, London, SW8 5DT
Telephone orders 071–873 9090
General enquiries 071–873 0011
(queuing system in operation for both numbers)

HMSO Bookshops
49 High Holborn, London, WC1V 6HB   071–873 0011 (Counter service only)
258 Broad Street, Birmingham, B1 2HE   021–643 3740
Southey House, 33 Wine Street, Bristol, BS1 2BQ   (0272) 264306
9–21 Princess Street, Manchester, M60 8AS   061–834 7201
80 Chichester Street, Belfast, BT1 4JY   (0232) 238451
71 Lothian Road, Edinburgh, EH3 9AZ   031–228 4181

HMSO's Accredited Agents
(see Yellow Pages)

and through good booksellers

ISBN 0 11 250035 8

Printed in the United Kingdom for HMSO
Dd 240094   C65   7/90 (4316)

# Foreword

The past, the present and the future are brought together spectacularly in the restoration of the famous Palm House of the Royal Botanic Gardens, Kew.

The restoration brings to our attention again the enormous skill of the Victorian architects and engineers. The exquisite balance of the design and form, the precise siting of the building with regard to vistas and light, the rhythm of its arches and the intricate details of the mouldings, spiral staircases and balcony serve as a monument to the greatness of the Victorians.

Although the edifice is beautiful and valuable of itself, its purpose reminds us of the Victorian love of collections, museums and objects of interest. The house was constructed for the purpose of growing and displaying trees and plants which for most people would otherwise be only fabled curiosities. This Victorian intention still enriches us today, linking the past with the present and even the future of our planet.

With strangely prophetic wisdom, when the restoration of the Palm House was planned ten years ago, it was modified to house samples of the two most species-diverse habitats on earth: the tropical rainforest and the coral reef with its associated marine environment; since that time we have become more and more aware of the threats to our ecosystems caused by man's destruction and degradation, be it of the North Sea, the tropical forest, the coral reef or the hedgerow.

So, in the present we are privileged to recreate in the Victorian Palm House something of the wonder of the tropical rainforest and of the coral reef. Wonder can lead us to respect and to value such environments. The displays so elegantly housed also prove to us the economic value of many of the plants and organisms, for our lives are touched daily by products of other ecosystems even when we are ignorant of the source.

Are we only preserving a Victorian legacy to pass to future generations? No, for while we will pass on our forefathers' gift of a spectacular building filled with plants and organisms from around the world, we are also safeguarding another inheritance for unborn generations. That inheritance is a genetic material of plants and organisms whose habitats are threatened by pollution and greed as well as an inexorable sequence of destruction and degradation.

It will be a hundred years before the Palm House needs refurbishing and a hundred years is longer than the tropical forests will last unless their destruction is slowed or halted. To visit, to look, to learn, to wonder; these are our privileges, but we must also act to conserve the ecosystems.

To all who have made this reopening possible, architects, builders, engineers, collectors, curators, gardeners and workers of every kind, we are indebted.

GHILLEAN T PRANCE
Director
Royal Botanic Gardens, Kew

TO THE MEMORY OF MY PARENTS
Norah and Harry
and to Penny

ontents

ACKNOWLEDGEMENTS

I would like to thank a large group of people who, in their various ways, contributed to the coming together of this book. To the contributing authors: Chris Jones of Posford Duvivier, Supervising Engineer, Peter Riddington of the Property Services Agency and Peter Morris, Marine Display Manager at Kew, thank you for becoming part of the whole story. Several taxonomists contributed in the way of detailed checking, including Dr John Dransfield, Susyn Andrews, Mike Lock and Jim Keesing. Ray Desmond gave much historical advice. Dr Linda Fellows of the Jodrell Laboratory at Kew assisted on the section on medicinal plants, as did Professor W Jacobson of the University of Cambridge Clinical School.

From the Information and Exhibitions Department at Kew, Dr Brinsley Burbidge gave initial encouragement, Dr Pat Griggs was meticulous in copy checking and Valerie Walley administered deadlines and payments. The library staff at Kew were patient and helpful. The Curator, with his long association with the Palm House since student days, made several suggestions, as did Sue MacDonald and Hans Fliegner, the Assistant Curator of the Temperate Section. David Barnes assisted with research. Mrs Brind, Ann Lucas and their team typed the words. Milan Svanderlik, Andrew McRobb, David Cooke, Dr Dransfield, Penny Hammond, Peter Riddington and Chris Jones assisted with photographs and picture research, as did the Bartlett School of Architecture. Philip Glover at HMSO was tolerant of delays and Anne Muffett did much to show that editors always improve what is in their care.

Much credit is due to Richard White of Posford Duvivier who, as Resident Engineer, ensured that between the design team and the contractor (Balfour Beatty Building) there emerged a workable restored building to form the subject of this book. His firm tact and thoughtful foresight were a godsend.

Putting together the plants and the building was accomplished with remarkable speed by David Cooke, who also had the satisfaction of planting many of the young palms he had collected and raised as propagator while the building was being restored. Working with him were Richard Weekly of the Palm House staff and a team of Kew Diploma students: John Chesters, Andrew Gaynor, David Barnes and Jo Jones. David Walley and Steve Ketley looked after the plants in storage and Martin Staniforth and his staff assured the good quality of the pool of plants from which the final selection was made. Stewart Henchie acquired the gantry without which the replanting would not have been possible and Neil Harvey and his team kept the compost coming. Without all these people my scale plans would have remained as drawings and the 'greening' of the Palm House after its architectural restoration would not have occurred.

Finally, my thanks to Penny Hammond and Marilyn Senf for listening when many others couldn't or wouldn't.

Introduction

'THE GREATEST GLASSHOUSE IN THE WORLD' is a phrase frequently applied to the Palm House at Kew. Its greatness means different things to different people. The first glimpse of its striking curved outline, especially when seen reflected in the still waters of the lake, is a sight that stops many visitors in their tracks. Tourists arriving in London by air may look down on a clear day to see its key site in the gardens, centred in the middle of radiating vistas designed by the distinguished Victorian landscape architect, William Nesfield.

The Palm House is not great in size by comparison with Kew's Temperate House or the Princess of Wales Conservatory (each of which occupy twice its floor area) and it was far smaller than the Great Conservatory at Chatsworth, Derbyshire, upon which it was originally modelled. It does, however, survive to this day, unlike the cast-iron frame of the Chatsworth conservatory, which was dynamited (on the sixth attempt) in 1920, and unlike many European conservatories of its time which have not found the budgets, or the political will, for their restoration. The garden historian would note that it is the largest surviving curvilinear house, while to the lover of things Victorian, it has been one of the greatest glasshouses to conserve. To the Americans, with their tradition of wooden buildings, it is remarkable in being iron at all.

For the structural engineer, the Palm House is a milestone in the history of building design. It represents the first use of wrought iron to span such widths without obstructive supporting columns. This was substantially the contribution of the Irish ironfounder, Richard Turner and, although it nearly bankrupted him, it presaged the use of this material in the vast railway termini of industrialised Victorian Britain. Remarkable in its functional simplicity, the Palm House is very much an engineer's building and it is the largest of Turner's glasshouses.

To the horticulturist it was built to house the tallest of the palms and came to house the greatest palm and cycad collection in Europe. Today it still houses such a collection, now augmented genetically with much plant material of valuable wild origin displayed to interpret the habitat under greatest threat worldwide, that of the tropical rainforest.

The origin of this book came in my desire to put together the various different ways in which this building might be appreciated and to link the disciplines of history, architecture, engineering and horticulture in a holistic approach. There are people here too, for although gardeners and horticulturists are often not good at documenting their work, glimpses remain of their particular social and workaday world in old photographs, long memories, the odd memoir and, further back, the hand-written archival notes which list the first introductions of (say) breadfruit, coffee, rubber or cocoa and many other species with which we are now familiar.

The conservation of plants, as well as the building fabric, is a strong theme in these pages. A remarkable trend since I produced the first draft of this book two years ago is the enormous growth of public concern about the environment. This has been paralleled by a change in political will on a national and international scale. Warnings that I thought would fall on relatively uncomprehending ears have become widely debated in the quality press and on national political platforms. The 'Greens' have come in from the cold and global warming through the 'greenhouse effect' is now an everyday phrase. This is enormously encouraging and signals hope for a grassroots appreciation of our responsibility towards delicate ecosystems. All life on earth is based on plants. The engineers have done their best to conserve the environment which the Palm House enshrines here in London, but we all hold responsibility for the future of the tropics of this ever-shrinking world.

SUE MINTER
September 1989

Greenery among the iron: the Palm House and its collections

1 The birth of the Palm House

WHEN THE FOUNDATION WORK for the Palm House was begun by the firm of Grissell and Peto in 1844 there had already been over a decade of discussion on Kew's need for a house for palms. The reasons behind this were much concerned with prestige. In 1840 Kew had been transferred to the authority of the Commissioners of Woods and Forests. A year later Sir William Jackson Hooker became Director and in 1843 the gardens were expanded from 20 to 65 acres. With these three events Kew had effectively become a national botanic garden as well as one enjoying many royal connections. It was thought fitting that such a garden should have a prestigious glasshouse tall enough to house palms, the 'principes' (princes) of the plant kingdom, whose culture was limited at that date to the gentry.

The major palm house of the 1840s, that of Conrad Loddiges' Hackney Botanic Nursery in Mare Street, Hackney, had been built by W & D Bailey using Loudon's patent wrought-iron glazing bars. The nursery's catalogue of 1830 listed 105 palm species belonging to 36 genera. The customers for such a nursery would have needed considerable resources: 'The culture of palms, as Mr Loudon justly observes, is less a matter of nicety than expense. They require a powerful moist heat, a large mass of rich earth in the pot, tub or bed and ample space for the leaves . . . it would require to have the roof elevated by degrees to sixty, eighty, or a hundred feet.'[1] Kew's collection at that time was relatively poor and confined to what is now the Aroid House, with a ridge height of only 7 metres. Sir William Hooker and his son set out to change this because, according to Berthold Seemann, there was considerable 'rivalry for pre-eminence observable in this respect amongst the various horticultural establishments'.[2] By 1882 Dr Hooker could report that Kew held 420 species:

The Kew collection of palms is the oldest of any note, it was eclipsed altogether between the years 1820 and 1845 by the famous collection of the brothers Loddiges at Hackney, which in the latter year contained upwards of 200 kinds but which was dispersed shortly afterwards.

Now it has but two rivals, a European and Asiatic one, namely, the magnificent collection made chiefly by Herr Wendland, in the Botanic Garden at Herrenhausen, Hanover; and the Palmetum of the unrivalled tropical garden at Buitenzorg in Java.[3]

The initial plans for a Palm House drawn up in 1834 by Sir Jeffry Wyatville had made no headway at Kew and the Commissioners of Woods and Forests received plans from Decimus Burton, a classical architect in his early forties, the son of a building contractor. The ground plans were at first similar to his Great Conservatory at Chatsworth, the largest conservatory then built, which had a cast-iron frame. They met with firm opposition from the Curator, the first John Smith, who records in his 'History of the Royal Gardens at Kew':

John Smith (right) was the first Curator of Kew, from 1841 to 1864, and it was he who supervised the movement of the plants into the Palm House. He correctly predicted that the boiler houses would flood and urged the use of green glass to shade the plants.

On his coming to Kew, he had not been more than half an hour in the Grounds when he fixed upon the site where it now stands. Being present, I thought it my duty to say it would never do here, for where we now stand is a bog the greater part of the year, and water was always to be found within a few feet of the surface . . . I found that there was so many pillars and they were so close together that there would not be room for the full expansion of the leaves of the large palms. On my calling attention to this, Sir W Hooker was of the same opinion, and on calling Mr Burton's attention to it he said he would try another way. With this our interview ended . . . About this time Mr Richard Turner of the Hammersmith Iron Works, Dublin, having heard of the intended erection of a large hothouse at Kew, came over to see about it, and having obtained an introduction to the Commissioners of Works they requested him to furnish a plan and estimate for an iron structure in conjunction with Mr Burton, which he obligingly did. On his informing me of this, I said, 'I hope you will not have so many pillars in the centre as in Mr Burton's plan'. 'Oh, no,' he said, and took a piece of paper, and drew a pen and ink profile of the Palm House as it was to be erected, being quite different from Mr Burton's plan, having no pillars in the centre.[4]

Richard Turner was an ironfounder who operated from the Hammersmith Iron Works at Ballsbridge, Dublin from 1834 until the business was taken over by his son, William, in 1857. He had recently expanded into glasshouse construction, having built the wings of the Belfast Palm House (1839–40) and tropical houses in County Fermanagh and at Killakee, County Dublin (1842–50). In 1842–6 he was also engaged in erecting the Winter Garden for the Royal Botanic Society in Regent's Park (demolished in the 1930s) in partnership with Decimus Burton. Turner's method was to insist on his expertise on projects at the tender stage and to become very influential in the adaptation of the work as it was built. This he did at Glasnevin (where the original plans of Duncan Ferguson were abandoned and where Turner later contracted to do much work in iron in 1848) and also with Burton at Regent's Park, where Turner won the tender and influenced the design.

A daguerreotype taken during the construction of the Palm House, probably in 1847. Decimus Burton and Richard Turner are seated centre, Turner being the more portly figure of the two. The building opened with only one spiral staircase.

His most important contribution at Kew was to substitute wrought-iron 'deck beam' (used in shipbuilding) for the much heavier cast iron suggested by Burton for the main arches; the first time deck beam had been used in this way in the history of building design. As it has a greater tensile strength when curved than cast iron, Turner was able to use it to span great widths of unsupported space, much to the Curator's delight and to the benefit of the broad crowns of the palms. So it is not inappropriate that the house has been compared ever since to the upturned hull of a graceful liner. Unlike Chatsworth, the Palm House was entirely of metal and used curved glass rather than the 'ridge and furrow' design invented by Paxton. In using wrought-iron glazing bars he was following in the steps of J C Loudon, who had first developed a wrought-iron sash bar which was exclusively used by the firm W & D Bailey. The chimney for the house, the campanile, followed on Loudon's realisation that a remote chimney removed the source of soot from the glass. A similar stack design had been used at Chatsworth and at Bretton Hall, Yorkshire, where there had been a circular house (demolished in 1832). The principle of the delivery of coke for the boilers by an underground railway was not unique to Kew either; it had operated successfully at Chatsworth. So had the use of the columns as drainage pipes, an idea first used in Sir Jeffry Wyatville's Camellia House at Wollaton, Nottingham, in 1823–4 (recently restored). Thus the Palm House combined many traditional ideas with brilliant use of a new structural material, making it a landmark in glasshouse design.

For many years Turner's contribution to the Palm House at Kew was not recognised at all. The matter became controversial in 1880 when Thomas Drew of Dublin wrote to *Building News* giving an intimate portrait of Turner 'in his vigorous days when he was ubiquitous, with a stock of daring and original projects always on hand, remarkable for his rough-and-ready powers of illustration of them, and eloquent, plausible, and humorous advocacy of them'. Drew claimed that Turner had designed the house, 'although carried out under the supervision of Mr Decimus Burton' and that through various lobbying, 'He was permitted, at his own risk and expense, to submit a portion of the structure full size, which was accordingly done and submitted to test in the yard of Messrs Grissel and Peto; the result being a triumph for Mr Turner, who was permitted to carry out his own design.'[5] The following day John

This engraving in the archives at Kew shows that the smoke stack for the Palm House, the campanile, was built some distance away. Turner's square Waterlily House, built in 1864 for the giant waterlily, was his last architectural contribution at Kew.

Smith wrote to confirm Drew's view but this did not become the accepted version of events, perhaps because Burton's initials were on the plans. Burton is credited as the sole author of the building in W J Bean's history of Kew (1908), which is unfortunate, as the author had been a Sub-Foreman in the Palm House itself. In 1941 the Assistant Director of Kew attributed the house solely to Burton[6] and this view was not challenged again until 1954 by Professor Hitchcock in his *Early Victorian Architects*.[7]

In 1982 in the *Journal of Garden History*, Edward J Diestelkamp wrote a most exhaustive examination of the subject, revealing conclusively the complex collaboration between Turner and Burton.[8] As it was the largest contract Turner had undertaken and he could not provide sufficient financial guarantees, Turner was listed as the subcontractor for the ironwork. He was very much a tradesman and still had to prove himself, whereas Burton was an established architect. Diestelkamp makes the shrewd speculation that it was this difference in status which made it impossible for Turner to claim more of the credit for the building, a difference in status clearly expressed in the tone of the Commissioners' correspondence with the two men. Turner later claimed he had lost £7000 on the contract, largely through his use of wrought iron. However, it did provide a testing ground for him and he went on to even greater things, successfully spanning a width of 153 ft 6 in (46.7 metres) in the wrought-iron roof of Lime Street Station, Liverpool (1850), over one-third as much again as the centre span of the Palm House.

The erection of the building was less a technical problem for Sir William Hooker than a matter of resources. On 30 December 1844 he pleaded for more money from the Treasury to erect the wings[9] which, if it had not been forthcoming, would have left us with a building of a radically different shape. In 1845 his report to the Commissioners reported that the centre was proceeding well and that the furnace chambers and subterranean chimneys had been built. 1846 was a good year and Hooker reported that:

Considerable progress has been made in the Palm Stove, since last year; so much, that the great outer scaffolding is almost entirely removed. The framework of the vast central portion may be pronounced complete, and much of the side walls, containing the ventilators, is finished: the gallery is formed, together with a good part of the balustrade; and a substantial yet ornamental spiral staircase, leading to the gallery, is appended. A further grant having been made last year, the two wings are commenced, the concrete foundation laid, and several of the granite blocks; and of one wing, several ribs are fixed. The terrace, around the edifice, is likewise in progress.[10]

In 1847 the walks around the house were completed and the pond dredged to deepen and enlarge it and obtain the reflection of the building in the water which had been a key objective in Burton's controversial choice of a site. That year saw the whole of the garden's budget devoted to completing the house: 'a structure so noble, and in all respects so worthy of the garden and the nation, that scarcely any sacrifice could be deemed too great for its accomplishment. This edifice', wrote Hooker on 7 February 1848 in his Annual Report 'is now happily in a very forward state, and a few weeks will assuredly witness its completion, and its fitness for the reception of plants.'

In fact the first plants did not go back into the house until September 1848. The Curator freely expressed the dislike of iron structures common among horticulturists at the time and his scepticism at being required to grow plants in it:

for in looking up nothing but iron was to be seen in every direction in the form of massive iron, rafters, girders, galleries, pillars and staircase, and the hot iron floor on which we stood and the smooth stone shelves and paths round the house had the appearance of some dock-yard smithy or iron railway station than a hothouse to grow tropical plants in, but there it was, and I was to make the best of it, and to be responsible for the good cultivation of the plants which were commenced to be put in.[11]

Smith moved the largest plants into the centre transept with the help of two engineers with tackle from the Deptford dockyard:

The first being the large palms *Sabal umbraculifera* from the old palmhouse . . . One plant weighed 17 tons the other not quite so much. They were then conveyed on rollers to the Palmhouse, a distance of nearly ½ a mile, and drawn up the steps of the east centre door by a windlass. Their leaves occupied the whole width of the doorway . . . They were followed by the two large plants of *Phoenix dactylifera*, one of *P. reclinata*, two of *Chamerops martiana*, one large *Pandanus odoratissimus* a tall *Strelitzia Augusta* . . . also two tall *Cocos* two *Caryota* and others from the No. 1 Conservatory. They were all placed in the centre of the house and although some distance apart they made a goodly appearance.

Still sceptical, he observed 'it occurred to me that if they could speak, they would say that they were not happy in this dry air, and iron domicile erected for us the principes of the vegetable kingdom.'[12] At first he was short of plants because the glasshouses from which the plants were drawn constituted only a quarter of the floor area of the new house. The wings of the Palm House were initially left empty.

An engraving taken from the Illustrated London News of 7 August 1852 shows the luxuriance of the Palm House, with fruiting bananas, pawpaw and yams. Victorian families thronged to the house to see the vegetation of the expanding British Empire.

Despite Smith's misgivings, the public approved of the new house. Certainly the arrival of barge-loads of ironwork on the Thames during its construction must have caused considerable interest. In his *Book of the Garden*, Charles M'Intosh praised it as 'the most complete specimen of hothouse architecture that this or any country can boast of.'[13] In 1844 the number of people visiting the gardens was 15,114. By 1847 this had risen over fourfold to 64,282, by 1848 to 91,708, by 1849, when the house was opened, to 137,865. In 1851, the year of the Great Exhibition, the figure was 327,900.[14] Hooker was enthusiastic: 'In the Palm Stove the growth and vigour of the inmates attest the excellence of the structure for cultivation, the foliage of some of the plants already extending to 60 feet from the ground. The palms and tree ferns are among the finest ever reared in Europe.'[15]

Those of us who have always thought of the Palm House as a perfectly symmetrical structure will be surprised to learn that it had been opened with only one staircase. This was common in Victorian houses and even today, some of them (for example, Liverpool's Palm House at Sefton Park) still have only one spiral staircase. By 1851 it was clear that the Palm House could not cope with the influx of visitors and Hooker took action: 'The crowds of visitors to the gallery of this stove house have necessitated the erection of a second spiral staircase for their accommodation'.[16] The crowds of people were soon followed by crowds of plants and in his report for 1852, only four years after plants were admitted, Hooker reported that:

Some of the palms have grown so rapidly as to reach the highest span of the roof (66 feet), and two of them we have been obliged to let down into sunk compartments underground, thus to retain them a few years longer.

The building is becoming too full, and the beauty of some of the finest specimens is concealed by the space around them being occupied by other plants.[17]

Despite the lush growth above ground all was not well below. Smith's misgivings about Burton's choice of a 'boggy' site for the house were well founded, and the basement boiler houses flooded. A well was installed with fire-engines to pump out the water and then in the summer of 1853 the floor of the furnace rooms was raised by 20 in (51 cm). This led to further problems because it reduced the draught to the flues. In fact the first two decades of the operation of the house were dogged by heating problems. On 18 November 1865 the Curator wrote to Dr Hooker proposing that more skilled heating tradesmen should be employed. This was not an entirely surprising request because heating by hot water was a comparatively new technology. Throughout the eighteenth century heating was provided by charcoal stoves and ducted under the floors. Steam heat, which had been used at Bretton Hall, had been proposed for the Palm House but was potentially dangerous. Hot water had been used in Russia for the Tsar's glasshouse ranges but not in England until 1826. And the specification for the Palm House demanded 'a temperature of eighty degrees during the coldest weather.'[18] On 6 August 1867 a full report on the deficient heating in the Palm House was submitted by Messrs Eyles and Ingram.[19] Two days later Hooker wrote to the First Commissioner of Works giving a dire picture of the conditions in the house:

Joseph Dalton Hooker (Dr Hooker) succeeded his father, Sir William Hooker, who had been Director of the gardens from 1841 to 1865. He presided over the house during its Victorian heyday and by the time he retired in 1885, his many achievements included advances in palm taxonomy.

My Lord, I have given my best attention to your Lordship's verbal instructions respecting the Palm House, namely, 'to go on this winter as was done last'.

This I regret to say, is not possible, for the evil is progressive. As the plants have died, or been removed to warmer houses, or have lost their foliage, so is the heat and moisture that these intercept now dispersed; as the climbers on the rafters have been successively killed, so has the radiation of cold from the iron and glass increased . . . The plants have made no growth, and very few and small leaves this summer. The leaves are already turning yellow, and are so sparse that the pots and tubs are everywhere seen; and a person standing outside the north wing can see the museum building through it all along, that is to say, through 16 parallel rows of plants . . . During the last two winters the thermometer in the Palm House sometimes stood at 42° . . . I have removed all the most tender plants into the other houses, which we have crowded to excess, and have filled up with about 1,500 greenhouse plants instead,[20] for appearance's sake; till now there is not a single young palm on the shelves, and the term palm-house is a misnomer . . .

Not only was the Palm House unfit for palms, but, lamented Hooker, 'many most interesting tropical plants (as the Mango, Cocoa-nut, Chocolate, Breadfruit etc.) can no longer be cultivated in it.'[21] He recommended closing the house to the public from November to April.

The solution was the introduction of two flue chimneys in the wings of the house, thereby rendering the campanile superfluous. This saved a quarter of the fuel and gave an extra 10°F (roughly 5°C), although the chimneys did interrupt the smooth outline of the building.[22] Further improvements to the heating system have continued to this day. A circuit of pipework around the gallery was installed at Dr Hooker's suggestion in 1877 to prevent draught at high level. This was so successful that another was added to the north wing lantern. The pipework in the north wing was renewed and upgraded in 1895 and that of the south wing in 1896, with pipework being carried all the way around at high level. Further renewal of the boilers took place in 1934–5 and extra piping was added. The heavy manual labour of hauling coke through the tunnel from the Shaft Yard to the basement boilers (which had always been assigned to gardeners who had committed some misdemeanour) finally ended when the railway was electrified in 1950. In 1961 the boiler houses were moved to the Shaft Yard, leaving the Palm House basements empty. The boilers were converted to oil and the campanile came back into use as a chimney, with the tunnel serving only as a duct for the heating pipelines. The two chimney stacks in the wings were removed several years later.

The Victorian gardening staff who managed the plant collections in this building throughout its various crises did so with some ingenuity. The iron floor had never been popular with them. It had been laid in order to improve the circulation of heat, relying on the experience of Turner and Burton in flooring the Regent's Park Winter Garden (1842–6). It did have the horticultural advantage of circulating heat around the plant roots but it committed the staff to growing everything in pots and tubs. Most of the more tender tropical plants needed hotbed cultivation and for the taller palms to reach the full height of the building some planting beds were needed. The climbers also required good rooting depth to rise to their full height. Smith records that

it was with a degree of horror that I learned that the floor on which the plants were to be grown was to be of perforated cast iron squares with hotwater pipes underneath it. It consisted of 4 ft squares of cast iron, a single square is said to have cost £3 – the whole nearly £3000. On calling Sir W Hooker's attention to this to endeavour to prevent it he would not interfere, he considering that whatever Mr Burton did was right. The only concession I obtained and that with difficulty was a small space for soil at the foot of each pillar, for planting climbers in to train up the pillars, but I could get no space for soil to plant climbers to train up the rafters.[23]

Smith was soon proved right and in the winter of 1859–60, three years before he retired, he saw the first great Victorian Director of the gardens arrange for large beds to go into the Palm House:

The arrangement of the inmates of the Palm Stove is at this time undergoing a change that has already proved highly advantageous, both for the noble Palms and for the general effect of the interior of that vast building; for all the largest Plants (a few of them 60 feet high) are being removed from their huge and unsightly tubs and planted in the ground under the great dome, so that the Visitor now walks among them on a level with their lofty but yet graceful trunks, and obtains such an idea of their magnificence as has no parallel in Europe.[24]

In 1865 other tropical plants were interplanted among the palms – for even in its earliest Victorian days the Palm House has never been *solely* a house for palms, largely because Kew did not have enough palms of sufficient size to fill it. In 1868 a hot bed 54 ft (16.4 metres) long was built for the coconut, mango and other delicate tropical plants.[25] It is now clear that what was special about the initial design of the Palm House is that it was *not* landscaped. However, it was designed without planting beds for reasons to do with the heating system, at Turner's insistence, and not with the needs of cultivation in mind. In this it differed from most other Victorian conservatories, which were landscaped; including Chatsworth, which had four beds with large rock formations, pools and tropical fish; and a whole host of European houses including the Winter Garden at Berlin–Dahlem (*c*.1820), the Jardin d'Hiver in Paris (1848), the Palm Garden at Frankfurt (1869), the Palm House at Herrenhausen (1846–9), the Great Palm House at

Munich (1860–65) and Ludwig II's winter garden at Munich (1867–9). The plant shelves were not popular either and were not used as intended (as propagation benches) after 1862, when the reserve stovehouses Nos. 19 and 21 were used instead. Too cold for propagation, the shelves carried a sad display of normally vigorous plants, whose roots had had to be contained. Most of the shelves were removed in the recent restoration and today the visitor to the Palm House can see a tribute to two traditions: the apse ends, with the plants in teak tubs on gratings and in clay pots on shelves, which recall the way the interior of the house was designed, and the system of plant beds, which are a tribute to what Victorian horticulturists did to parts of the centre of the house in order to provide better conditions for growing the plants.

It was unfortunate that during this early period of management of the house the Curator, John Smith, did not get on better with the Hookers, and particularly with Dr Hooker, who had been made Assistant Director to his father in 1855. Smith had a poor opinion of the younger Hooker's competence, a prejudice which was entirely unfounded, as Hooker was soon to become an eminent palm taxonomist and also made many practical improvements to the house. The problem was possibly one of communication and approach. Smith complained that Hooker's 'rearrangements' of the house (mainly to illustrate the principles of systematic botany to the public) involved him and his men in an enormous amount of work.[26] During the period 1857–60 it was obvious that the house had become seriously overcrowded and that many management decisions needed to be taken. There then followed a hard time for Smith as a result of Hooker's 'destructive policy':

the first act of which was to cut down the climbers which occupied the whole of the staircase pillars and gallery rails, thus leaving the iron work bare as it was left by the architect ... thus making out that ... the public was more interested in the iron construction which constitutes the 'Glory of the Garden' than in the beautiful *Passifloras* and *Aristolochias* which had hitherto hung in tassels overhead.[27]

Dr Hooker felt that the house should be more ventilated than it was and his father had a ruthless approach to thinning, which Smith protested was

wanton mischief ... The mode of proceeding was, Sir W Hooker would fix his eye on a plant, ask its history, then say 'Away with it' and in a moment the foreman's big knife made the bark hang in ribbons. This was the signal for the men to break it up, and convey it, and the box in which it was from to the rubbish yard. Plant after plant followed in the same way with apparently as much indifference as if they had been common laurels ...[28]

This distressed Smith, who produced a list of five pages mentioning 46 specimen plants which had succumbed to the 'away with it' policy. He particularly mourned a 15 ft (4.5 metres) mango which had been at Kew since 1826 and had produced 16 fruits in 1857, one of which had been sent to the Queen; an 11 ft (3.3 metres) tamarind tree and a 22 ft (6.6 metres) litchi tree in full fruit. Smith felt that he was never given reasons for these removals, but it is obvious from the list that the Hookers were clearing sizeable plants and quick-growing species (rather than irreplaceable ones) in order to contain the sheer volume of growth. It is indicative of their overall plan that the list contains no irreplaceable palms and that when ordering the destruction of one specimen, Hooker noted, 'Oh! we can soon get a young one up.'[29]

Smith resigned in 1864 when he had become nearly blind. He wrote his history of the gardens resentful that his hopes for the Palm House collections had never been realised. He was succeeded by another, younger, John Smith, whose experience had been gained at Syon Park and who enjoyed a much better relationship with Dr Hooker. Under his aegis in 1868 the plants on the shelves around the building were arranged geographically and in 1875 the palms in the central transept were arranged geographically as far as possible. But the old problem of overcrowding remained: in 1876, 4319 plants were cultivated in pots in the Palm House. Hooker proposed, in a remarkable turnaround, that the two staircases should be replaced by one and that it should open under the gallery floor to give greater accommodation for the taller palms.[30] This was never done for structural reasons after a report by the Board of Works. Many palms were felled in 1875–6, including large plants of *Arenga saccharifera*, *Livistona inermis*, *Sabal umbraculifera* (one of the first plants into the house), *Phytelephas macrocarpa* (the rare ivory nut palm which had flowered in 1855) and *Areca alba*. They were replaced by younger plants of different species.[31] In the next two years, attention was paid to the pandans in the north wing, where 'one side of them alone is exposed to the light. Cross alleys have been made in the wings and various of the larger and more umbrageous plants destroyed, with the view of bringing more of the medium sized specimens to the light.'[32]

With the resolution of the worst of the heating problems and the addition of further planting beds the management of the house became a matter of containing its successful growth. In nature, Darwinian principles would have ruled and the most vigorous species would have choked the rest. But the Palm House was a managed jungle and Victorian gardeners felled, replanted, pruned and rearranged potted plants to retain the diversity of the collections and ensure access by the public. That principle prevails today.

2 The growth of the Victorian plant collections

THE PLANT COLLECTIONS OF THE PALM HOUSE have, for over a century, concentrated on limited plant groups. The largest representation has been that of woody monocotyledons, particularly the palms and pandans, and of the cycads, an ancient group of gymnosperms related to both the conifers and ferns. Along with these groups are included many tropical dicotyledonous trees, some of them important as timber crops, for their fruits or simply as ornamentals. The uniting factor between all these is that they are woody plants. Many of them are interesting economic plants which are important crops in the tropics. Kew has had an important contribution in introducing some of these from one continent to another.

The palm collection in the Palm House grew greatly during its Victorian heyday. According to the first Curator, the original collection of palms in England was that of Lord Petre at Thorndon Hall, Essex, who grew them in soil beds under a house 30 ft (9 metres) high. Six palm species were grown at Kew in 1768, ten by 1787 and 20 in 1813. The plants were plunged in beds of bark into which the roots grew as their tubs decayed. By 1830 the collection had grown to 40 species but by 1882 the total was 420. A year later Dr Hooker joined with George Bentham in publishing *Genera Plantarum*, in which he classified the known palms into 132 genera. This took palm taxonomy from its early beginnings in the work of Linnaeus (1753) and Martius (1824) through to many of the subfamilies accepted today.

Apart from the collection at Kew there were many others in private hands, at Schönbrunn in Vienna, at Pfaueninsel in Berlin, at Biebrich, and in England, of course, the collection of the Duke of Devonshire, for which Paxton and Burton built the Great Conservatory at Chatsworth. Palms had an almost anthropomorphic appeal to the gentry:

The thief palm, Phoenicophorium borsigianum, *was given its name after a plant was stolen from Kew in the 1850s. It is a beautiful palm from the Seychelles, much planted as an ornamental but vulnerable in the wild.*

the palm tree resembles man in many respects because of its straight, slender, upright shape, its beauty, and its separation into two sexes, male and female. If one cuts off its head it dies; if the brain suffers, then the whole tree suffers with it; its leaves if broken off will grow again as little as the arm of man will; its fibres and surface mesh cover it like the growth of hair covers man . . . This distinguished form of the palm, superior to all other plants, the noble bearing, the stem striving to reach the skies . . . its nourishing fruits, the materials for clothing and shelter – all these combined to create the sense of a higher being inherent in it, if not a godhead then surely the dwelling of the same.[33]

Undoubtedly the finest collection was that of an ex-Kew man, Hermann Wendland, at the Berggarten in Herrenhausen, which grew from 22 species in 1846 to 224 in 1854. Wendland published his *Index Palmarum* in 1854, describing 192 species, and was always on the look-out for new accessions for his collections, often exchanging material with Kew.

In the autumn of 1855 Wendland was to become unfortunately involved in the extraordinary episode of the thief palm. The background to this is as follows: On 4 October 1855 Mr James Duncan, the Superintendent of the Royal Botanic Garden in Mauritius, had sent two plants of a new species of palm.

These he was later to recommend should be called *Stevensonia grandifolia* 'after our Governor' Stevenson.[34] On the back of the collector's paper relating to the delivery John Smith wrote some interesting comments:

The first palm in the list is the *Stevensonia* in the autumn M Whenland [*sic*] visited Kew, and was very anxious to get a plant of the new palm, being rare. I at first hesitated about letting him have one but after consulting Sir W Hooker we agreed he should have one. On taking Mr Whenland to the [?] in order to show him the plant I intended to give him, it was gone. Whenland immediately coloured up upon the supposition that I might think he had stolen it, this however was not the case for it was afterwards found that it had been stolen by a german [*sic*] gardener by the name of Voellner and he, Whenland said that it had been sold to a nurseryman in Belgium and afterwards became the property of an amateur plant grower in Berlin where a few years ago I learned it was a splendid plant. This circumstance . . . led to Whenland calling it by the abominable name . . . [illegible].[35]

The 'abominable name' was *Phoenicophorium* (thief palm), and the species name is *borsigianum*, after August Borsig, the 'amateur plant grower in Berlin' who ended up with the plant in his private palm collection. This very tender palm probably succeeded well because Borsig's glasshouses were well heated by steam from his own ironworks at Moabit, Berlin. This was not the first rare plant to be stolen from Kew but Hooker was furious at the commemoration of such infamy in a generic name. Wendland wrote an extremely apologetic letter to Hooker on 18 April 1865 claiming he had no knowledge of the name 'Stephensonia' and querying its spelling. On 8 August Wendland wrote again to Hooker offering to alter the name if 'anyhow indecent to Kew Gardens or to science in general' but his name stuck and is now accepted as the validly published legitimate name.[36] The species has flowered at Kew, notably in 1892. A young plant of *Phoenicophorium borsigianum* is now planted in the south wing, a testimony to the excesses of plant enthusiasts.

One of the rarest palms seen in collections, and cultivated at Kew since 1850, is the double coconut or coco-de-mer (*Lodoicea maldivica*) which comes only from the Seychelles. This tender and very slow-growing palm produces such huge two-lobed nuts, the largest in the plant kingdom, that it became the focus of the most bizarre folklore. Much of this was based on the fact that the nuts were carried long distances by sea. Berthold Seemann refers to a description of the plant by Rumphius:

The Double Cocoa-nut is not, he assures us, a terrestrial production . . . but a fruit probably growing itself in the sea, whose tree has been hitherto concealed from the eye of man. The Malay and Chinese sailors used to affirm that it was borne upon a tree deep under water, which was similar to a Cocoa-nut tree, and was visible in placid bays, upon the Coast of Sumatra, etc., but that if they sought to dive after the tree it instantly disappeared. The Negro priests declared it grew near the island of Java, where its leaves and branches rose above the water, and in which a monstrous bird, or griffin, had its habitation, whence it used to sally forth nightly, and tear to pieces elephants, tigers, and rhinoceroses with its beak, the flesh of which it carried to its nest . . .[37]

Such was the fame of this plant that in the Maldive Islands all nuts found were the property of the king. Chinese traders thought that water kept in the shell was life-preserving and that the albumen inside could be used as an antidote to all known poisons. Kew received a plant late in the year 1850 specifically for the Palm House. In his Annual Report for 1852 Hooker mentions it as a great rarity

The double coconut, Lodoicea maldivica, *is a huge palm from the Seychelles producing separate male and female plants. The two-lobed fruits contain the largest seed in the plant kingdom. Dr Hooker had obtained a plant for the Palm House by 1852.*

which our Garden alone possesses in a living state . . . a healthy young Double Cocoa-Nut (the Coco de Mer of French navigators, the Lodoicea Sechellarum), a Palm of the highest interest, whether botanically or historically, for it inhabits only one spot in the whole world, a single islet in the remote Seychelles group; and this treasure he (Prof. Bojer of Mauritius) . . . offered to our splendid Palm-House. The difficulty was to have it conveyed, in its great tub, a Sugar Cask, to England. It was conveyed to England free of expense by the Screw Propelling Steam Company in their ship the Queen of the South.[38]

Unfortunately this plant is so tender that it has never been grown under glass at Kew beyond its first few juvenile leaves. In the wild it is a huge tree palm, a great tourist attraction for the Seychelles. A young specimen is now planted in the south wing. Greater success has attended Kew's true coconuts, which are also tender species. On several occasions they have flowered in the Palm House, but they have never set fruit and are unlikely to do so under glass in temperate regions. Further information on palms and Kew's collection is given in chapter 5.

The second important collection of plants which developed in the Victorian heyday of the Palm House was that of the cycads. These primitive, palm-like plants were often colloquially referred to as palms because of the structure of many of the species, with a single trunk and crown of leaves. Unlike palms they are strictly either male or female. They were introduced to Britain slowly. Loddiges' nursery catalogue of 1830 lists four species of *Cycas* and 22 *Zamia* (although these might have included some *Encephalartos*). By 1845 he listed five *Cycas*, 12 *Encephalartos*, one *Dioon* and 14 *Zamia*.

Kew's collection started with the efforts of plant collectors sent to the Cape. The first and most famous of these was Francis Masson, who initially went out in 1772. In 1775 he sent back the famous male plant of *Encephalartos longifolius* now correctly identified as *E. altensteinii*. This produced a cone in 1819, such a notable event that Sir Joseph Banks visited the Palm House to see it, reputedly his last visit to Kew. But the bulk of the *Encephalartos* collection was formed from stems sent back by James Bowie, who had been appointed Botanical Collector in 1814 to succeed Masson and worked diligently until 1823. *E. woodii*, the rarest species and now extinct in the wild, was sent to Kew in 1899 as an unnamed species by its discoverer, J Medley Wood, and named after him by the firm of Sander and Son in 1908.

The collection of *Encephalartos* became the finest in Europe and it was largely under the watchful eye of Dr Hooker that the cycad collection expanded to be almost 'complete' by 1881. In the 1870s fine specimens of Australian cycads were sent by Sir Ferdinand Mueller in Melbourne, and many others arrived from Africa and East Asia.[39] By 1947 the collection had grown to occupy almost the entire south wing, and it was fully completed in terms of genera when the rare Cuban *Microcycas calocoma* was obtained from Fairchild Tropical Garden, Florida, in 1977.

This large collection has been recorded in terms of growth and the production of cones since 1972. The productivity is remarkable. In 1979, for example, 47 plants produced a total of 182 male and female cones, most of them being on *Zamia* (20) and on *Encephalartos* (11).

The genus *Pandanus* (screwpines) was also represented in the Palm House. Kew held 15 of the 17 species listed as available in the Loddiges' nursery catalogue of 1845. Two very large plants pre-dated the Palm House. One was *P. reflexus*, a male plant introduced by Wallich in 1818, which found a home near one of the Palm House staircases. By 1876 this had reached nearly 7 metres across. The other was a female plant then known as *P. odoratissimus*, which was one of the first plants moved into the building. In 1876 it was lowered into a brick pit to give it an extra 5 ft (1.5 metres) of headroom and it commenced

fruiting for the first time in 1883, producing heads 1 ft (30 cm) long. By 1894 it had 40 branches and reached 30 ft (9 metres) with a spread of 40 ft (12 metres). It was said to weigh around 6 tons. For years this had been a fine feature in the apse end of the north wing. It had to be cut down in 1894 because it had totally outgrown its position.[40] Many other species were obtained as seed from the island of Rodriguez in the Indian Ocean in 1874, sent by Professor Bayley Balfour during his attachment to the Transit of Venus Expedition.

By the 1980s the collection of cycads had grown to fill the south wing, giving a vision of the type of vegetation common in the age of the dinosaurs.

The fourth plant collection in which the Palm House has always been rich is that of the climbers, which was the first collection to be planted out, at Smith's insistence. Loddiges' nursery catalogue of 1830 lists 145 climbing species from 18 genera in his 'stove' (tropical) section. The largest groups then introduced were *Bignonia* (36 species), *Passiflora* (34), *Piper* (15) and *Clerodendrum* (12). The Palm House climbers were grown in beds in the centre transept and at some point later beds were provided round the walls under the side shelves to allow climbers to ascend the main arches.[41] In the 1950s many of the box vents in the dado wall were blocked up to allow brick containers to be built for this purpose. The beds were resoiled and the whole collection was renewed whenever the interior of the house was painted. One of the floral glories of the house was the collection of *Bougainvillea* cultivars held in the 1950s and 1960s, a collection now much reduced because of the current emphasis on growing true species of natural source and plants of conservation value. The collection in general is, however, still very floriferous. Particularly good displays are produced on *Allamanda*, *Aristolochia*, *Passiflora*, *Jasminum*, *Thunbergia*, *Clerodendrum* and on the jade vine (*Strongylodon macrobotrys*).

13

Of the various economic plants in the house, none was so popular with the Victorians as the banana. A number of the true species were introduced very early. At least six were available by 1830: *Musa coccinea* (the spectacular scarlet-flowered banana), *M. discolor*, *M. × paradisiaca* (the plantain banana), *M. × sapientum* (*M. rosacea*) (one of the parents of the edible banana) and *Ensete superbum* (then known as *Musa superba*).[42] One of the first plants to go into the Palm House was *Ensete ventricosum* (then known as *Musa ensete*), a huge, dramatic plant. Since it was only temperate in its heat requirements it coped well with the early problems of inadequate heating and formed a valuable feature throughout the 1850s:

the most extraordinary Plant in all our Collections, the gigantic Abyssinia Banana (Musa Ensete), described and figured by no author, save the celebrated Bruce, and now first introduced to Europe through W C M Plowden, Esq.; the British Consul at Mussonah. This striking Herbaceous Plant has attained in the Palm Stove, in five years' time, a height of more than 30 feet, with a stem of 7½ feet in circumference, and leaves, of which the blade, independent of the stalk or petiole, is 16 feet long![43]

There was considerable rivalry about the cultivation of bananas, as there had been earlier with pineapples. Edinburgh Botanic Garden had a particularly good collection from the 1840s onwards under the cultivation of Mr McNab. Sir William Hooker was wont to present bunches to the Queen, a habit which nearly led to the undoing of a young gardener in the late 1840s. Thomas Meehan described

how I first offended Sir William Hooker. It was on the occasion of a visit of the Queen to Kew. A very fine bunch of bananas had been cut that morning, and Sir William thought to present it to her. I was working near, in my shirt-sleeves, when he asked me to go as hastily as possible and get the bunch before the Queen left. Without waiting to get my coat, I tore away and came up with the bananas near the entrance gate. It was a very heavy bunch; I held the bunch in one hand and my hat in the other, while Sir William explained to her Majesty facts in its history. I found it impossible to keep it up with one hand, so put my hat on my head and used both. Subsequently Sir William sent for me, and asked how I dared to appear before Her Majesty without my coat and to wear my hat in her presence.[44]

The Victorians loved to cultivate bananas, both fruiting forms and those with ornamental flowers and foliage. Musa coccinea, *the scarlet-flowered banana, had been a prized plant in Britain since 1830. The Palm House contained a wide-ranging collection of* Musa *and* Ensete.

Luckily this *faux pas* did not damn the young man forever, and he later became botanist to the Board of Agriculture in Philadelphia.

At around the turn of the century about 20 species of banana were grown at Kew in a bed of rich loam and cow manure built on the north-east side of the centre transept. The bed was doubled in size in 1976. Some of the fruit produced has traditionally gone to the staff, cut green and allowed to ripen off the plants to produce the highest proportion of invert sugar.

In the period from 1927 onwards, while the Palm House displayed tropical crop plants to the public, Kew became a quarantine station for bananas, cocoa, rubber and other tropical crops in transit between continents. The money for the first quarantine house (1927) was provided by the Empire Marketing Board and for the second (1951) from Colonial Development and Welfare, the names of these bodies giving a clear idea of Kew's role. Banana germplasm from Africa was

One of the most historic plants in the Palm House is the hybrid Brownea × crawfordii. *(See p. 108.) The parents of this plant originate in the rainforests of Venezuela. It was raised by an Irish enthusiast, Dr Crawford, and was donated to Kew on his death in 1889.*

quarantined before being shipped for breeding purposes to the Imperial College of Tropical Agriculture in Trinidad, as were cultivars being shipped from the West Indies to stock new plantations in Queensland, Ghana and the Cameroons. Of particular concern was wilt (Panama disease). In the 1940s this work was under the charge of a Danish woman called Else Jensen, who was known throughout Kew as the 'Banana Nurse'.[45]

Many other tropical crop plants were introduced around the world through the agency of Kew. One of the earliest was the breadfruit, *Artocarpus altilis* (*A. communis*). Sir Joseph Banks was responsible for sending the young botanist David Nelson, to join Captain Bligh's expedition, which had the specific purpose of introducing the species from the South Seas to the West Indies. Banks was responding to a direct request from George III, who had been petitioned by the West Indian planters for a direct food source for their slaves. Presumably with this in mind, Banks called the ship the 'Bounty'. Bligh left from Spithead, Hampshire, on 23 December 1787, sailed around the Cape of Good Hope and arrived in Tahiti ten months later. Five months were spent in propagating plants and on 4 April he left with 1015 rooted breadfruit. In less than a month into the crossing Fletcher Christian led the famous mutiny on the *Bounty*, casting the loyal crew into a small boat. But Bligh survived, amid much public interest, and led another voyage in 1791–2 with the collector Christopher Smith and this time succeeded in introducing the species into St Vincent and Jamaica. Here they were grown on by an old Kew man called James Wiles. The species is now cultivated around the tropics and has been grown at Kew at various times since at least 1844. A plant can be seen in the north wing.

15

Quinine (*Cinchona succirubra*) was received at Kew from the Andes around 1850 and was introduced to Sikkim and the Nilgiri Hills in India in 1861 to help the British in the lowland tropics cope with malaria. The operation was directed by Sir Clements Markham of the India Office. Markham also attempted in the years following 1875 to introduce rubber, *Hevea* species, from its native Amazon to Asia, to ensure continuance of supply. This object was successfully achieved by Sir Joseph Hooker, who asked H A Wickham to collect the short-lived seed. Wickham chartered SS *Amazonas* to take the seed to Liverpool and thence by train to Kew on 14 June 1876. Two thousand eight hundred plants were grown and in August they were despatched to Ceylon packed in 38 Wardian cases. These plants prospered but others sent to Singapore did not. Singapore Botanic Gardens planted nine of Wickham's plants sent a year later, in June 1877, and there is a memorial to them still in the gardens. These first steps toward a rubber industry in Malaya were dogged by lack of interest from the peninsula's coffee planters until the turn of the century. This was despite all the efforts of the Director of the Gardens, H N Ridley, who earned the name 'Mad Ridley' as the result of his repeated promotion of the crop and his study of its growth, culture and tapping methods. Ridley's persistence paid off when the first plantation was made in 1898, and when coffee prices fell, the rubber boom of 1910 gave Malaya her prime position in world production.

Cocoa (*Theobroma cacao*) is another South American plant introduced to Asia via Kew, namely into Ceylon in 1880. However, the main areas of production are now Ecuador and Brazil in the New World and Ghana and the Ivory Coast in the Old World. This plant has always produced its pods freely in the Palm House and until recently Kew has quarantined much material in transit between South America and Africa. In 1936 a batch of cocoa seed from Brazil arrived in Europe in a particularly unusual way – in the airship *Graf Zeppelin*! They resulted in a batch of particularly healthy seedlings at Kew.[46]

On 5 August 1876 an author writing in the Supplement to the *Gardeners' Chronicle* gave a vivid overall picture of all these plant collections in the house nearly 30 years after planting and he made some interesting suggestions. It is the only vivid description we have of the plantings at that date, so is quoted at some length:

Entering the building at the north end, we are at once struck with the desirability of providing a porch or vestible [*sic*] to protect the plants from the currents of air inevitable in a building whose doors are so frequently opened . . . A fine Date Palm forms a striking object on entering, but its foliage is frequently injured by the draught . . . Near to the Date Palm just mentioned is a remarkably fine Pandanus odoratissimus whose grand proportions have, till lately, been concealed by overcrowding. The spirally arranged leaves and the aerial roots are finely developed. Not far off is a worthy companion, in the shape of P. reflexus, some 20 feet in diameter.

Near the centre of the building we find groups of Pandani and Bromeliads. The central bay itself is occupied on the outer side with small Palms, overtopped by Musas. A fine plant of Carapa guineensis, with bold pinnate foliage, climbs up one column; the elegant Calamus asperrimus mounts another . . . We are now in a very thicket of noble PALMS . . . Kentia Canterburyana, represented by a noble illustration, is one of the finest species that will succeed in a low temperature; Corypha australis, another Australian cool-region species, is here represented by a good specimen; Sabal glaucescens, Sabal umbraculifera, are striking examples of the vegetation of Ceylon and Malibar; Cocos plumosa, from Brazil, has its head almost touching the roof, 66 feet in height; Caryota urens, the Wine Palm of India, also stretching up to the roof, and now blooming is another denizen of the tropical forest. Areca Baueri is noticeable for its noble pinnate foliage, beneath which are produced its clusters of berries . . . Phoenix dactylifera, P. silvestris, and P. reclinata are represented by large specimens. A fine Monstera twines around the stem of the last named. Good examples of Livistona humilis and borbonia should be noted, as also Astrocaryum rostratum, a pinnate-leaved Palm, remarkable for its dense investiture of stout spines. Some of the Palms are in tubs, others are planted out in beds or troughs edged with slate, while a delightful effect is produced by an undergrowth of Aroids, Ferns, Selaginellas, and, in some cases, by draping the stems with Epiphytal [sic] Ferns, Bromeliads, etc. By the side of the staircases leading to the gallery is a Bamboo, Dendrocalamus giganteus, which serves to give an idea of the dense growth of these plants. A fine collection of arborescent draceanas [sic] and Cordylines, overtopped by a superb plant of Musa Ensete, must not pass without notice.

By ascending to the gallery the visitor is enabled to get a bird's-eye view of some of the smaller Palms and Pandani, while the taller ones still soar above him. From hence the massive head of Phoenix reclinata is seen to the best advantage, and the plumy inflorescence of the gigantic Sabal umbraculifera. Here the noble proportions of the Seaforthia elegans, Corypha australis, and Caryota urens may best be estimated . . . Descending from the gallery and proceeding along the western wing . . . we can but be struck with the impressiveness of the large foliage plants, and more especially with the many noble Cycads . . . At the extreme southern end is a glorious group of these plants, with a fine Encephalartos Altensteinii in the centre, backed up by Cycas revoluta, which has lately flowered, and which is now sending up a new crown of foliage . . .

Of the side stages we have not yet spoken: they run completely round the building, and accommodate a large number of plants of different families arranged in geographical order, according to their native countries. Generally speaking, the plants are too insignificant for their position . . . One of the side stages on the north-eastern side of the house is devoted to BROMELIADS, and a most striking assemblage it is . . .

Before quitting this house, and remembering its main educational object, we may offer a suggestion that at certain prominent points should be placed a label-board, descriptive, in general terms, of the contents of the building and explanatory of the method of arrangement, together with the names of a few of the more striking and interesting plants with indications of their uses. Again, some of the larger specimens, especially those seen from the gallery, require additional labels so placed as to be seen from that point.[47]

Many of the author's suggestions have since been carried out. A porch at the north end was added in 1929 and a south porch (to balance the outlines of the building) in 1988. The slate side stages were blinded over with ferro-concrete in 1934–5 and then removed in the 1980s restoration, leaving a much smaller area of benching which could be better maintained. As to the author's comment on the educational object of the building, we leave it to the visitor's judgement as to the adequacy of the current interpretation of the plants. Certainly it is something which has received much thought. The policies behind the current plantings are described in chapter 17.

3 The workday world of the Palm House

THERE IS NO DOUBT that the Victorian gardening staff who looked after the collections of plants had a long and hard job, felling, replanting or retubbing the plants, pumping rainwater and carrying heavy watering cans, not to mention hauling coke through the supply tunnel to maintain the boilers. The working hours in the 1890s were from 6 a.m. to 6 p.m. six days a week for the greater part of the year, with three-quarters of an hour for breakfast and one hour for lunch. On the dark mornings of winter, work started at 7 a.m. and ended at 4.30, with breaks at 8 o'clock for breakfast and 12 noon for lunch. (It was not until after the Second World War that the current starting time of 7.50 a.m. was introduced.) Wages were only 18 shillings a week.[48] Of course these were not uncommon working hours in Victorian Britain but the work was arduous and the heat enervating. 'No one who has not experienced it can have any idea of the nature of the gardener's work in such houses as the Palm House' lamented one gardener. 'Ten hours a day for six days in the week, seven days in every fourth week, in a tropical temperature, often doing heavy work, trying to keep plants healthy under the most artificial, often unfavourable, conditions, is an experience without parallel in horticulture at any rate.'[49]

Heavy work in the Palm House was never popular. The boilers in the basements were supplied with coke via an underground tunnel and railway, as at the Great Conservatory at Chatsworth. Nowadays the tunnel is used to pipe heat from remote boilers. It also doubles as a fire escape.

It was common for new staff to the gardens to be sent to a large glasshouse to work with several men in order to be tried out.[50] Many staff progressed through the Palm House. 'I did not take kindly to the work,' wrote William Dallimore, who arrived at Kew from Chester in 1891 and spent nine weeks in the Palm House before moving eventually to the Arboretum.

I was given a section of the house to look after, and apart from watering and damping down, much of the work was sponging plants, with an occasional job connected with the annual reconditioning of the nearby Water-lily House. Six men worked in the Palm House and a good deal of our time was spent in waging war against mealy bug and scale insects; the large house and large plants made cleaning a long and monotonous occupation. There was a very good collection of the *Cycadaceae* and the plants were difficult to clean. I still remember some plants of *Cycas revoluta* that were badly infested with scale insects, which I was instructed to clean; before I had finished I felt that I never wanted to handle a *Cycas* again . . .[51]

William Dallimore went on to become Sub-Foreman in the Temperate House, Sub-Foreman in the Arboretum and later Keeper of Museums, but his initial memories of the Palm House must have stayed with him, for in his writings on the development of the gardens he never once mentioned the building of the Palm House!

As Dallimore indicated, one of the main problems in the house was pest control, and the management of pests by hand was obviously unpopular.

18

He also gave a vivid picture of the use of nicotine fumigation in the Temperate House in the 1890s, a practice which had been first used in the Palm House. The process used contraband tobacco which had been confiscated by customs officers and supposedly treated to make it unfit for smoking, though several gardeners were wont to add it to their pipes nevertheless. In a procedure which would have horrified today's Health and Safety Executive, the staff remained in the houses to stoke the nicotine pyres for the entire period of up to two and a half hours, with no form of protective clothing. It is lucky no one was killed. A R Gould, who left Kew in 1910, wrote back 63 years later to say he remembered being pulled out of the Palm House legs first by his mate, Jack Watts, when he was quite overcome by the fumes.[52] Such experiences made deep impressions and Captain Digoy of the 14th Infantry Regiment, who endured mustard gas in the First World War, wrote back from Toulouse in 1915, 'We had a very hard summer, with several gas attacks that made me think of the fumigating of the Kew Palm House.'[53]

During all this work the gardeners wore clogs, as indeed did most Victorian workers. But it must have made the Palm House a noisy place when all six of them were walking on the gratings at once. Clogs were very useful in plant houses, where the floors were constantly wet, as they kept feet drier than boots. Every gardener was issued with a pair on beginning work and could claim a replacement after 12 months' service. According to Dallimore the gardens used to abound with 'clog stories', usually at the expense of some naive newcomer:

One extra large pair had remained in the stores for a long while, until a young man arrived whom Nature had endowed with very big feet. The storekeeper gave him no choice but handed him the large pair. He was sent to the Palm House to work and a story was soon current that when he was in one of the narrow paths between raised beds, he had to back out as his clogs were so large that they prevented him from turning round.[54]

In 1936 clogs were adapted to have a leather infill and lacings around the ankle, but nowadays it is more common to see gardeners in sandals, except when doing heavy work needing safety boots.

The work in the Palm House was supervised by a Sub-Foreman, subsequently regraded to Foreman in 1935 and then to Gardens Supervisor in 1968. Forty people have held this job during the 140 years that the house has been in use. Some have served for only a year but some have obviously loved it and stayed. These include James Walker, Sub-Foreman for 12 years in the 1860s to 1870s, George Anderson, Acting Temporary Foreman and then Foreman for 18 years from 1946 to 1964, and Ruth Storr (later Henderson), the first woman Supervisor of the house, for 11 years from 1971 to 1982. Several Sub-Foremen have gone on to greater things, for example William Watson, who was Curator from 1901 to 1922, and John Coutts, who became Deputy Curator in 1929. But the most distinguished was William Jackson Bean, Sub-Foreman in the 1880s, who became Curator between 1922 and 1929 and later showed his versatility by writing the standard and definitive *Trees and Shrubs hardy in the British Isles*, a work affectionately known to generations of horticultural students as 'Bean'.

Women never worked in the Palm House in Victorian times. The first women were employed at Kew in 1896 under the directorship of Sir William Thistelton-Dyer. He must have been under considerable pressure to take graduates from

The longest-serving Foreman in the Palm House was George Anderson (1946–64). He presided over the restoration of the house in the 1950s, during which many huge plants were lifted or successfully propagated by air-layering into pots.

Swanley Horticultural College in Kent, which had opened to women in 1891. The furore this caused is commemorated in the ode 'The lady in knick-knacks who gardened at Kew'. In 1913 the suffragettes turned their attention to Kew, breaking into the orchid houses and destroying plants on 8 February 1913 and burning down the tea pavilion a fortnight later. Between 4 March and 7 April various parts of the gardens were closed in response to their window-smashing campaign, a precaution which led the editor of the *Journal of the Kew Guild* to speculate what would happen 'if the Suffragettes had started on the Palm House at Kew'.[55] Thereafter the opportunities and performance of women closely followed that of women in the economy in general, that is, employed when labour was short – as during both wars – and encouraged (or required) to relinquish their jobs for men at other times. Women replaced student gardeners in the First World War, mainly in the Decorative Department under Mr Coutts where they were somewhat indecorously called 'Coutt's harem'. By 1917 there were four female Sub-Foremen and 27 gardeners. The closest women got to the Palm House was to work on the adjacent parterre, which in 1917–18 was trenched to grow an excellent crop of onions for the war effort.[56] In 1944 Miss E V Paine became the highest-promoted woman at Kew, appointed Temporary Assistant Curator in charge of the Decorative Department. She left in 1947 to teach horticulture. Thereafter the number of women declined in the gardens, with only four in 1949 and none by 1952. It seemed easier for women to succeed in pure botany than in practical horticulture, for at this time the Deputy Keeper of the herbarium was a woman, Miss E M Wakefield, OBE. However, in 1954 women became eligible to take the student gardeners' course and one took up the offer. This must have started a trend and for the past 18 years the Palm House has been supervised by women, two of them ex-Kew students, though women still remain under-represented in the gardens.

One of the reasons that the work led by the Foremen in the Palm House was so difficult was that the house had been painted green and glazed in green glass, factors which by the 1890s were radically reducing the light the plants received and producing sickly growth. Various authors have seen this as nothing more nor less than a mistake in the original design, forgetting that air pollution in London created conditions in 1890 quite different from those prevailing in 1848. The plants had also grown up to establish their own shade. Curvilinear glasshouses had originally been designed to maximise light for the ripening of exotic fruit. From 1832 the development of larger panes of glass no longer tinted with green and thinner-sectioned metal rather than wood structures caused rates of light transmission to soar. This was a matter of some concern to practical cultivators of tropical plants other than fruit, and much debated, especially in the 1840s.[57] Kew noticed scorching on orchids and ferns after clear glass was installed.

John Smith records his discussion with Turner on the subject:

I then asked Mr Turner what glass was to be used, he said holding up his hands, 'Glass, you won't see there is glass it will be so clear.' I said this will be very pretty, but how are the plants to be shaded in summer? For if not shaded by some material the plants will be likely to be scorched and called his attention to the plant-houses in the garden being covered with canvas shades during bright sunshine in summer. Both he and I saw that it would be difficult to shade the palmhouse with canvas and I suggested the only way of getting over the difficulty would be to use green glass. 'Green glass,' repeated Mr Turner with some degree of astonishment, 'Yes', I replied, 'the glass originally used in glazing the fruit and plant houses at Kew which Mr Aiton called 'Stourbridge Green' which was in general use until the duty was taken off glass in 1845, on repairs being required in the hothouses, the contractors for glazing substituted clear glass, which led to the necessity of using canvas shades.[58]

Decimus Burton and Sir William Hooker consulted Mr Robert Hunt, Keeper of the Mining Records in the Museum of Economic Geology, who was keenly interested in photography and light transmission and who had presented a paper on glass for glasshouses to the British Association. Smith was asked to provide some samples of palm leaves, which he sent over to Turner's lodgings at the Rose and Crown tavern for him to take to Hunt. The bizarre experiments involved 'spreading the expressed juice of Palm leaves over paper and exposing it to the action of the spectrum' so as to identify the burning rays.[59] Hunt then gave a special recipe of copper oxide to Messrs Chance of Birmingham, the glass supplier for the house.

Many gardens emulated Kew and the installation of coloured glass became standard practice at, for example, the Berlin Palm House (1859) and Glasgow's Kibble Palace (1873). John Smith reported that his successor as Curator considered the glass 'in every way a success.'[60] However, cleaning rapidly became a problem with any glass in London. William Dallimore gave his impressions on his arrival at Kew in 1891:

The Aroid House – the first seen – was not inspiring; it looked as though it was covered with slates instead of glass, but it was not until I saw Ferneries, Greenhouse, Succulent House and T-Range that I fully appreciated the dirt. The glass had not been washed after the fog and it was black with filth . . . [I] was not prepared for the many leafless and flowerless plants that should have been in first rate condition.[61]

From 1886 the use of green glass at Kew declined and, one learns from the *Kew Bulletin*, it was abandoned in 1895 due to air pollution:

Of late years at Kew the object aimed at in the use of green glass has been attained in great measure by the increasing haziness of the sky, due to the smoke produced by the rapid extension of London to the south-west. The extreme obscurity of the winter of 1885–6 showed that no available sunlight could possibly be spared. It became obvious that for the future the plant-houses must be so constructed as to exclude as little of the available sunlight as possible.[62]

At the turn of the century the house must have presented a strange, patchy sight, as it was progressively reglazed. As the result of a complicated oxidation process involving manganese and iron, the green glass had faded and some panes had even become pink! The problem of fog, however, remained, even with clear glass, and the resemblance of glass to slate could be clearly seen until after the 1950s restoration. (See picture on p. 142.) Many of the Palm House plants were severely damaged by fog but the problem receded in the 1960s after the Clean Air Act (1956) established Smoke Control Areas, assisted by the closure of the Brentford Gas Works in 1963.

During this century the Palm House has survived several storms and two wars. All glasshouses were fitted with electric horns as air-raid sirens and out of 23 bombs and hundreds of incendiaries dropped on the gardens the Palm House was hit only by the sleeve of a rocket gun.[63] The Temperate House suffered severely by comparison. Far more damage has been done to the Palm House by natural causes; both by rust and decay and also by hail – on the morning of 3 August 1879, 4558 panes in the house were broken by hailstones, some of them 12.5 cm in circumference.[64] Today it also suffers from

Horticultural staff at Kew have favoured the planting of large specimens in beds since the building of the house. However, palms and cycads in teak and brass tubs can still be seen in the apse ends of the house.

being on a major flight path into Heathrow airport, receiving unwelcome quantities of excess aviation fuel.

Throughout the life of the house its immediate surroundings have been continually improved. William Andrews Nesfield (1793–1881) landscaped the terrace on which the house stands, with its sloping banks, vases and steps. His original wall (1847) was replaced by an iron fence at some point in the 1870s and Irish ivy (Hedera helix 'Hibernica') was planted and trailed in swags between the posts. This became a standard way of decorating the top of a bank but it gradually thickened, to become a solid hedge during the 1950s. It is now one of the oldest arborescent ivy hedges in the country, though some people feel it obscures the view of the lower part of the house. During the building of the house the pond was deepened and in 1856 Museum No. 1, designed by Decimus Burton, faced it across the water. Nesfield's complicated designs of box-edged flower beds on the parterre in front of the house, never installed in their entirety, were progressively replaced after 1881 but his vistas, all centring on the Palm House, were a great success. W J Bean saw the Palm House as 'the central point of Kew, the spot upon which all the main routes converge.'[65] Syon Vista and Pagoda Vista, both nearly 1000 metres long and originally gravelled, were turfed over under the direction of Dallimore when he was Foreman of the Arboretum. In the winter of 1908–9, 60 trees weighing between 3 and 6 tons were moved to complete these avenues, using Barron's Transplanting machine, popularly known as 'the devil' and now restored for the public to see near Kew's tea bar. Much of the preparation of the trees for this work was done by an Irishman called Jack Cotter, renowned for his eccentric appearance, a true 'Kew character'.[66] The Palm House terrace, also originally gravelled, was turfed in 1896 to make it more pleasant to walk upon and less hot and arid to the eye in summer.[67] The hedge around the present Rose Garden was originally of yew but this too succumbed to London's pollution and was replaced with holly after about 50 years. Although not totally devoted to roses until after 1908 this area still suffers from impeded drainage, being on the site of the old lake of George III's time, which once extended under what is now the north end of the Palm House.

Over the years many improvements have been made to the Palm House's heating and water supply. Originally the gardens were supplied by a well near the present Cumberland Gate. In 1855 water was taken direct from the Thames (via the Lake near the Temperate House) which covered the palms with a 'minute crust of dust' from the alluvium.[68] In the drought of 1921, increased salinity in the river caused considerable damage to plants. River water from the Metropolitan Water Board was supplied via the Richmond Park reservoir from 1931 and treated mains water from Petersham Pumping Station from 1973. The introduction of alkaline mains water off the Chilterns caused problems with acid-loving plants, and expensive deionisation equipment has been installed to complement the rainwater saved from the glasshouse roofs. In 1961 a system of overhead automatic watering was installed in the Palm House by the Ministry of Works in association with Long Ashton Research Station. This simulated rainfall and imitated a system originally installed when the house was built, which operated off a pressure tank at the top of the campanile. Unfortunately the pressure was only adequate in the centre transept but the same system was very effective in the Aroid House. It was not renewed in the 1980s restoration, when a new humidification system was introduced. The attempts which were made in 1969 to reduce the labour of applying water by heavy-duty hose by introducing a sprinkler system to the beds in the centre transept, unfortunately resulted in inadequate water distribution. It is now hoped that humidification will help to lessen the amount of watering needed, by reducing the transpiration of the plants.

In 1968 the Palm House was moved from the Tropical to the Temperate Section to help balance the spread of responsibility between the two. Thus the most famous 'tropical' house at Kew is now part of the Temperate Section. The rationale for this is that Temperate looks after 'tender woody' plants and Tropical 'tender herbaceous'. Unfortunately this does not accord well with ecological plantings at Kew, which demand the planting of all layers of vegetation, woody and herbaceous, in the same house.

Since the gardens first opened in 1841 there has been a steady increase in public provision. Sunday opening started in 1853 and entry was entirely free until 1916. The gardens began opening to the public at 10 a.m. in 1913, but the Palm House, and all other houses, were traditionally closed for maintenance, botanical research and instruction all morning until the 1970s. The issue of public access was one of great controversy under the Hookers. Today, work in the glasshouses is often done with the public in close attendance from 10 a.m. onwards.

Promenading around the Palm House was a popular pastime for Victorians. In 1976 a ramp for the disabled was added to the south bank of the terrace to increase public access and several concerts were held. On 15 July 1977 the house was lit externally and internally to celebrate the Queen's Silver Jubilee and a military band with trumpeters accompanied picnickers. A firework display followed, just as Concorde flew overhead. The success of the concert was repeated on 5 July 1979 when 4000 people gathered to celebrate the 'Year of the English Garden' and the Orangery's exhibit on 'Kew's Historic Greenhouses'.

It is hoped that the Palm House will continue to be a site of public interest, education and of unique public events. Certainly the paths in the house are now wider, to allow for easier access, though they are trodden by far fewer gardeners than in Victorian times. You will not hear the sound of clogs except once a year, when the new intake of diploma students race down the Broad Walk wearing clogs and apron, the historic uniform of the gardener.

4 The structure of the rainforest and the Palm House plant collections

IN AN ATTEMPT TO GROW THE PLANTS of the Palm House more successfully, horticultural staff at Kew have been growing more and more plants in beds, and fewer in tubs ever since the 1860s. As the number of glasshouses at Kew has grown, so the collections have been rationalised, in order to match the plants more effectively to the environments we can provide. Various technical developments have enabled a greater degree of environmental control and the 1980s restoration has seen the installation of humidification equipment into the Palm House for the first time.

The plant displays of the Palm House of the 1980s are the result of an increased interest in plant ecology and the functioning of plant communities along with an understanding of the urgency of conservation. As far as is possible under glass we have created a tropical rainforest – a constantly humidified, warm environment of predominantly woody plants growing in the ground. Kew has always been in the forefront of tropical botany – in plant collection and exploration, in introducing economic plants to the tropics and in the setting up and staffing of botanic gardens there. The later part of the twentieth century is a period when the flora of the tropics and in particular the rainforest flora is under great threat, a threat which our Victorian ancestors could not possibly have foreseen. At the time of writing, over 40 per cent of all tropical forests have been destroyed and, in the Amazon region, which contains a third of the flora of the entire humid tropics, the destruction by logging and burning is destroying an area the size of England and Wales every year. The smoke produced is the only result of human activity (apart from the Great Wall of China) which can be seen from outer space. All primary rainforest has been destroyed in India, Bangladesh, Sri Lanka, Ghana and Haiti, with that of Malaysia likely to follow by 1990 and Nigeria by the year 2000. Losses like this, which equate to the area of ten football pitches every minute, will, it is estimated, completely destroy or seriously disturb *all* the world's rainforests by the year AD 2135. If this should happen, it would be the most severe ecological disaster of the past 65 million years. Today we consider it part of our educational role as conservationists to show the palm-rich rainforests of the world, in microcosm, to the public who visit the Palm House. This is the underlying theme of the present plantings and is more fully described in chapter 17.

The plants now in the beds are no longer grouped according to the principles of systematic botany but in mixed communities, as they would be in nature. This enables us to interpret the house to the public ecologically and to show the structure of the rainforest. We have also divided the plants into three groups to represent the rainforests of the different continents: the American in the centre transept, the African in the south wing and the Asian, Australian and Pacific rainforests in the north wing. It is obvious that there are many structural differences between these plantings, such as the paucity of palms in Africa, the richness of the forest floor in Asia and the presence of the epiphytic family Bromeliaceae only in the Americas. This is an educational feature in itself.

The visitor to the Palm House might like to reflect that to fully enshrine a real part of the rainforest the Palm House would have to be four times its height. The tallest woody trees of the families Dipterocarpaceae and Leguminosae which form the upper rainforest canopy frequently reach 90 metres, growing as they do in optimum conditions 12 months of the year. However, we can show the layered structure of the forest and many of its detailed features, although not in full scale.

At a distance, primary, undisturbed rainforest has a dense, mounded appearance, with the crowns of the upper canopy trees fully visible. Some botanists have compared it to the head of a cauliflower, mounded with individual florets. Trees in the rainforest are frequently grouped into three strata or storeys. These are often discontinuous and may be difficult to define. In undisturbed forest some of these storeys may join up and form closed canopies, which radically reduce the light reaching the forest floor. When disturbed, more light is admitted and may provide a niche where climbers can establish themselves. Climbers exist wherever they can compete successfully by rapid growth to the canopy: growth more rapid than the time required for the canopy to grow over. This is why climbers flower mainly on young tip growth, that is, growth which has emerged into the light on top of the canopy. In the wild, climbers sometimes form dense mats over the crowns of trees or hang down from them at the margins of the forest or wherever the forest canopy is broken by a water course. In the Palm House the climbers are expected to get very vigorous with an unrestricted root run. They usually hang down under their own weight over the paths as they would along water courses in the wild. Sometimes, under closed canopy conditions, the only indication of the presence of climbers are fallen flowers on the ground.

In the Palm House, the gallery in the centre transept allows the public to walk around as if in among the forest canopy. In the wild, botanists often construct aerial walkways in order to carry out studies of the canopy and the flowers and fruits which only appear there. In this multi-layered world each stratum has its own botanical characteristics, its own light and humidity levels and its own fauna. Where the layers are disturbed or destroyed, secondary forest develops, with an impoverished mixture of species. Many secondary forest trees have huge palmate leaves, soft wood and a very fast growth rate, to maximise their chances in the competition of vegetation to re-establish. Examples of these in the centre transept are the balsa wood tree (*Ochroma pyramidale*) and *Cecropia*. Bananas and plantains (*Musa* and *Ensete* species) and the related genus *Heliconia* in tropical America, are similarly only giant forest weeds (though herbs rather than trees) making use of cleared ground just as stinging nettles do in the waste ground of temperate areas.

Outrun in the competition for light, understorey shrubs, palmlets and herbs on the forest floor make a virtue of their small stature and exploit an evolutionary niche. Adapted to low light and high humidity they live out their entire life cycles without need for the full light of day.

The ecosystem represented by these different storeys is often balanced on a very thin and impoverished soil. Nutrients are recycled not through a deep soil profile but through a very effective system of surface rooting. The forest floor is frequently matted with surface roots. In addition many trees send down aerial roots to absorb moisture directly from the air rather than via the soil. Epiphytes, which live perched on the bark of trees, do the same by collecting moisture in a central cup. This also forms a trap for debris, which rapidly turns into a kind of nutrient soup. Such plants often have a very rudimentary root system. Some of them are well known as houseplants, particularly the bromeliads and some *Asplenium* (birds nest's ferns) and orchids.

A feature of this mass of life above the soil level is the insidious phenomenon of strangulation, common in rainforests with populations of *Ficus* and *Clusia*. Fruits of these genera establish themselves in debris in the crowns of trees and then send out roots which descend the trunks, often growing tens of metres down to the ground, where they establish themselves as normal roots. As the strangler grows, the host tree becomes more and more constricted until it dies away and rots, the strangler having become self-supported. Many *Ficus* and *Clusia* are planted throughout the house in the ground, showing that strangulation is not a necessary lifestyle, more an opportunistic way of getting a 'leg up' into the canopy.

The tallest and most vigorous of the rainforest trees frequently grow by a series of spurts, reaching for the sky and then branching, in a habit called 'pagoda growth'. Many *Terminalia* species do this, and so do many of the family Bombacaceae, including *Pachira aquatica*, the Guinea chestnut, which can be seen in the centre transept. Many rainforest trees also produce huge plank buttresses at the base of the trunk as if to support themselves on the thin soils, though the precise function of these structures has never been satisfactorily demonstrated. A forlorn feature of many areas cleared of primary rainforest are the stumps of these buttresses, left because of their hard timber, which is resistant to fire, which serve as a persistent memorial to the vegetation that has been lost. In Malaysia they are sometimes seen scattered under the rubber plantations. In the Palm House, buttressing is developing on some of the *Ficus* and on *Pachira aquatica*.

The Palm House contains the vegetation characteristic of a tropical rainforest. This ecosystem develops layered growth, with different species occupying different storeys. Here the fan palm Licuala ramsayi from northern Queensland, though tall, is acting as an understorey palm below the forest canopy.

26

Visitors to the Palm House often lament the lack of flowers. Rainforests, however, are predominantly green, the green lungs of the world in fact, generating huge amounts of our global supplies of oxygen. Apart from the ferns and cycads, however, they are nevertheless composed of angiosperms: flowering plants. The flowers are there, but they are frequently found in odd places, growing directly out of trunks, for instance. This phenomenon is known as cauliflory and is commonest among understorey shrubs and trees. It is thought to be an adaptation to pollination by the insects which are found in the stiller understorey atmosphere. It is also true that many cauliflorous plants produce heavy fruits, which need to be supported by woody trunks rather than by more flexible tip growth. Examples of cauliflorous plants in the centre transept are the anchovy pear (*Grias cauliflora*), *Herrania balaensis* and *Goethea strictiflora*. The

Many tropical trees produce flowers and then fruits growing directly out of the old wood, a phenomenon called cauliflory. Several tropical fruits do this, including cocoa, the Asian durian and the American calabash tree, Crescentia cujete, *shown here.*

27

calabash, *Crescentia cujete*, and the cannonball tree, *Couroupita guianensis*, are both cauliflorous trees which produce fruits the size of a baby's head and which we hope will fruit once they have been planted out. Besides the floral displays produced by the climbers, the brightest flowers in the Palm House are mainly shrubs of forest margins or open areas, such as *Hibiscus* and *Ixora*, important horticulturally in tropical and subtropical landscaping and needing bright light to flower.

People in temperate regions are used to seasons and the usual leafing in spring and leaf fall in autumn. In tropical zones the forests shed leaves and releaf at less seasonal times, or sometimes many times a year. Frequently the new growth is spectacularly colourful, in shades of red and pink, before it darkens into the mature leaf. Sometimes this growth is lax and almost as soft as butter. In the centre transept, this can be observed on some of the *Brownea* hybrids which have lax, chocolate-brown growth for several days. The phenomenon is common amongst the Leguminosae. It is thought to be a protection against scorching.

It is well known that rainforests absorb a huge amount of rainfall, with parts of the Amazon and monsoonal Queensland receiving 4 or 5 metres a year. Much of this is collected by the canopy and runs down the trunks or drips off the leaves. In the Amazon area 90 per cent of the rainfall is known to be recycled. Many rainforest trees bear leaves adapted to shedding water with a long funnelling 'drip tip'. This is common among many genera, especially in the genus *Ficus*. The tree sacred to Buddha, *Ficus religiosa*, has spectacular drip tips. It is planted in the north wing.

All the characteristic features of the rainforest are features of a self-sustaining but very fragile community. Even if only part of it is destroyed, the whole web comes apart with disturbing results. At best, secondary forest develops, with its usual reduction in richness of species. At worst, the loss of canopy reduces the ability of the area to moderate its rainfall, producing catastrophic floods in lower areas accompanied by silting of waterways. Once cleared of vegetation, rainforest soils are not fertile for long, because the nutrient investment is in the vegetation and not in the soil; so much so that some rainforest ecologists have called them 'wet deserts'. The effort in clearance for agriculture is a poor investment.

This fragile community is very old. Unlike temperate floras, which have been successively impoverished by the harshness of the ice ages, the tropics have been left climatically untouched apart from transient phenomena such as hurricanes. In this environment speciation has advanced unhindered, producing a richness well understood by the forest peoples and of much potential in economic crops for the rest of the world. Tropical forests are five to twenty times richer in tree species than are temperate forests and contain half the total number of plant and animal species on only 7 per cent of the land surface of the globe.

Kew puts great value on its tropical collections for several reasons. We maintain collections of living material (as opposed to pressed specimens) in order to hold a gene bank of value for research, development and possible reintroduction into the wild. As the tropics and subtropics contain 65 per cent of the world's flora these zones are correspondingly important in our collections, simply on a numerical basis. Secondly, because the tropical floras are more threatened (and tropical botanic gardens are few and often badly resourced) we hold a responsibility for *ex situ* conservation of rare plants here. A high proportion of the plants grown in the Palm House are threatened in the wild, 25 per cent of the palms and 50 per cent of the cycads. The categories of threat used in the following chapters are those of the International Union for the Conservation of Nature, a worldwide organisation based in Switzerland. These range from the most pessimistic, 'extinct' (i.e. in the wild), to warning categories such as 'vulnerable', which indicates that a species is likely to become 'endangered' if no action is taken.

The drenching rain of rainforest ecosystems is easily shed from the leaves of trees with well developed drip tips. Top row, left to right: the African yam, Dioscorea sansibarensis; the Buddhist peepul tree from Asia, Ficus religiosa.
Bottom row, left to right: the South American Brownea coccinea × latifolia, Dioscorea sansibarensis, Ficus benjamina, Ficus religiosa.

5 *Palms*

DAILY LIFE IN THE TROPICS revolves around the use of palm products. Palms are one of the most diverse families within the monocotyledons. They are as important to the economies of the tropics as that other great group of monocots, the grasses, are in our temperate zones. Linnaeus believed that human life started in the verdant tropics and that we are so dependent on palms for food, shelter and clothing that we should be called 'palmivorous'. Paying respect to their importance, he called the order of palms 'principes', or princes of the plant kingdom. They are a truly ancient group, the most advanced of the arboreal monocots and, judging by fossil records, appeared on earth during the Upper Cretaceous period of 65 million years ago.

All palm leaflets are folded but the leaflets are usually arranged in feather form, as in coconuts, or in fans like the Bismarckia nobilis *shown here. Fan leaves radiate like fingers from the 'palm' of the hand, an arrangement after which all palms are named.*

Palms are distributed in a great swathe across the humid tropics and subtropics from 44°N to 44°S. Few genera creep into the temperate zones, though some have developed within the semi-deserts of the dry tropics. Their distribution in world terms is very uneven. Of roughly 2800 species, about 1102 exist in the New World. The greatest diversity is in South-east Asia. A notable feature is the paucity of palms in continental Africa, a poverty perhaps compensated for by the plenty in Madagascar, which separated from mainland Africa around 100 million years ago and where around 14 endemic genera have evolved. The palms of each continent tend to be restricted to that continent. Within the great continental masses there is also a high proportion of palms (up to 90 per cent) which have evolved with a limited local distribution. These so-called 'local endemics' are often very threatened. There are no true pantropical palms, the widest in distribution being the coconut, the fruits of which are adapted to distribution by water and which have been further spread by humans. Certain subtribes of palms have evolved with a strong bias towards either the southern or northern hemisphere. In addition there is much fossil evidence to suggest that palms once had a much wider distribution during the Eocene period and even occurred in the Thames Valley. Their present distribution is probably a reflection of climatic cooling in the Miocene and Pliocene periods.

A palm is a monocot which produces a shoot crowned by a bud which produces a crown of leaves. Many tree palms which produce a single stem grow to their full diameter before the stem elongates and gains height. This method of growth is an obvious way in which a plant lacking cambium to produce wood as it grows upwards (like the dicotyledons), can produce adequate girth to sustain it as it becomes older. The 'rosette' stage can be seen on many of the palms in the Temperate House. It is these palms which inspired the building of the Palm House to its current height, in order to accommodate as much as possible of their lives before the single bud is carried into the glass and they have to be cut down. Other palms produce a cluster of such shoots and can be effectively divided, while others produce procumbent stems. An important group of palms climb, sometimes to 180 metres or more. These 'rattans' grapple into the canopy by viciously effective thorny adaptations of their leaves or flower spikes using a 'fast growth to the canopy' strategy in a competitive response to the availability of light. Other palms have developed minature form and live happily on the murky forest floor. These two groups, the climbers and the understorey group, represent 50 per cent of all palm species. Despite this diversity, however, some growth forms are absent from the family, notably the herbaceous habit, the deciduous habit, the parasitic and the epiphytic habit. The closest palms get to an aquatic adaptation is in *Nypa*, the mangrove palm, and the South American swamp palm, *Mauritia*. Few palms branch, an example being the semi-desert genus *Hyphaene*.

By far the great majority of palms have either palmate or pinnate leaves. This basic division into palms with a fan-shaped leaf (called 'palmate' after the shape of the palm of the hand, after which all palms are named) and pinnate palms (with a leaf like a bird's feather) has only a few modifications. A few genera have a simple, undivided leaf, which may be of dramatically large proportions, as in *Johannesteijsmannia*. One genus, *Caryota*, has bipinnate leaves with fringed leaflets like fishtails. Some fan palms have leaves whose midrib extends through the body of the leaf. Such leaves are called costapalmate. Most palms when they are young also have leaves which differ from those of the mature palm. As a general rule there are more fan palms in the northern hemisphere and more feather palms in the southern. Further taxonomic characters include the way the folded leaves split as they open out; those which are V-shaped in cross-section are called 'induplicate' and include practically all the fan palms, while those which are shaped in cross-section like an upturned V (which is far more common) are termed 'reduplicate' and include all feather palms with the notable exceptions of the dates, *Phoenix*, and the sugar palms and their relatives (*Arenga*, *Caryota* and *Wallichia*). Palm leaves vary in size from 15 cm long to the huge structures of *Raffia* palms which, at 25 metres, are the longest in the plant kingdom.

The nature of the leaf base has an important effect upon the appearance of the stem, either abscissing cleanly and leaving rings or persisting and leaving a fringe of leaves which is often cut back in cultivation to leave a cross-hatched trunk. Stems of great beauty develop in the Arecoid group of palms, whose leaf bases sheath to some length – in some a metre or more – between the stem and

Some palms have huge, undivided leaves, as does this South-east Asian understorey species, Johannesteijsmannia altifrons. *The leaves make excellent thatch and impromptu umbrellas.*

In Arecoid palms the sheathing leafbases form crownshafts of spectacular beauty. Roystonea hispanolana *is one of the so-called royal palms. These are commonly planted in avenues for formal effect.*

the crown, leaving a smooth 'crownshaft'. The finest examples are the royal palms, *Roystonea* spp., which make fine avenues in the tropics and have green crownshafts. Others include the Asian *Ptychosperma*, the South-east Asian *Cyrtostachys renda*, the sealing wax palm, in which the leaf sheaths are brilliant red, and the Mascarene *Hyophorbe*. Some palms develop complex fibre on their stems from the leaf sheaths, as in *Arenga*. In most species of *Coccothrinax* and *Thrinax* these are as complex as in the weft and warp of fabrics and may indeed have inspired the development of weaving. Other genera, particularly *Bactris* and its relatives, produce forbidding spines on their trunks, leaves, flowers and fruit.

The flowers of most palms are small, usually white and usually profuse, sometimes extraordinarily so. They are arranged on simple or branched inflorescences, often within a sheathing bract. These arise on the plant in three ways. Usually they appear between the leaves (interfoliar). In Arecoid palms, however, they often appear below the crownshaft (infrafoliar) and, where many appear at once, give these palms a dramatic white frill. Rarely, as in the talipot palm (*Corypha umbraculifera*) and in the sago palm (*Metroxylon sagu*) the inflorescence is suprafoliar and towers above the palm, which pours all its energy into the process and then dies. This is a similar growth habit to that of some of the annual grasses and bamboos. In the case of the talipot, the national floral emblem of Sri Lanka, the inflorescence may be 7 metres tall. With around 60 million flowers it is the largest inflorescence in the plant kingdom. In the fishtail palms, *Caryota* and related species, inflorescences are produced successively all down the stem, quite a sight sometimes in the Palm House.

At the time the Palm House was built it was thought that most palms were dioecious, that is, producing separate male and female plants. This is true for some genera, of which *Chamaedorea* is well represented in the Palm House. There are also hermaphrodite palms. However, most palms are monoecious and bear flowers in several ways, the commonest being in groups of three, two male surrounding a central female and generally maturing first so making self-pollination unlikely. It was also believed in Victorian times that all palms were wind-pollinated, but recent research shows that a huge range of insects may be involved (often species-specific in the case of weevils) or even mammals, such as bats.

Reproduction by vegetative means is uncommon in palms. Some clustering species can be reproduced in cultivation by division and some, particularly *Chamaedorea*, by air layering. However, propagation from seed is the usual method. Seed is generally borne singly in brightly coloured fleshy fruit, probably adapted to dispersal by animals. The family contains the largest seed in the plant kingdom, that of the double coconut from the Seychelles. The fruits sometimes weigh as much as 18 kg. On the other hand, some small understorey palms bear tiny fruits of 4–5 mm across. Thereafter palms grow at a varied rate, very slowly in *Lodoicea*, which can reach ages of 350 years or more, and very fast with others (especially if well nourished); the African oil palm, for example, can begin to bear fruit in under three years from seed.

Palms live in a great variety of habitats but the greatest concentrations are in the tropical lowlands, and on islands, where many species are endemic. Some species exist in vast stands which totally dominate the landscape. This is particularly common in swamp palms such as *Nypa* and *Metroxylon* in South-east Asia and *Mauritia* in the Amazon basin, but also occurs in areas subject to seasonal drought as with *Copernicia* in Brazil and Paraguay and *Hyphaene* in Africa. More often palms exist as one element of the mixed flora of a vegetative type but they are always richest and most diverse in the lowland rainforests of South-east Asia and South America. Mountain palms probably evolved from lowland communities. The richest montane palm flora exists in the South American Andes, where the tallest of all palms, the wax palms (*Ceroxylon*), are found. They form a community with *Aiphanes*, *Prestoea*, *Euterpe* and *Chamaedorea*, all of which are represented in either the Palm or Temperate Houses at Kew. Further evolution in the Americas is represented by the stemless palms of savannah areas such as *Allagoptera* and some species of *Syagrus*, and palms of sand dune areas such as some species of *Sabal*, which are able to withstand drought.

Apart from the semi-desert palms such as *Phoenix* and *Hyphaene*, most palm genera grow on moist, acidic soils. Some genera exist on limey soils, rarely in South-east Asia but more commonly in the New World. A whole bed in the centre transept of the Palm House is devoted to these tropical palms, species of *Gaussia*, *Coccothrinax* and *Thrinax*, which are adapted to seasonal drought, limey soil and higher light conditions. Their more subtropical counterparts such as *Brahea* are planted in the Temperate House. Many of these have attractively glaucous leaves, perhaps an adaptation to reflecting some of the harsh light of their environment.

Tree palms are used widely in the tropics and subtropics for landscaping. This is because many species with compact root systems transplant well. Using modern tree spades and winches, avenues can be created quite quickly and new roots often form above the level of the old.

About 30 palms are very useful to humankind. For food uses the kernels of many fruits or the fruit flesh itself yield oil which is important in the manufacture of margarines and other edible fats and cattle food. The main species involved are the African and American oil palms, *Elaeis guineensis*, *E. oleifera* and hybrids between them, which are grown as plantation crops. Many species yield carbohydrates of local importance to subsistence communities, particularly the Papuasian sago, *Metroxylon sagu*. The terminal bud or 'cabbage' of some species is edible, but harvesting kills the stem. The resulting 'hearts of palm' are expensive and sometimes called 'millionaire's salad'. The profuse pollen of most palms is important forage for honey-bees, again of some local importance. Local communities also ferment sap to produce palm wine or toddy, or distill it into alcohol called arrak, or reduce it by evaporation to produce a brown palm sugar like maple candy, called jaggery. Coconuts yield milk and flesh which, when dried, is called copra, the greatest production being in India and Sri Lanka. In Central and South America the fruits of the peach palm, *Bactris gasipaes*, are a feature of local markets.

Manufactured palm products include soap, cosmetics, glycerine and synthetic rubber (from palm oils) and polishes, carbon paper and gramophone records (from palm waxes). Fibre from various species yields raffia and also piassava, used in street brooms (mainly from Brazilian and West African wild sources), and coir from coconuts, mainly from Sri Lanka and India, is used for matting and doormats, rugs and cable coverings. The seed of the ivory nut palm (*Phytelephas*) is very hard and is used to make high-quality buttons. The leaves of various species are used for thatching, fans, basketry, hats, ropes,

Palm products are part of daily life in the tropics. These baskets were photographed in the Kalimantan Barat province of Indonesian Borneo.

brushes, forage for livestock, cigarette papers, writing materials and impromptu umbrellas. The trunks are useful for building piles, and as a source of tannin, as well as providing rough fibre for wallboard, cork substitutes and stuffing for upholstery. Various palm fruits are used as sources of dyes.

The rattan palms are an important economic group in South-east Asia, where they are used to produce basketry and form the raw material of the cane furniture industry. Most rattan is harvested from the wild, but attempts are being made to grow it as a plantation crop for smallholders, particularly in Indonesia. This decade has seen a steady increase in demand. A world trade of over 1 billion $US, traditionally operated via Singapore and Hong Kong, is increasingly being carried out by the producing countries themselves. Several species are grown in the Palm House, although their extreme thorniness makes them hard to handle.

The five palms of highest economic importance overall are the African oil palm, *Elaeis guineensis*, the coconut, *Cocos nucifera*, the date, *Phoenix dactylifera*, which is the oldest cultivated palm, the carnauba and ouricury wax palms of north-east Brazil, *Copernicia prunifera* and *Syagrus coronata* and the betel nut, *Areca catechu*, which is commonly chewed by the peoples of South-east Asia and India.

Kew's collection of palms is currently rich in sizeable species from the Americas, in common with most European collections. It is also rich in younger plants of South-east Asian species, particularly forest-floor palms, and rare palms of Madagascar. Over the past century more and more temperate palms have been transferred to the Temperate House, while some small tropical palms have already been planted in the Princess of Wales Conservatory, where they are enjoying the humidification system. These understorey palms are considered an evolutionarily advanced group. However, they are also threatened, naturally by falling trees, but also by the rapid clearance of tropical rainforest. This not only causes plant loss but also reduces regeneration, because these species need a dense canopy to provide the shade to which their seedlings are adapted. Kew's aim is to demonstrate the diversity within palms as a whole and to maintain a stock of endangered species grown from wild collected seed from those areas most threatened by loss of habitat due to population pressure, shifting cultivation and logging.

Note

The recent taxonomic classification of palms by Dransfield and Uhl (1987) recognises six subfamilies of the family Palmae, most of them showing a distinct northern or southern hemisphere bias in distribution. These have 14 tribes between them. The Coryphoid palms have three tribes, two of them mainly from the northern hemisphere and one from the southern; the Calamoid palms (predominantly South-east Asian) have two; the Nypoid are represented by one genus with one species only, *Nypa fruticans*, the mangrove palm; the Ceroxyloid palms of the southern hemisphere have three tribes; the largest group, the Arecoid palms (mostly southern hemisphere) have six tribes and the Phytelephantoid is represented by only three South American genera. This classification is used in the following descriptions of palms planted in the restored Palm House.

Palms of the Americas

The American flora contains about 1102 palm species. The following are displayed in the centre transept.

Acoelorraphe wrightii, the Everglades palm, is a clump-forming fan palm native to the Everglades swamps of southern Florida and the only species in its genus. It is also found in the West Indies and Central America. In full sun it will grow fairly slowly to 12 metres, producing reddish-brown matted trunks, bright green leaves with orange, spiny stalks and handsome, orange, pea-like fruits which turn black when ripe. This is a Coryphoid palm. It grows in the shallow island 'hammock' vegetation of the Everglades along with mahogany and the lily-like *Crinum americanum*. It is also widely planted as an ornamental.

The Everglades palm, Acoelorraphe wrightii, lives in the swamplands of southern Florida in the United States.

Aiphanes is a genus of around 38 species, mostly from northern South America. They belong to the Cocoid tribe of the Arecoid subfamily and are feather palms with sharp black spines on the stem and leaves (presumably to protect against predation by herbivores). Some have rather ruffled leaves. The chonta palm, *A. caryotifolia*, from Colombia, Venezuela and Ecuador grows rapidly to 10 metres, as does the coyure palm, *A. acanthophylla*, from Puerto Rico. Both of these have red fruits. The chonta palm needs the moisture and shade of the tropical rainforest understorey, especially when young. The coyure palm is now rare in Puerto Rico.

Allagoptera arenaria is a small, stemless Cocoid palm growing in clumps to around 1.8 metres and has feather leaves which are silvery underneath. This is a seashore palm which grows in the sand dunes of eastern Brazil in full sun. It is a highly specialised member of the Cocoid group and is vulnerable in the wild.

Astrocaryum mexicanum is a small Cocoid palm of the lowlands of Mexico and Central America, growing to 2–4 metres. Its trunk and leaf stalks are covered with black spines, as are the fruits, the kernels of which are edible, with a flavour like coconut. The leaves are dark green on the upper surface and whitish underneath. This species has been the subject of extremely detailed and prolonged ecological research in Mexico. The genus is closely related to *Bactris* (q.v.) and *Aiphanes* (q.v.).

Bactris is a large Cocoid genus of 239 species, second only in size to *Calamus*, but is entirely New World in distribution, with species from Mexico and the Caribbean southwards, but with most in Brazil. They are almost all very spiny and all so far studied are pollinated by beetles attracted by the musty smell and heat produced by the inflorescences. The most important economically is *B. gasipaes*, the peach palm or pejibayé, which is now only found in cultivation. It produces apricot-sized fruits which are prepared by boiling in salted water and have a high nutritional value. This crop is the subject of breeding programmes from selected germplasm in Costa Rica to produce stock for plantation cropping. The 'cabbage' also makes good eating. The peach palm reaches 20 metres but the related *B. guineensis* from the landward side of mangrove swamps in Central America reaches only 4 metres. The latter is a clump-forming understorey palm producing purplish-black fruits.

Chamaedorea is a Ceroxyloid genus of about 100 species from Central America southwards to Bolivia and Brazil. Most of them are understorey plants of moist soils, with one or two being more tolerant of sun and preferring limestone. Kew has a particularly good collection of these, with around 25 species, and they grow well in the Palm House (with a few in the Temperate House) taking up little space and fruiting very successfully. Most species are small and tend either to form a single stem with a small tuft of terminal leaves or to form dense clusters. One species (*C. elatior*) is a climber, while a few have a creeping habit. All are dioecious, i.e. they produce separate male and female plants. Some produce brilliant cream-coloured inflorescences, those of one or two species being fleshy and edible. We tend to know this group from *C. elegans*, the parlour palm, which is probably the commonest palm sold as a houseplant, though it is vulnerable in the wild. Many others have commercial potential because of their ease of cultivation, relative cold-tolerance and ability to enjoy the low light of room conditions. Their inflorescences also make colourful material for flower arranging. All the following species are Mexican unless otherwise noted:

C. cataractarum is a clump-forming species with profuse finely pinnate leaves.

C. concolor, to 3 metres, develops large terminal leaflets and an orange inflorescence up to 60 cm long. Its fruits are red.

C. ernesti-augusti, to 1.8 metres, has simple oblong leaves and a prominently ringed trunk which sometimes develops aerial or bracing roots. The male inflorescence is green, the female green when young, becoming orange in fruit. Distribution extends into Guatemala and Honduras.

C. erumpens grows to 2–4 metres in a multi-stemmed clump of rather bamboo-like habit with pinnate leaves. Inflorescences burst through the sheaths and are orange, contrasting with the black fruits.

C. falcifera is a Guatemalan species with solitary stems 1–6 metres tall with a tuft of shiny pinnate leaves. The sickle-shaped fruits are orange, turning black.

C. fragrans is a Peruvian clump-forming species with two-pronged (bifid) leaves. It is unusual in the genus in needing sandy, poor soil and low humidity as well as low light. Its flowers are intensely fragrant.

C. glaucifolia is a relatively sun-tolerant species with thinnish, glaucous grey-green leaves. It forms a single stem up to 7 metres with pinnate leaves up to 2 metres long. Male inflorescences are green, the female orange-red in fruit and spectacular. Fruits are green turning black. This species also develops stilt roots. Distribution extends from South Mexico into Guatemala.

C. klotzschiana forms a single trunk to 2.5 metres. The pinnate leaves have attractively wide, glossy leaflets grouped together and held in different planes. Female inflorescences are orange in fruit while the fruits themselves are black.

C. metallica is a highly ornamental species with great potential as a houseplant but endangered in the wild. Its leaves are wedge-shaped, leathery and with a metallic bluish hue. It grows fairly slowly to 1.8 metres. Fruits are black on orange infructescences and are easily produced following hand pollination.

C. microspadix is similar to *C. erumpens* in having a multi-stemmed, open, bamboo-like habit. It grows to 3 metres and produces yellow inflorescences and orange-red fruits. This eastern Mexican species is moderately cold tolerant. It is common in collections but vulnerable in the wild.

C. oblongata is a single-stemmed species growing to 3 metres with orange inflorescences and dark green fruits turning black at maturity.

C. radicalis is a creeping species from eastern Mexican oak and cedar woods, tolerating limey soils and some dryness. It suckers in cultivation. Fruits ripen to orange-red. This species is vulnerable in the wild.

C. stolonifera is a species which suckers in such a way as to make it almost a groundcover palm. It reaches 1 metre. Most plants in cultivation seem to be female and it is now thought to be extinct in the wild.

C. tepejilote is a fast-growing species reaching 3 or even 7 metres and has rather erect pinnate leaves from stems with swollen joints and aerial roots. It is cultivated for its edible cream-coloured inflorescences. Fruits are green, ripening to black.

×⅓

×1

Coccothrinax is a West Indian genus of about 49 species of Coryphoid fan palms, most of which are found in conditions of bright light and dryish limestone soils. Like *Thrinax* (to which they are closely related) they are grown in the Palm House because of their heat requirement though they are not plants of the rainforest. All are slow-growing, most have beautiful stem fibre and are grown as ornamentals. Several species are used for thatching and making brooms. The species we hold are *C. alta*, from Puerto Rico, *C. dussiana* from Guadeloupe and *C. fragrans* and *C. martii*, both from Cuba, which is a centre of diversity in the genus.

Copernicia hospita represents a genus of 25 species from South America and the Caribbean. These Coryphoid fan palms are very slow growing but some ultimately become very large. They are locally important in making hats, brooms, panniers and for thatching. One of the South American species, *C. prunifera*, is of great economic value as the source of carnauba wax, which can easily be flaked from the leaves. As wax is basically a protection against sunlight it is not surprising that these are sun-adapted palms mostly from dryish savannah areas, like *Thrinax* and *Coccothrinax*. *C. hospita* is endemic to Cuba, where it grows to 8 metres and produces a magnificent fragrant inflorescence up to 2.5 metres long. It is the waxiest of all the Cuban species. When mature these palms produce massive trunks, also greyish, rather like solid concrete pillars.

The genus Chamaedorea *(see pp. 36–37) is an important group of understorey palms from the Americas. Several are already common in the pot plant trade; others, such as the glaucous-blue* C. metallica, *have great ornamental potential.*

Cryosophila nana, the rootspine palm, is a Mexican species of the Coryphoid group, growing on limestone soils in dryish woods. A distinctive feature is the development of much-branched root spines on the solitary stem. Where stilt roots develop they too are prickly. The fan leaves are densely woolly felted underneath and the fruits are white. This palm is vulnerable in the wild.

Elaeis oleifera, the American oil palm, is a Cocoid palm from central and northern South America, where it grows in swampy soils and sandy areas of impeded drainage. It is a less important source of oil than its African relative (*E. guineensis*, q.v.) and only grows to about half its size, 8–10 metres. It is unusual for species of one genus to be distributed over more than one continent. It is thought to be vulnerable in the wild.

Euterpe edulis is an Arecoid palm of South America, important economically as the source of the sweetest 'cabbage', used as a local food and tinned as 'hearts of palm'. It is a tall, fast-growing palm with a distinct crownshaft, vulnerable in the wild because of over-exploitation.

Gaussia is a Central American and Caribbean Ceroxyloid genus of four species, all of them adapted to growing on limestone.

G. attenuata from Puerto Rico reaches 7–9 metres and develops a trunk which tapers markedly from an enlarged base from which emerge woody roots which creep over the surface of the soil between the rocks

38

in which the plant grows. This palm produces a long inflorescence (1.3 metres) and bears cherry-like fruits.

G. maya, the Maya palm, grows in association with the Mayan Indian archaeological sites in Guatemala and Belize. It grows fairly rapidly to 20 metres, producing a ringed trunk also swollen at the base. This palm may produce up to 17 inflorescences at once all along the trunk, at various stages of development from bud to fruiting stage.

G. princeps, the llume or sierra palm, from Cuba, closely resembles *G. attenuata*, except that it is shorter (5–7 metres). It is rare in the wild.

Orbignya phalerata, the babassu palm, is a massive Cocoid feather palm closely related to *Attalea*, *Scheelea*, and *Maximiliana*, with fronds which emerge nearly vertically from the ground and form narrow crowns to 9 metres or so before any trunk appears. The taxonomy of these genera is not yet resolved but all species bear male and female flowers on separate inflorescences or together in one, both on the same plant, an unusual arrangement. Most species bear fruit, which is an important local source of oil. *O. phalerata* may reach 20 metres and comes from Brazil.

Polyandrococos pectinata, the buri palm, is a Cocoid tree palm from the Mato Grosso, Brazil. It grows to 7–10 metres and produces a large, unbranched inflorescence up to 1.2 metres in length with showy yellow stamens. The deep orange fruits are edible and are locally important as livestock feed. The trunks may be used as building material. This species is distinct from *P. caudescens*, which was once thought to be the only species in the genus.

Prestoea montana, the mountain cabbage palm, is an Arecoid palm from the Lesser Antilles where it occurs in large stands in wet montane forest, usually on limestone. It attains 3–17 metres and usually develops aerial prop roots at the base of the swollen stem. The fruit is black and forms a food source for flocks of parrots. The 'cabbage' is edible and much sought after. This palm is rare in cultivation.

Sabal is a genus of about 14 species of Coryphoid fan palms mostly found on islands in the Caribbean and on the land which fringes it, but it also extends into Texas and Pacific Central America. Most species have costapalmate leaves and all have, as juveniles, subterranean stems, which grow downwards before ascending, supposedly an adaptation to protect against fire. Most species of *Sabal*, like many *Thrinax* and *Coccothrinax*, are palms of dry areas and sandy coastal fringes and need good light. However, unlike them, most are fast growing and massive. We accommodate two species in the Palm House:

S. bermudana, the Bermuda palmetto, grows slowly to 5–8 metres, often with a leaning stem. Unlike most *Sabal* species, it grows in moist, acid soils and is now threatened in the wild by the expansion of tourism. In the eighteenth and nineteenth centuries it was an important source of material for making hats.

S. minor, the dwarf or blue palmetto, has a bluish palmate leaf. It rarely forms a trunk and tolerates dry and cool conditions. The arching inflorescences grow up to 2 metres long and produce glossy black fruits.

Syagrus is now recognized as a genus of 32 South American Cocoid palms closely related to the coconut and mostly from dryish areas.

S. amara, the overtop palm, from the shores of the Lesser Antilles, grows fairly rapidly to 20 metres, producing orange fruits containing a bitter milk. Until recently it was included in a separate genus, *Rhyticocos*. It is rare in the wild.

S. flexuosa from the savannahs of Brazil develops a very slender trunk and arching fronds of narrow leaflets.

S. romanzoffiana, the queen palm, from Brazil, Paraguay and Uruguay has been grown under many names, including *Cocos plumosa*, but more recently as *Arecastrum*. It is a quick-growing, moisture-loving species much used as a street tree in southern California and Florida because it transplants easily. In South America the orange fruits are used for pig food and the trunk for construction. We also have the variety *australe*, which may reach 25 metres in height.

S. schizophylla, the arikury palm, also from Brazil, produces a short trunk, 2–4 metres tall. It yields edible orange fruits and grows in full sun in very sandy soils in 'cerradão' type vegetation – vegetation of open savannah and transitional forest.

Thrinax are a group of Caribbean fan palms closely related to *Coccothrinax* and, like them, adapted to dryish soils of limestone areas. They are known as thatch palms as they are widely used for roofing material. Many are species of the shoreline which are adapted to wind pollination and most have stem fibre which is used in basketry.

T. floridana, the peaberry palm, is a slow-growing species eventually reaching 9 metres; it produces fruits like white peas.

T. microcarpa, the brittle thatch palm, grows occasionally to 10 metres with leaves silvered underneath and tiny white fruits.

The tallest tree palms

In the two large beds beneath the dome we grow tall tree palms from throughout the world, rather than just from the Americas. These species are described below. It is from these that we hope to recreate in years to come the superb silhouette of palm crowns which were cut down prior to the 1980s restoration. The tallest palm restored to this area in 1989 was an 8-metre *Ptychosperma* from Samoa.

Actinorhytis calapparia is a tall tree palm native to New Guinea but widely planted in Malaysia and South-east Asia, where it reaches 13 metres or more. It is a highly ornamental Arecoid palm with arching feather leaves up to 3 metres long and a slender crownshaft, below which are produced large branched inflorescences. The red fruits are remarkably large, usually bigger than hen's eggs, and have local medicinal uses as well as being a substitute for the betel nut (see *Areca catechu*). This is one of the most beautiful of the palms of lowland rainforest and develops masses of roots at the stem base.

The sugar palm, **Arenga pinnata**, is an important source of sugar, palm wine, fibre, sago and leaves for thatching. The dense mass of this palm produced quite an effect in the Palm House in the mid-Victorian period with its huge (2-metre) inflorescences. Being a solitary palm this species dies when its successive flowering is completed. It is a very important economic plant in South-east Asia.

Borassodendron borneense is a massive Coryphoid fan palm from Borneo with a stout single trunk. Male and female flowers are borne on separate trees. The leaves are carried on long stalks, producing a heavy crown. The interfoliar inflorescences hang down, the female bearing large three-seeded fruit. The 'cabbage' of this species is sought after by local people and the young leaves are relished by orang-utan. It is vulnerable in the wild.

The coconut, *Cocos nucifera*, is economically the most important of all palms worldwide both in terms of commercial cropping and export and on account of a host of local uses. It is a fast-growing Arecoid palm, providing it is well fed, and is also one of the palms which is most demanding of heat. It is a plant mainly of the coastal strands of the tropics and warmer subtropics from 20 to 25° each side of the Equator. Its origin, long disputed, is now generally thought to have been in the western Pacific and eastern Indian Ocean islands. Coconuts will grow to 30 metres or so and usually develop a characteristically leaning trunk, even as small specimens. They flower continuously in the tropics, though rarely under glass, at least in Europe, and will fruit when only five years old, the fruit taking eight to ten months to mature. A good tree will yield up to 75 fruits a year. The main crops are the fruit, which is used locally or exported, and the dried kernel (copra), used in cooking and for the manufacture of coconut oil. This oil is then used to produce soap, shampoo, detergent, synthetic rubber and brake fluid. Copra meal is used as a livestock feed and as fertiliser. The husk of the nut, coir, is used to make matting and the palm is often planted as an ornamental, especially in coastal areas. There are several races of coconut which have been bred for resistance to disease, the most serious of which is lethal yellowing, caused by a mycoplasma-like organism. 'Lethal Yellows' became a serious problem in the Caribbean in the early decades of this century and spread through Florida in the 1970s, attacking many species of palm besides the coconut. These, and coconuts themselves, are subject to strict quarantining. The susceptible cultivar, 'Jamaica Tall', has now mainly been replaced by the resistant 'Malayan Dwarf', of which the most ornamental is the yellow form with golden leaf stalks and fruits.

Plectocomia elongata var. *philippinensis* is a massive climbing rattan of the Calamoid subfamily from poor soil sites in the Philippines. It is extremely fast growing and a different variety of the same species was the first palm to reach the top of the Palm House in 1850, two years after planting! The palm suckers freely and produces pinnate leaves up to 4 metres long ending in an extended midrib which is viciously armed with black spines, which function for the plant like grappling irons. The pendulous inflorescence is up to 1.2 metres long and very beautiful, though signalling the death of that particular stem. Unfortunately this rattan is useless for furniture making, having a very soft pith, though it is used for rough basket work and making coat hangers.

Ravenea moorei is one of ten species of a genus of Ceroxyloid palm from Madagascar and the Comoros, mostly from tropical rainforest. It has a robust solitary stem and rather erect pinnate leaves, interfoliar inflorescences and brightly coloured fruit. This is currently our largest specimen of Malagasy palm.

Roystonea oleracea, the Carib royal palm from the Caribbean islands, is a fast-growing Arecoid palm of the type used to form avenues in the tropics. It has a fine green crownshaft.

Veitchia winin from Vanuatu represents a group of around 18 species of fast-growing Arecoid palms, most of which are elegant ornamentals popular for landscaping. Most come from Fiji and other islands in the south-west Pacific, but one species occurs in the Philippines. *V. winin* reaches 21 metres and is one of the tallest. All species have elegant green crownshafts; they are rapid-growing and produce attractive clusters of red fruit. Several have edible 'cabbages' and the trunks are used in house-building and boat-building. The genus is closely related to the Australian *Carpentaria acuminata*, planted in the north wing.

The beautiful stilt-rooted palm Verschaffeltia splendida *is a threatened species from the Seychelles and is not commonly seen in European botanic gardens.*

Verschaffeltia splendida is an Arecoid palm from the Seychelles, where it grows on steep rocky slopes not higher than 600 metres above sea level. It will grow to 10 metres, producing huge undivided leaves up to 2 metres long and forked at the tip. The stem is densely covered with black spines and is supported by a mass of prominent stilt roots up to 2 metres long. This dramatic palm, which is usually solitary in the wild, is tender and is therefore common in cultivation only in very tropical gardens where it is sometimes planted in avenues, or in groups (as at Singapore). It is vulnerable in the wild.

Palms of Africa and Madagascar

Visitors to the south wing of the Palm House will notice fewer palms here than anywhere else, showing clearly the impoverishment of the palm flora in the continent of Africa. Various authors have attributed this phenomenon to the extinction of genera caused by climatic change.

It is also noticeable that the palms which are displayed here originate from the Seychelles and Madagascar. The flora of Madagascar is extremely rich in endemics, as are so many islands where evolution has pursued a line of separate development. Madagascar separated from Africa some 100 million years ago. Several new genera have recently been discovered on the island including *Marojejya* (1955), *Halmoorea* (1984) and the forest coconut *Voanioala* (1986), which has been shown at Kew to have more than twice the number of chromosomes of any other monocotyledon. In addition five genera and 11 species are endemic to the volcanic Mascarene Islands near Madagascar: Mauritius, Réunion and Rodrigues. In time we hope to display more of these if we successfully raise them beyond seedling stage.

Dictyosperma album, the hurricane or princess palm, is a fast-growing Arecoid palm often grown as an ornamental. It comes from the Mascarenes, where it is endangered in the wild on all three islands and nearing extinction. It is a lowland species needing good soil moisture to attain 12 metres. It produces an attractive whitish-green crownshaft, reddish-yellow flowers enclosed in a paddle-like bract and purplish fruits. This is a genus of one species and three varieties; var. *aureum* is smaller and more slender, with yellow-flushed petioles and veins.

Elaeis guineensis, the African oil palm, is the most commercially important oil-producing plant of the tropics. It is an Arecoid palm of the Cocoeae and has a less commercially important relative in the Americas (see *E. oleifera*). This is a very fast-growing palm, flowering and cropping at three to five years old. It will reach 16 metres and produces a dense head of pinnate leaves 4 or 5 metres long with saw-toothed stalks. The male and female flowers are produced in separate bunches but on the same tree and usually in phases of three to six months, which is an uncommon feature in palms. The fruits develop in compact spiny clusters between the leaves and take up to six months to ripen. Huge plantations of this crop are spread throughout the tropics, often of named commercial clones. Locally its leaves are used for thatch and it can be tapped for wine. After the oil is expressed the waste is used for cattle food.

Hyophorbe is a remarkable and highly endangered Ceroxyloid genus endemic to the Mascarenes. All species have arched pinnate fronds and prominent, handsome crownshafts below which appear stubby, upward-pointing inflorescences.

H. lagenicaulis, the bottle palm, is so-called because it normally produces a trunk swollen to twice its width or more at the base. It only grows to 2–6 metres and produces characteristically few leaves, often just three, which are arching and laterally twisted. It produces a fringe of inflorescences at about eye level, making it highly desired in ornamental collections, where it is usually planted in groups. The flowers are mignonette-scented. In the wild only a few plants remain, on Round Island.

H. verschaffeltii, the spindle palm, is taller at 5–10 metres and has a spindle-shaped trunk with a waxy crownshaft bearing few leaves at a time. It grows in dry and salt-laden soil on the island of Rodrigues. It bears purple fruits and is also highly sought after by collectors. As a young plant the crownshaft is often rather triangular, above a fine grey trunk attractively ringed by the leaf scars.

Latania is a genus of three species of Coryphoid fan palms, also native to the Mascarene Islands. Two of them are endangered in the wild and one, *L. verschaffeltii*, is rated as vulnerable. All species are highly ornamental and are common in botanic gardens. They prefer sun and seasonal drought in the winter. All have separate male and female plants.

L. loddigesii, the blue latan, from Mauritius, grows fairly rapidly to 11 metres, producing a swollen stem base and large costapalmate leaves of a fine glaucous-blue hue. The young petioles are reddish but develop a brownish wool with age. The male inflorescence is long and pendent, the female very dense and erect and the fruits are pear-shaped.

L. verschaffeltii, the yellow latan, produces denser leaf growth with deep orange petioles and leaf veins, especially when young.

The poverty of palms in continental Africa contrasts with the wealth of palms found on the island of Madagascar where there are numerous endemic species, and probably many more still to be discovered. This is a palmlet of the forest floor, Dypsis mocquerysiana.

The coco de mer or double coconut, **Lodoicea maldivica**, is a huge Coryphoid fan palm from the Seychelles, the only species in the genus. It is not native in the Maldive Islands, the species name being based on *Cocos maldivica*, the first name published from nuts washed up there. This extraordinary palm grows slowly to a majestic 30 metres, although it is so difficult to transplant and so sensitive to cold that it is rarely seen in botanical collections beyond the juvenile stage, where it produces one or two arching and almost triangular leaves. It is reputedly easier to grow if germinated *in situ* rather than transplanted. At maturity the leaves are costapalmate and reach 6 metres by 4 metres across. Male and female flowers appear at the age of 14–30 years on different trees. The female flowers are the largest in palms. The nuts are two-lobed, remain on the tree for five to eight years and contain the largest seed in the entire plant kingdom. In the wild the palm grows on the low slopes of Praslin and Curieuse Islands and is considered vulnerable. The Seychelles government has declared a national park to conserve it and is the sole distributor of the remarkable fruits, an important source of tourist revenue. Every part of the plant was once used – the leaves for thatch, the trunks for building materials and water troughs, the leaf down for upholstery and pillows, while the seeds make a good vegetable ivory. The plant has been the source of many legends. (See pp. 11–12.) In the Palm House we are attempting to grow this beyond the juvenile stage by warming the rooting zone to 25°C with an electrically heated soil warming pad. This may also help with *Nephrosperma vanhoutteanum*, another of the six monotypic genera endemic to the Seychelles, which is tender, uncommon in cultivation and vulnerable in the wild.

Neodypsis is an Arecoid genus of 14 species from the rainforests of Madagascar. It is closely related to *Chrysalidocarpus*, of which *C. lutescens*, the yellow bamboo palm, is one of the commonest palms sold as a houseplant. The genus varies between single-stemmed tree palms and clustering palms. More work is needed on the taxonomy, distribution and conservation status of these palms.

N. decaryi, the triangle palm, is a fast-growing tree species reaching only 6 metres but producing a three-sided arrangement of leaf bases, which accounts for its common name. The leaves are stiffly erect in growth and the inflorescences arise between them. This is an important landscape palm of moderate size. It is severely threatened in the wild by overcollection of seed for the international horticultural trade.

Phoenicophorium borsigianum, the thief palm, is a species of lowland origin on the Seychelles, where it is vulnerable in the wild. It is a solitary palm of moderate size with large undivided bright green leaves marginally lobed. The entire plant bears black spines when young. This is valued as an ornamental in the Seychelles and the leaves are used as thatch. The story of the theft of this palm when first introduced to Kew and the controversy of its naming is described on pp. 10–11.

The Madagascar triangle palm, Neodypsis decaryi, *is named after its three-ranked arrangement of leaves. The demand for seed from nurserymen supplying the landscaping trade has led to severe pressure on the limited native stands.*

Palms of Asia, Australasia and the Pacific

The north wing houses the palms distributed through Asia and the Pacific. These areas are rich in palms, particularly in understorey species and in rattans, the climbing palms.

Areca is a genus of about 60 species, widely distributed throughout India and South-east Asia. Most are dwarf understorey palms or moderate-sized rainforest species, some with very limited local distribution and precise habitat requirements.

A. catechu, the betel nut, one of the larger species, forms a slender trunk topped by a fine green crownshaft. This produces a nut which is sliced, mixed with lime and the leaves of *Piper betle* and chewed. The alkaloid in the nut is a mild narcotic. The mixture stains the mouth orange and chewing it can be a ceremony for which elaborate silver betel-chewing kits are sometimes seen on sale. The palm is frequently seen by the roadside or in gardens but is also cultivated as a plantation crop. The fruits are a source of tannin for dyeing and the 'cabbage' is edible. It is a fast-growing species and a good ornamental.

A. triandra from India, Malaysia and Indo-China grows to 7 metres and suckers to form a clump of slender stems, occasionally with stilt roots. The trunks are green and attractively ringed, terminating in a smooth green crownshaft. The fragrant white flowers are followed by orange-scarlet fruits. It is a variable species with many local forms.

The genus **Arenga** contains about 17 species with a wide distribution throughout South-east Asia. They are moisture-loving rainforest palms which grow in deep soils, frequently clustering in habit and many with densely matted black stem fibre. They flower like most species of *Caryota*, producing inflorescences successively down the trunk, the stem then dying, or, with multi-stemmed species, then being replaced by a sucker. The fruits of most species contain irritant crystals.

A. engleri from Taiwan and the Ryukyu Islands is a dwarf understorey palm growing to a maximum of 3 metres but often spreading considerably. It produces several stems covered with black fibre and the long-stalked leaves are white underneath as in all other species of the genus. The fruits are purplish-red. This species has an edible 'cabbage' and orange flowers.

A. microcarpa from New Guinea and some of the Indonesian Islands is another clustering species and grows to 7–10 metres. It is a very important local source of sago.

A. porphyrocarpa from Sumatra and Java forms a dense cluster of slender stems growing to 2 metres. The leaves are unusual, with widely spaced, rather jagged leaflets. The interfoliar inflorescences are creamish-green and the fruits are purple.

Calamus is the largest genus in the palm family with around 370 species, all of them dioecious and many either vulnerable or rare in the wild. Around 90 per cent are climbing species of rattan and this is the genus which yields most of the commercially important 'cane' used in the cane furniture trade and often mistaken for bamboo. *Calamus* is distributed throughout India, South-east Asia and the Malay Archipelago to Queensland and Fiji, with one species in Africa. The greatest number of species occur in west Malaysia, Borneo and New Guinea. Their habitat requirements are variable – from monsoon forest to rainforest to littoral mangrove swamps. Most species grow fast to the canopy by internodal elongation, and climb or grapple into it by whip-like hooked growths modified from sterile flower spikes or from the leaf midribs. The leaf sheaths are also very spiny and must be removed to reveal the smooth cane inside. To many people this makes them awkward forest weeds. In Queensland they are called wait-a-while vines or lawyer canes. They are not common in botanical collections due to these growth habits. They are commercially important as the raw material of a forest industry (from wild harvested plants) and also as a small-scale plantation crop. The genus is undergoing study at Kew by Dr J Dransfield. The representative of this genus in the Palm House is *C. longipinna*, which suckers freely from the roots. The most important commercial species are *C. caesius*, *C. manan* and *C. trachycoleus*. Other rattan genera planted in the Palm House are *Ceratolobus* (north wing) and the giant *Plectocomia* (centre transept).

Carpentaria acuminata is a handsome Arecoid palm from the moist lowland rainforests and salt-water swamps of the Northern Territory in Australia. It is the only species in the genus but is closely related to *Veitchia*. This palm grows quickly to 13–20 metres and develops a long crownshaft below which the inflorescences appear. The crimson fruits that then develop are very handsome and the palm is often planted as an ornamental in Darwin, in Queensland and also in the United States, in southern Florida. It is vulnerable in its wild state.

Carpentaria acuminata
*produces abundant crimson
fruits in its native Australia.
It is vulnerable in the wild.*

The talipot palm, Corypha umbraculifera, *is a monocarpic palm which produces a vast inflorescence of up to 10 million flowers and then, exhausted, dies.*

The fishtail palms, **Caryota** species, are immediately distinguishable because of their bipinnate leaves, unique in the palm family. In the most recent revision of palm taxonomy they have been included as Arecoid palms but in their own subtribe (Caryoteae). There are about 12 species, some growing very tall (*C. urens, C. no, C. rumphiana*), which are mostly very useful in local economies because they yield sago, timber, thatch and leaf wool for wadding.

C. urens of south India and Sri Lanka is an important source of toddy and is known as the kitul or jaggery palm. *C. mitis* is grown in the Palm House. It is a multi-stemmed species which is found from Indo-China to the western part of the Malay archipelago, where it is common, especially in secondary forest. The plant grows to 7 metres and flowers appear at the uppermost node and then successively downwards, as in *Arenga*. The stem then dies, usually after five to seven years.

Ceratolobus pseudoconcolor represents another genus of rattan, and is one of six species, all found in South-east Asia. It is distributed in western Java and southern Sumatra, where it is found in lowland tropical rainforest dominated by trees of the Dipterocarpaceae. The plant produces attractively pink-tinged young growth and climbs by a cirrus, an extension of the midrib. The wood is too weak to make it an economically useful rattan. It is endangered in the wild from population pressure in Java and from forest disturbance in Sumatra.

Chambeyronia macrocarpa is a rare Arecoid palm endemic to the rainforests of New Caledonia, where it reaches 20 metres. The outstanding ornamental feature of this palm is the colouration of the young leaves, which are a russet red when young, greening up in about a week. This is a spectacular event, though not common as leafing occurs only once or twice a year. The palm produces arching pinnate leaves with hardly any petiole and a short but well defined crownshaft. The inflorescences are rather stubby and are followed by large red fruits up to 6 cm long. This species is both rare in the wild and uncommon in cultivation.

Corypha umbraculifera, the talipot palm, is one of eight species of massive Coryphoid palms. It is native to southern India and to Sri Lanka, where it is the national floral emblem. This palm is extraordinary because of its monocarpic flowering. When it is about 30–40 years old and about 25 metres tall, with a trunk 1 metre in diameter, the stem elongates into a pyramidal inflorescence above the leaves which may add another 7 metres to its height. This huge suprafoliar inflorescence is the largest found in any flowering plant and may contain anything up to 10 million white flowers. There is some evidence of synchronous flowering in these palms, as in some bamboos. Slowly the palm then dies, relying upon its seed to perpetuate the species.

This palm grows very slowly when young, later producing massive costapalmate leaves up to 5 metres across, the largest of any fan palm and an important local source of thatch and material for tent- and hat-making, umbrellas and writing materials. The seeds are a good source of vegetable ivory. The uprush of sap which occurs just before flowering can be tapped at the base of the inflorescence to ferment into wine. With so many uses it is not surprising that this palm is quite common in villages in Sri Lanka and India. Like *Lodoicea* it can never be expected to flower within the confines of the Palm House and is planted as a botanical curiosity. To see this palm in flower would make any trip to the tropics worthwhile.

Cyrtostachys renda (*C. lakka*), the aptly named sealing wax palm, is a highly ornamental Arecoid palm from the coastal peat swamps of west Malaysia, Thailand, Borneo and Sumatra. It forms an erect clump up to 5–10 metres high by suckering from the base. Its leaf sheaths and petioles are brilliant scarlet. No other palm produces such spectacular crownshafts and the species is a commercially important ornamental, much used for landscaping in Singapore. When it flowers, the infrafoliar inflorescences also develop red stalks. The flowers are green and the fruits black. This palm is endangered in the wild in Thailand and in peninsular Malaysia, but is locally abundant in Borneo and Sumatra.

Hydriastele microspadix is an understorey Arecoid palm from New Guinea, requiring very moist soil and a hot and humid still atmosphere. It occurs on rich soils in lowland rainforest. It is tender with a slow-growing habit and a tendency to scorch in bright light or draught. The palm forms tall slender trunks often clustering at the base and has slender crownshafts. The overall effect is a very erect, columnar clump. This palm has good ornamental potential for shady areas in the warm tropics.

Iguanura wallichiana is an Arecoid palm of the understorey of undisturbed tropical rainforest in Sumatra and in peninsular Malaysia. It rarely reaches 4 metres and has few pinnate leaves without a crownshaft. The leaves are often tinged with a striking brownish-red when young. The flowers are pollinated by various insects, particularly ants, and the fruits are bright red. They are supposed to have contraceptive uses. This is an ornamental understorey palm, uncommon in collections and not easy to grow.

Laccospadix australasica is one of several palms representative of the palm flora of the tropics of Queensland, Australia. This is an Arecoid understorey palm from the montane tropics of north-eastern Queensland, where it is known as the Atherton palm. There is only one species in the genus. It grows to 3 metres (often less) with few leaves on long stalks and with no crownshaft. The most ornamental aspect of the plant are its long spikes of red fruits up to 1 metre in length. The palm is used to deep shade and it prefers a drop in temperature at night.

The genus ***Licuala*** is a Coryphoid genus of about 108 species ranging from India through Malaysia to Queensland, Australia, some of which are rare in the wild. Most have leaves which are circular in outline but are divided into wedge-shaped leaflets. The most dramatic in shape have undivided, circular leaves (*L. grandis* and *L. orbicularis*). *L. grandis*, from Vanuatu, is a spectacular plant with a solitary stem 2–3 metres high and a crown of undulating circular leaves between which the long flower spikes emerge, later developing crimson fruits. In Singapore it is widely grown as a slow-growing pot plant for shady conditions. All licualas are plants of the understorey of tropical rainforests in low-lying areas, including swampy areas subject to flooding. One of the most extraordinary experiences of my life was being taken to a reserve of *Licuala ramsayi* in Queensland where cyclones had taken out the upper storey of the forest, leaving these palms exposed in a huge stand. Below them in the swampy ground the dead fronds could be crunched underfoot while above, the disc-like leaves formed extraordinary silhouettes. Besides the ornamental use of licualas, local people cut the stems as walking-sticks or use the leaves to wrap food.

The sealing wax palm, Cyrtostachys renda, *is endangered in its swampland habitat in Thailand and peninsular Malaysia. The attraction of its brilliant red crownshafts makes it common in the landscape trade operating out of Singapore.*

Nenga is a genus of five South-east Asian species of dwarf understorey palms from undisturbed tropical rainforest. They are Arecoid feather palms which usually develop crownshafts and stilt roots. *N. gajah* grows to 2 metres in the dipterocarp forests of Sumatra, where it is rare. *N. pumila* var. *pachystachya* from Sumatra, Thailand, Malaya and Borneo grows to 2–3 metres in primary forest. These palms are not commonly seen in cultivation.

Phoenix is a genus of 17 species of mainly sun-loving and semi-arid adapted palms displayed, for historic reasons, in the north apse end of the Palm House in their original pots. They are not rainforest plants and prefer dry air. *P. dactylifera,* the date palm, is a very important economic plant, especially in Africa, the Middle East and California, the forms grown being the result of human selection over the centuries to produce fine varieties. In all *Phoenix* the fruits are produced on female trees only if a male is nearby. *P. loureirii,* the pygmy date, grows to 2–3 metres and is used as a landscape plant from eastern India to southern China. Its small fruits are inedible.

4584.

Reeve & Nichols imp.

Wallichia densiflora *is an unusual understorey palm from the Himalayas needing moisture and shade. The flowers appear in cycles, alternating with long periods of vegetative growth.*

P. roebelenii, the roebelin date, is a slender species attaining 3–4 metres from Laos and Vietnam, with an attractive trunk covered with the stumps of old leaf bases. Typically the trunk is wider at the top than the bottom and often leans. The leaves are much softer and more pendent than in other species and it is more shade tolerant. This species is grown commercially as a pot plant. *P. canariensis*, the Canary Island date and *P. theophrasti*, the Cretan date, are grown in the Temperate House. The latter is vulnerable in the wild.

Pinanga is a genus of around 120 mainly Indo-Malayan species of understorey Arecoid palms. Many have great potential as ornamental pot plants, where an adequate temperature can be provided, as most are cold-sensitive. They are not commonly seen outside collections in the tropics. Most species are small, sometimes with many reed-like stems and attractive crownshafts. Some are stilt-rooted. One ornamental feature is mottling on the young leaves of some species, another is the bright colouring of the petioles, infructescences and fruits.

51

P. coronata from Java and Sumatra forms a clump up to 5–8 metres tall of fairly erect-growing fronds. The fruits are dark red.

P. densiflora from Sumatra grows to 2–4 metres in a dense clump and with very broad leaflets. The inflorescence is pink and the fruits black.

P. disticha is a very small clump-forming palmlet from peninsular Malaysia, Thailand and Sumatra reaching 1–2 metres. The leaves are bifid (or irregularly pinnate) and often yellow-mottled. The fruits are black, borne on a bright red spike.

Pritchardia is a genus of 37 species of Coryphoid fan palms from Hawaii, Fiji and surrounding islands. They are known as loulu palms. Thirty-three are endemic to Hawaii, where a high proportion are either endangered or have become extinct in the wild. Mostly they are large, sun-loving fan palms forming stout trunks. They are grown in the Palm House in their original teak containers along with *Phoenix* both as a historical display, commemorating the way palms have been grown in the north wing and because *Phoenix* and *Pritchardia* demonstrate the two main types of palm leaf: feather and fan. All species of *Pritchardia* have beautiful costapalmate leaves, sometimes glaucous, and protected when young by a woolly indumentum. Local people use them as umbrellas and fans. All species are sensitive to cold.

P. arecina is endemic to Maui, where it grows to 11 metres, producing leaves covered underneath with a light yellow wool.

P. hillebrandii is endangered in Hawaii, where it grows to 7 metres, producing a dense crown of grey-green leaves on leaf stalks at least a metre long. Flowers are profuse in this species and the fruits are black. *P. kaalae* from Oahu is also endangered and grows to 10 metres with light green leaves.

P. pacifica from Tonga and Fiji grows to 10 metres with leaves covered with white down when young.

P. remota is endangered on Hawaii. The greyish-green leaves have attractively pendent tips.

Ptychosperma species are Arecoid feather palms, with about 28 occurring in New Guinea and the surrounding island groups and some in northern Australia. Many are fine ornamentals, known in cultivation for over a century in collections or as landscape plants. They currently represent some of our largest Palm House specimens. Some are solitary species and some are clump-formers. All have prominent crownshafts with infrafoliar inflorescences and profuse red, orange or purplish-black fruits. Their native habitats are lowland and coastal rainforests or montane valleys where they are protected from wind. Most are understorey palms requiring good soil moisture. Many species hybridise in cultivation.

P. elegans, the solitaire palm, is a slender tree palm from the understorey of what is left of the rainforests of north-east Queensland, Australia. It grows to 8–12 metres, often in communities, and produces large clusters of bright red fruits. The leaves are few and strongly arched. This species is commonly used in landscaping.

P. macarthurii, the Macarthur palm, is a clump-forming species from Cape York, Queensland and from New Guinea but is now widely distributed around the tropics as a landscape palm due to its relatively restricted size (7 metres, often less). It also has bright red fruits.

P. salomonense from Vanuatu, Bougainville Island and Guadalcanal closely resembles *P. elegans* though with larger leaves.

P. sanderianum from New Guinea or Australia (the precise location is unknown) is another clump-former reaching 3–7 metres in height.

P. waiteanum from New Guinea was first described as a species in 1956. It develops a solitary stem to 5 metres and its red flowers and inflorescence form an unusual feature. The fruits are black.

Rhapis species or lady palms are a group of small clump-forming Coryphoid palms from southern China, Indo-China, Thailand and north Sumatra, poorly known in the wild. All have slender, cane-like stems covered with fibre and fan leaves deeply divided into radiating segments. They sucker from underground rhizomes. The genus produces separate male and female plants and comes from the forest floor of dryish evergreen forests.

R. excelsa, sometimes called the bamboo palm, grows to 2 or 3 metres and produces pinkish flowers and small white fruits. In Japan many cultivars have been developed and are highly prized, particularly the variegated forms. These are all slow-growing, dwarfer than the true species and make particularly good houseplants. They must have shade. In the Palm House we grow several on the north apse end bench, including the dwarf 'Daruma'; 'Koban', which has large oval leaves; 'Kodaruma', which is very dwarf with small twisted leaves; and 'Tenzan', which is the tallest cultivar, with very slender canes and stems. 'Chiyodazuru' is variegated with delicate white stripes on the leaves.

Wallichia densiflora is a dwarf Arecoid palm of the understorey of the forests of Assam and the Himalayas. It has wedge-shaped leaflets of a type which relate it to *Arenga* and *Caryota*. It produces purple and yellow flowers in cycles, often growing for periods of 10–15 years and then flowering for four to six years. Its flowering is similar to that of *Caryota* and *Arenga*, with inflorescences appearing at the top of each stem and then successively downwards. The first inflorescence is always female, the later (lower) ones male. This is a very specialised understorey palm needing moisture and shade. All of the genera to which it is related are well represented in the north wing of the Palm House.

Wodyetia bifurcata, the foxtail palm, is an Arecoid palm from the Melville Range of north-east Queensland, Australia, where it forms the upper canopy in the monsoonal rainforest. There is only one species in the genus and it was only botanically described in 1983, though discovered five years earlier. It grows to 6–15 metres and produces a slightly swollen, light grey stem, a whitish crownshaft and fronds which are very bushy in outline (plumose), explaining its common name. The fruits are reddish-orange. This palm has considerable ornamental potential as a landscape palm.

6 Cycads and pandans

CYCADS

KEW HAS A VERY IMPORTANT COLLECTION of cycads, with some of the largest plants grown in tubs in the world. Walking among these plants it is easy to be transported in spirit to the Jurassic period, around 180 to 135 million years ago, when cycads literally covered the earth, sharing it with tree ferns and the predominant fauna of that period, the dinosaurs. What is left to us now (ten genera of three families with around 150 species) is a mere remnant of a huge deceased flora which, like the dinosaurs, was wiped out by climatic and other ecological changes, their identity known to us only through the fossil record and the work of palaeobotanists. Living cycads are often referred to as 'living fossils' not only for this reason but also because individual plants may be many hundreds of years old. The oldest plant we have predates the building of the Palm House and is currently thought to be the 'oldest pot plant in the world'. This specimen, long known as *Encephalartos longifolius*, was brought to Kew from Cape Province, South Africa, by one of our earliest plant collectors, Francis Masson, in 1775. It flourished at Kew through the French Revolution, the Napoleonic Wars, the Great Reform Bill, the foundation of Kew as a national botanic garden and then found a home in the south wing of the Palm House, where you can still see it today.

The cycads are an ancient group of cone-bearing plants related to the conifers and, like them, they are gymnosperms or plants that bear naked seeds. The rest of the plants in the Palm House belong to the angiosperms, which bear their seeds in ovaries. Their name derives from the Greek *cyckos*, meaning 'palm-like', referring to the overall shape of many genera, with a solid, usually unbranched trunk and a crown of leaves. They are not palms although their common names (bread palm, mujaji palm, etc.) show that local peoples are unconcerned with such botanical niceties.

Cycads bear cones and all species are strictly dioecious, that is, with separate male and female plants. The most primitive genus, *Cycas*, bears undeveloped reproductive structures showing the evolutionary link between cycads and ferns. The female is formed of a number of reduced leaves which bear seeds on the margins just as ferns bear spores under their fronds. All cycad cones have developed from leaves, the spines in the cones of *Macrozamia*, for example, being remnants of leaf midribs. All the genera except *Cycas* bear well developed cones on the axis of the plant, which is known as the 'cone dome'. Some are brightly coloured, normally yellow or orange. The female cone is composed of a series of scales or sporophylls arranged spirally, each bearing two seeds. Large cones may contain as many as 500 seeds, that of *Dioon spinulosum* being the largest cone of any known gymnosperm living or extinct. The male cones are more slender and bear prolific pollen in sacs under the scales. At maturity these cones elongate to open the scales and release the pollen, which is normally carried to the females by the wind or by beetle activity. Summer is the best time to see cycads coning at Kew. The total collection has in the past produced as many as 182 cones a year.

Cycads are palm-like plants, remnants of the vegetation which covered the earth in the age of the dinosaurs. Some species withstand severe drought, as does Cycas media, *photographed here in Queensland, Australia. The Palm House is now mostly reserved for the species from tropical rainforests.*

These extraordinarily long-lived plants are very slow-growing. In fact everything in their life span is prolonged. The process of pollination and fertilisation of the cones takes up to seven months and the embryo then develops for six months before the seed is released from the stalk of the cone. The seeds are spread by various species, including monkeys, baboons, fruit-eating bats, birds and marsupials, and are then very slow in germinating, the seed coat being very hard. The young seedlings produce tap-roots and as the plants age, many species slowly build up a columnar stem of spirally arranged leaf bases, which has enormous strength and weight. In the most advanced species this stem is pulled below ground by contractile roots, a process which is probably an adaptation to drought. Other species develop massive above-ground trunks, as seen in the Palm House. In nature, and because of their limited root systems, these may lean under their own weight or become procumbent and give rise to offsets along their stems. In the Palm House we support their stems to prevent them tipping out of their containers.

Although they grow slowly overall, when they do decide to produce leaves the event is very rapid. In a spurt of growth a new whorl can emerge in a couple of weeks. The growth is very soft and easily damaged but hardens rapidly, normally within a month. All cycad fronds consist of a central rachis with numerous leaflets. In *Cycas* the leaves emerge like the croziers of ferns, curling over at the tips. This process of circinate vernation again shows the evolutionary link with ferns. Full leaf whorls appear only when the plants are 15 to 20 years old and plants may go through resting periods of some years when no leaves appear at all. The reserve of energy in the stems is enormous, so a defoliated stem is not necessarily a dead plant.

Cycads develop a tap-root system from a young age. They also develop a remarkable root adaptation to assist their nutrition in arid and infertile environments. When the plants are still seedlings, coralloid roots develop, growing upwards towards the soil surface. These knobby accretions contain the cyano-bacteria *Anabaena* and *Nostoc*, which fix nitrogen and provide nitrates for the plant. These cyanobacteria are thought to be more abundant in cultivation than in the wild and in young rather than old plants. This phenomenon in cycads exists in no other gymnosperm. It is similar to nitrogen-fixation in peas, beans and other legumes and is currently the subject of much research into the possibility of gene transfer into crops without the ability to 'self-feed' in this way.

All cycads bear cones and the sexes are borne on separate plants. Zamia is a New World genus of small-sized species, some from the wet forest floor, some, like Z. furfuracea, from dryish woods.

In the nineteenth century all cycads were placed in the family Cycadaceae. The classification of cycads now used at Kew is that of L A S Johnson, published in 1959. Johnson recognised three families: Cycadaceae, with one genus (*Cycas*); Stangeriaceae, with one genus (*Stangeria*); and Zamiaceae, with eight genera (*Bowenia, Ceratozamia, Dioon, Encephalartos, Lepidozamia, Macrozamia, Microcycas* and *Zamia*). The world distribution of these genera is very similar to that of palms. The majority of cycads and all the Old World species (except *Cycas*) are from the southern hemisphere, whereas all the New World species (except *Zamia*) are from the northern. No genus is common to both the Old and New Worlds and most genera have very local distributions. *Bowenia, Lepidozamia* and *Macrozamia*, for example, are all Australian endemics. *Microcycas* is endemic to Cuba, and *Stangeria* to South Africa. *Ceratozamia* is mostly Mexican, as is *Dioon*, although the latter extends into Honduras and probably Guatemala. *Encephalartos* has a wider distribution, most species being South African but some existing in Zimbabwe, Tanzania, Nigeria, Mozambique, Uganda, Ghana, Malawi, Kenya, the Sudan and Zaire. The most widely distributed genus in the Old World is *Cycas*, with species distributed from Japan through South-east Asia to Australia, and from Madagascar through the east coast of Africa. The most advanced genus (*Zamia*) also has a wide New World distribution, from Florida and Mexico through the West Indies down to Brazil, Chile and Bolivia.

Cycads come from a wide variety of habitats, from the deep shade of rainforests to savannah or semi-desert. It is thought that cycads originated in rainforests and adapted to drier conditions very effectively as the climate changed. Their habitat preference is shown in their leaf adaptation. Semi-desert species (which are now in the majority) have xerophytic adaptations to withstand drought. Their leaflets are usually narrow and many have glaucous-green leaves with a high level of wax to protect against the sun. Many also have subterranean stems or large water-storing root tubers, and some have wool on the young growth and cones to reduce water loss. Most of the xerophytes are also very prickly, which is probably an adaptation against browsing by animals. Cycads from areas of seasonal drought have broader leaflets but are still protected by prickles and thick outer layers. In all these dry areas cycads are protected from fire by the tough leaf bases around the stem. Even if the foliage is destroyed, as is common in parts of Australia and South Africa, the stem regenerates a new crown. Cycads from rainforested areas generally have broader, dark green leaflets, often forming a lax head totally without prickles. *Bowenia spectabilis*, for example, from the forest floor of the Queensland rainforest, looks like a large, lush fern. *Zamia pseudoparasitica*, from the rainforests of Panama, produces verdant foliage which hangs down from the trees where it grows as an epiphyte. Along with all these morphological variations, cycads vary in their tolerance of different temperatures. The rainforest species are truly tropical but many of the xerophytes come from subtropical areas and together with the semi-desert species can withstand cold nights and occasional freezes.

With their varied tolerance to cold and diversity of natural habitat it is surprising that the bulk of the important collection of cycads at Kew has always been grown in the warm, humid Palm House. The reasons for this are historic. The nineteenth century was a period of great interest in cycads by botanists and 50 per cent of all known species were identified and described during this period. Kew's collection became famous. Being palm-like plants and demanding of space the Palm House formed their natural home, at least until the building of the Temperate House. Eventually the collection filled almost the entire south wing, standing on gratings above the heating pipes and accommodated in rot-resistant teak tubs and in clay pots on the south-west bench. The xerophytic species grew well, warmed and kept relatively dry from underneath by the heating pipes, but the rainforest species grew far less fast than they would have done in nature. The collection was managed by periodic resoiling of the tubs (many of which weighed over 2 tons) and was done by unbolting one side at a time, removing some of the soil, refastening and topping up with soil. This was standard practice with large plants in the nineteenth century, modelled on the cultivation of the large palms at Versailles grown in 'Caisses Versailles' which were hinged for this purpose. This is a popular job at Kew, and students usually feel rewarded when the cycads produce new leaves a month or so later. On the gratings of the south apse end we still grow a selection of cycads in this traditional way.

Since the 1980s restoration, in which soil beds have been introduced throughout the wings, it has been decided only to plant out those species which originate in rainforests. The xerophytic species will be accommodated in their tubs elsewhere, in conditions which will provide brighter light, less humidity and lower temperatures, more in keeping with the habitats they come from.

Kew's cycad collection is becoming richer and more varied, though this is not always apparent to the public, as many of the younger plants are held in one of our nurseries. Since 1971 the collection has also been recorded monthly to map the development of leaves and cones, forming a unique record of their behaviour under glass. This collection is probably more threatened in the wild (particularly in the New World and in Australia) than any other single group of plants at Kew. Fifty per cent of those currently in the Palm House have conservation ratings. The reasons for this are more complex than for palms, which are mainly threatened by habitat destruction. Cycads are threatened by plant collectors who see the possibility of forming a 'complete collection' of every species of this remnant group of plants. Secondly, some cycads are seen as a pest in Australia and in Mexico where the toxic glycosides they contain (macrozamin, cycasin, pakoein and neocycasin) cause liver damage and paralysis of limbs in cattle. In Australia government subsidies have been made available to eradicate them in cattle-grazing areas. Habitat destruction also threatens cycads in Florida, Cuba and Mexico. However, in South Africa cycads have been specially protected plants since 1971. The government requires owners to obtain permits and conservation ordinances apply in each province. There is now a flourishing nursery industry raising *Encephalartos* species from cultivated seed to protect wild stocks. The rarest plant at Kew is *Encephalartos woodii*, a single male plant of which was discovered by J Medley Wood, Director of the Natal Government Herbarium, in Zululand in 1895. Kew has one plant from this clump, Durban Botanic Gardens has two others and various offsets are now grown at gardens in the United States, including Longwood in Pennsylvania and Fairchild in Florida. No other plant has ever been discovered and, without a female, this lone plant is a real 'living fossil' with no possibility of sexual reproduction. Efforts at cloning the plant in micropropagation laboratories have so far failed.

Unlike palms, cycads have very few economic uses. Indeed, eating the seeds of many, especially *Cycas* species, has recently been identified as the cause of several neurological diseases. Nevertheless, *Encephalartos longifolius* has been called the bread tree because its pith has been used (after extensive detoxification by washing) as a source of starch by native peoples in South Africa. Native species have been a food source for aboriginals in Australia. *Zamia pygmaea* and *Z. floridana*, or Florida coontie, were collected for starch in Florida early in this century. *Cycas revoluta* is also traditionally the source of 'palm' fronds for Palm Sunday. The only other important use of cycads is in landscaping, particularly for *Cycas revoluta* and *C. circinalis*. The high prices made by many cycads on the horticultural market in fact contribute to collection from the wild and lead to erosion of international agreements on export and import restrictions.

In botanic gardens cycads are held as botanical curiosities, a testament to the world's vegetation as it once was, their seeds and pollen exchanged by enthusiasts. To see them in the wild, however, is a remarkable experience, their age and slow growth testifying that some parts of the world's vegetation at least remain undisturbed.

Cycads of the Americas

Of the four New World cycad genera, three are planted in the centre transept: *Dioon, Ceratozamia* and *Zamia*. The habitats of many are at risk and more species are probably yet to be discovered and named.

The genus **Ceratozamia** is distributed mostly in Mexico. Most of them are circinate in vernation like ferns and their natural habitat is shaded, moist woodland.

C. hildae from the state of Hidalgo is a recently described species of very distinctive habit. It forms only a short trunk but sends up very erect fronds with widely spaced leaflets whorled around the stem, unlike any other cycad, giving it the common name of bamboo zamia. In cultivation the fronds reach 1-1.5 metres but I have seen it grow 2–3 metres in deep soil in heavy shade. We hold both male and female plants and the cones they produce are 15 cm long. This is a moisture-loving species and it has been known to survive occasional freezes. It is endangered in the wild.

C. kuesteriana comes from deep calcareous soils in wooded mountain areas in northern Mexico, in the northernmost range of the genus. The fronds reach 1.8 metres.

C. mexicana, the Mexican horncone, develops a trunk to a maximum of 2 metres although most of it is usually buried below the soil. The strongly arching fronds have spiny petioles. We hold several male plants and a female, all of which cone freely. This species is rare in the wild.

C. zaragozae is an endangered species discovered and described to science in the early 1960s. It is similar to *C. kuesteriana* in habit but the leaflets are very narrow and twisted. They are arranged more or less spirally on the stems.

Dioon is a genus distributed in Mexico and Honduras. All species are sun-loving and xerophytic with the exception of the following two, which are planted out in the Palm House.

D. mejiae from Honduras has sharply pointed leaflets. When young the fronds are covered with a dense white tomentum, making it a highly attractive species. It is tolerant of shade and moisture. The local Indian population boil the seeds and grind them into bread flour.

D. spinulosum is the tallest of the New World cycads, with a slender trunk reaching 10–16 metres. The leaves are very spiny, resembling those of *Encephalartos*. The cones are the largest of any known gymnosperm, the female cone reaching up to 55 cm long and up to 13 kg in weight, which causes the whole structure to become pendulous. A large, well pollinated cone may contain up to 300 seeds. Mexicans make tortillas from flour ground from the seeds. Its natural habitat is mahogany forest on limestone soils in shade, but it is endangered in the wild. It takes more soil water than other species of *Dioon*.

Zamia is considered to be the most advanced of the New World cycad genera, and the most dwarf. The majority of species are forest-floor dwellers, with poorly developed or absent trunks or turnip-like subterranean roots and thin, fern-like leaves. Nearly all of them are tropical rainforest species, the exceptions being *Z. pumila* from Florida and *Z. loddigesii* and *Z. furfuracea* from Mexico. At least six species are threatened in the wild.

Z. fischeri from shady, moist forests in Mexico develops a small, spindle-shaped subterranean trunk. As with many rainforest plants the young growth is bronzed when it first emerges. It elongates to 45 cm or up to a metre in rich soil. The leaflets are thin and have serrated margins. Cones in this species are brown, up to 8 cm long, and the fruits ripen to red.

Z. furfuracea comes from dry sand-dune areas or shady woods in Mexico and is planted in the Palm House along with some of the palms which need seasonal drought. It is larger at maturity than most other zamias and bears stiff, rounded leaflets, thick in cross-section and with a tan-coloured scurfy surface. As young plants these are highly ornamental. It is vulnerable in the wild.

Z. muricata is a Venezuelan species from shaded rainforest with leaves reaching 1.2 metres long, unfurling a terracotta colour and then maturing to a shiny, bright green. It often clusters with several rosettes at a time.

Z. skinneri is a variable but highly ornamental species from the rainforests of Costa Rica, Guatemala, Panama and Peru. The fronds reach only 55 cm long, but they are finely corrugated and glossy green. It is vulnerable in the wild in Panama and Costa Rica.

African cycads

In the south wing are displayed representatives of all three African genera: *Encephalartos* and *Stangeria* (which are endemic), and *Cycas*, which has one species in this continent. Kew has always had a large collection of huge and very old specimens of *Encephalartos*, particularly *E. altensteinii* and *E. hildebrandtii*. Many of these African and South African species are no longer kept in the Palm House but have been moved to areas of drier air, lower temperatures and fuller light. The most famous Kew cycads, *E. altensteinii*, *E. woodii* and the male and female *E. ferox*, which produce their orange cones nearly every year, are kept on the south apse end grating in their traditional teak tubs, just as they always were.

Cycas thouarsii is the only representative of this mainly oriental genus in Africa, where it is distributed around Dar es Salaam in Tanzania, in Kenya and also in Madagascar, the Comoros and the Seychelles. It is endangered in Kenya and vulnerable in Tanzania, where the natural stands have been destroyed to make way for coconut plantations. This species grows to 10 metres with 3-metre leaves, up to 40 of them in a full head. The seeds become red at maturity and, as in many *Cycas* species, are very large, being the size of a good goose egg, but liable to shrivel if unfertilised. We hold a large female plant. This species comes from forest margins and it needs a high rainfall, good humidity and light shade.

Encephalartos is a genus endemic to South Africa and to parts of central Africa. Most are xerophytic plants needing a period of summer rainfall only, with huge and heavy water-storing trunks and prickly fronds.

Encephalartos *is an important African cycad genus. This is a female cone on* E. ferox, *a sight which can generally be seen every year in the Palm House.*

The 'oldest pot plant in the world', a specimen of *Encephalartos altensteinii*, was brought to Kew from the Cape by one of our first botanical collectors, Francis Masson, in 1775, having spent two years on its journey. Since then it has grown an average of 2.5 cm a year. This species, which is rare in the wild, normally reaches 4–5 metres when growing in full sun. In the wild it rarely leans or becomes procumbent through its weight, as ours has done. The cones are golden-yellow, the males reaching 40–50 cm long by 12–15 cm across. The female cones are 25–30 cm across. The story of the coning of our male plant is described on p. 12. Until very recently, this plant was called *E. longifolius*, but studies carried out by Dr Piet Vorster of Stellenbosch (in press) have shown it to be *E. altensteinii*. Although we hold a number of offsets from this plant, I always feel awed by the age of the parent. It seems a living memorial to the lives of a succession of gardeners and student gardeners who have cared for it for over 200 years. While at Kew it has probably received its sparse watering well over 8000 times.

E. ferox is a low-growing species with a rosette of holly-like leaves up to 4 metres across and comes from Natal (where it is of vulnerable status in the wild) and from Mozambique. We hold male and female plants which both produce multiple orange-scarlet cones in summer practically every year and form a spectacular feature. As is common in cycads, leaf production slows when coning is regular, especially in the females. Our female plant has not produced new leaves since May 1974, whereas the male did in May 1974, March 1978, May 1980 and March 1989. In September 1988 Jim Keesing of Kew succeeded in germinating seed from the female plant. It had been fertilised in October 1987 from pollen of the male which had been stored in a refrigerator for 2–3 weeks. He injected the pollen in a water suspension. It was a great success for cycad pollination at Kew, perhaps helped by the short time the pollen had to be stored, since the plants coned relatively close in time. Several seedlings germinated around the female plant and one, as often in nature, in its crown.

E. villosus is the one species of *Encephalartos* which we have planted out. It comes from shady, moist places in coastal and inland areas of the eastern Cape, Natal, the Transvaal and Swaziland, where it receives a good summer rainfall of 1000 to 1250 mm a year. This species forms a cluster of dwarf stems with subterranean tubers and glossy, dark green arching fronds which burn if exposed to too much sun. The cones are yellow in this species and it is rare in the wild.

E. woodii is one of the rarest plants in the world and probably the rarest at Kew. Its discovery is described on p. 12. No female plant is known to exist and the male is extinct in the wild. It is characterised by a stout trunk up to 6 metres tall and a strongly arching crown of leaves. The cones are bright orange and reputed to be 60–90 cm long. It is said to flourish best with ample moisture and a rich soil and it needs light shade under glass to prevent leaf-scorch. We were extremely lucky not to lose this plant in the hurricane of October 1987, when falling poplar branches broke about 270 panes of glass in the roof of the Temporary Palm House (mainly in the cycad section) and guillotined half the crown of a nearby *Cycas rumphii*.

Stangeria is a monotypic genus in the family Stangeriaceae from the eastern Cape and Natal. There is one species, *S. eriopus*, but this appears to have two ecotypes. The plant was originally described as a fern. It produces tuberous roots and has a subterranean stem which may branch. Coning then occurs simultaneously on the various heads. In open grassland subject to burning it produces short, hard fronds and may be deciduous. In forest districts it grows more lushly to 1–2 metres, with softer, more fringed leaflets.

Cycads of Asia and Australia

The north wing of the Palm House contains two genera of cycads, *Cycas* and *Lepidozamia*, which show their rainforest origin by their relatively soft leaves. All of them could be mistaken at a distance for tree ferns.

Cycas is the most widely distributed genus of all the cycads, ranging from southern Japan through Malaysia to Australia and out to India and the East African islands. It is the largest genus of Old World cycads, with around 16 species. It is also the most primitive and most closely related to its fern ancestors, the now extinct 'seed ferns'. This is obvious in the fern-like way in which both fronds and individual leaflets unfurl. The genus can be recognised by the prominent midrib along each leaflet, with no secondary nerves. Their seeds are some of the largest in the plant kingdom. Many yield starch or sago from their seeds and trunks which, despite being poisonous, is eaten during times of famine. This (hazardous) use is commemorated in their common names. The species planted in the Palm House are rainforest species but there are others which are xerophytes, including *C. media* from Queensland which grows in association with *Eucalyptus*, and *C. siamensis* which comes from the dry forests of Burma, Thailand, Cochin China and Yunnan. The latter is displayed in the Princess of Wales Conservatory.

C. circinalis, the queen sago, comes from India, Madagascar and New Guinea but is widely planted throughout the tropics as a landscape plant. It is also called the fern palm, which is a good visual description, although it is neither a fern nor a palm. The stout trunk of the species grows to 5–12 metres and the arching fronds form a lush and particularly graceful head to 5 metres across.

C. revoluta, the sago palm, is distributed from southern Japan to Java, showing its tolerance of a wide range of conditions. It is also used as a landscape plant, in Europe even as far north as Lisbon. It forms a short trunk to 3 metres, sometimes branching. The fronds are rolled downwards (revolute) at the margins and reach 1.5 metres long. In Japan many cultivated forms are grown, including some with curiously contorted growth.

C. rumphii, the bread palm, comes from northern Australia and Malaysia, where it grows to 6–15 metres with straight fronds 2 metres long. In Australia this species grows in coastal forests, in Malaysia in dipterocarp rainforest.

The three cycad genera endemic to Australia are *Lepidozamia* and *Bowenia*, both from monsoonal rainforest, and *Macrozamia*, which is extremely xerophytic from poor silicaceous soil sites in the dry forests or deserts of the Northern Territory, Central Australia and New South Wales. *Macrozamia* is not therefore represented in the Palm House although we have a nursery collection. In addition the range of several *Cycas* species also spreads into Australia.

Lepidozamia is a genus of two species from the rainforests of north-east Queensland and northern New South Wales. The plants develop single, erect stems and full heads of drooping fronds. Their cones are always solitary and the outer seed coat ripens to red.

The tallest species of cycad is the Australian Lepidozamia hopei, *here photographed in the wet coastal rainforest of northern Queensland, where it is rare. It can grow to 20 metres.*

L. hopei is rare in the wild. It is a magnificent plant, the tallest of any known cycad, reaching 20 metres. The fronds can reach 3 metres. In the wild it grows in coastal strand rainforest in shade or filtered sunlight or sometimes under stands of the endemic palm *Licuala ramsayi*. Both male and female specimens are planted in the Palm House.

L. peroffskyana is similar to *L. hopei* but has narrower leaflets and rarely exceeds 7 metres. It also extends further southwards in range, indicating that it takes slightly lower temperatures.

The genus **Bowenia** is represented at Kew by *B. serrulata*, the so-called Byfield fern. This is planted in the Australian House. There are two species, *B. serrulata*, coming from dry eucalyptus forest and

B. spectabilis, which is of the monsoonal rainforest and found growing with *Lepidozamia*. We hope to establish this species in the groundcover of the north wing of the Palm House as it is reputed to be difficult to grow in pots. *Bowenia* is interesting because it is the only genus with bipinnate as opposed to pinnate leaves and is rare in cultivation as well as being vulnerable in the wild. The leaf margins are serrated as in many *Zamia* species and in some ways this exploits a similar habitat in Australia to that of *Zamia* in the Americas – the forest floor. Good examples of *B. spectabilis* produce glossy fronds up to a metre tall and always produce abundant cones from a short subterranean trunk. Like *Cycas* its leaves unfurl by circinate vernation, showing its link with fern ancestors and underlining the antiquity of the group as a whole.

This is but a sampling of the cycads held at Kew. They are the main group of gymnosperms found in the Palm House. However, there is one other, *Gnetum gnemon*, which is planted in the north wing as a representative of an ancient order of cone-bearing plants, the Gnetales. This evergreen tree from Malaysia produces small fruits, the kernels of which are pounded, sun-dried and then fried with flour to produce a bitter biscuit. Other members of the Gnetales include the extraordinary two-leaved *Welwitschia* from the Namib desert, which can be seen in the Princess of Wales Conservatory.

PANDANS

The screwpines (*Pandanus* species) have always formed an important group in the Palm House. Their common name has a simple derivation, from the way the leaves spiral the stem, as in the thread of a screw, and from the pineapple-like fruits. There are around 350 species of *Pandanus* and more than 200 species of the climbing genus *Freycinetia* which, along with the genus *Sararanga*, together make up the family Pandanaceae. They are distantly related to the palms. Like palms they cannot gain much in width after a certain age, but unlike most palms, they branch freely, many producing a spectacular candelabra-like structure. Their root systems are similar to palms, but practically all pandans also develop huge prop roots as if to match their aerial branching. All pandans produce separate male and female trees, the male (staminate) trees producing huge amounts of pollen on very short-lived inflorescences. The female (pistillate) trees produce the pineapple-like fruits, which often take several months to enlarge and ripen, those of some species being edible, and some of which are produced without fertilisation (parthenocarpy). Fruit production may be irregular.

Nearly all *Pandanus* have long narrow leaves, deeply channelled at the midrib, pleated once on each side of it and covered with prickles on the leaf margins, midribs and pleats. Like the leaves of other monocotyledons, including the palms and grasses, they elongate by basal rather than tip growth. They are not a well-studied group perhaps because of their leaf armour. However, there are thornless cultivars which are important as landscape plants, and attractive variegated forms, all of which are propagated clonally by the offsets which are freely produced in this family.

Screwpines are so called because of the spiral arrangement of their leaves and their pineapple-like fruits, some species being edible. This is an Australian species, Pandanus spiralis.

The distribution of *Pandanus* is confined to the tropics of the Old World and the Pacific; not one is found in the Americas. There are two 'centres of speciation' where the genus has developed, one in Madagascar and the other in the Malaysian–Indonesian area. This accounts for all the species apart from a few in tropical Australia, two in the Hawaiian Islands and species scattered through Melanesia and Polynesia. In the Palm House this means that you can see pandans in the south wing (Africa) and the north wing (Asia).

Many screwpines are plants of marshy coastal areas or boggy upland savannahs needing good light. However, many west Malesian species are adapted to dark undergrowth. A very high proportion of the island species are endemic and many are threatened in the wild.

Pandans in Madagascar and the Mascarenes

The screwpines in the south wing represent one of the centres of speciation in the genus. They have evolved in geographical isolation in a similar way to the many rare and endemic palms of these islands. They are threatened by the drainage and reclamation of the marshlands which form their habitat and by the introduction of invasive foreign species or 'exotics'. Ninety-three per cent of the forests of Madagascar have already been destroyed. In the Mascarenes the government has set up a reserve and there is a good collection of species at Pamplemousses Botanic Garden.

P. pristis is a dwarf species from Madagascar. It forms a neat clustering rosette only 2–4 metres high. The short, stubby leaves are strongly recurved and have white marginal spines. Our plant is a male and flowers freely though only a metre high.

P. utilis from Madagascar is currently our largest plant, freely branching and with a good prop root system. It grows to 15 or 20 metres tall and has deep olive-green leaves with red spines. It is planted as a plantation crop in Africa and the Mascarenes for its leaves, which are woven into hats and baskets.

P. vandermeeschii is endemic to Mauritius, where it is threatened in the wild. It forms a clump or thicket up to 6 or 8 metres tall. The glaucous leaves have orange-red marginal spines and the bark of the trunk becomes pinkish-grey. The fruits ripen to yellow. Its habitat is on rocky exposed cliffs and beaches. In the early 1980s only two populations of this ornamental species remained in the wild, each of five plants.

The Asian pandans

South-east Asia is the second important centre of diversity in *Pandanus*. Papua New Guinea is also the only area where pandans are cultivated (as a high-altitude crop) for their fruits. Karuka nuts are an important supplier of fat and protein in the diets of the highland peoples, the trees fruiting at five to ten years old and continuing to produce several heads of around 7 kg each for up to 60 years. The species involved are *P. julianettii* and *P. brosimos*. The nuts are stored after drying, which covers people for the lean years of cyclic cropping. Generally speaking, fewer species are threatened in Asia than in the Mascarene Islands.

P. albifrons is a small species from Sumatra growing to 2 metres. It has very wide, deep green recurving leaves. The plant we have is male.

P. dubius comes from Malaysia, Vanuatu, the Bismarck Archipelago and tropical Australia. It will grow to 10 metres or so with a shortish trunk and favours riverine flats or tidal mangrove swamps. The leaves are very broad and are used to make mats. The seeds of this species are edible, having a mild coconut flavour. Male plants are rare. Their flowers are held in bright lemon-yellow spathes.

P. nitidus is from Java. It is a dwarf species reaching 3 metres with very narrow leaves 2 metres long. The fruits are green.

P. odoratissimus, the pandang or walking tree, is a widespread species of the sandy sea-shores of Hawaii, Polynesia, Vanuatu, Queensland and monsoon Asia. It branches to 6 metres and has grey-green leaves 1 or 2 metres long with stout marginal spines. The leaves of thornless cultivars are used for thatching and weaving after being dried, beaten, resoaked and sun-bleached. The aerial roots yield fibres for cordage and brushes while the fragrant male inflorescence is distilled in water and the vapour absorbed into sandalwood oil to make the perfume 'kewda attar'. The fruits ripen to orange and the seeds are edible. Our female plant fruits frequently in the Palm House. Some authorities consider this species to be synonymous with *P. tectorius*. There are various cultivars: 'Veitchii' is variegated, with leaves banded white along the margins; 'Laevis' is a variegated form without any spines and of great value as a land-scape plant, particularly in the Americas. It is displayed in the centre transept.

In the north wing we hope to build up a collection of *Freycinetia* species to represent this important group of climbing members of the Pandanaceae. These extraordinary plants climb up any host support with the aid of their aerial roots. In Queensland they cover the trunks of palms such as *Ptychosperma elegans* and *Licuala ramsayi*, producing fruits which ripen to red and then become soft. Some species are probably pollinated by fruit flies, which teem in the ripening fruit, others by bats.

Many Pandanus *are adapted to growth by watercourses and develop a system of stilt roots to anchor and support their branching growth.*

7 Tropical climbers

THE TROPICS ARE EXTRAORDINARILY RICH in climbing plants. While this is partly a reflection of the overall richness and diversity of plant life in the tropics, the competition engendered in this lush environment gives climbers an evolutionary advantage and makes them a notable part of the overall plant community. Ninety per cent of climbing plants live in the tropics, compared to temperate Europe with only 2 per cent. In the race of vegetation towards the light, climbers have exploited an ability to grow fast whilst using other plants for support, so wasting less energy in forming woody tissue of their own. Climbers are nature's 'hangers on' in more ways than one. Once they have attained the sunshine above the very tall canopy of tropical rainforest, climbers spread out and flower, often forming a dense mat over trees and festooning downwards under their own weight at the margins of streams. In the wild, large lianes may reach 70 metres and develop trunks as thick as a human thigh, with growth which descends from one tree only to ascend another or even bridge watercourses. In the Palm House you can see their flowers best from the perimeter paths. Here their growth hangs down and contributes greatly to the feeling of being in the tropics.

A climber may be defined as any plant which relies on others for support in the struggle for the light required to photosynthesise. Usually such plants have developed some sort of morphological adaptation to make their ascent, such as the growth of tendrils, recurved thorns or the twining habit itself. This is apparent when the plant is still small. In some genera, *Strophanthus* and *Combretum*, for example, the young plants behave as shrubs and then develop long climbing shoots, perhaps when they have developed the reserves required to do so. Anatomical studies show that the stems of many woody climbers are not made up of a single rod of wood, like normal woody stems, but of a rope-like bundle of several woody strands which can bend and slip over one another, thus combining strength with flexibility. In some families every member has developed the climbing habit. Examples are the mainly South American Passifloraceae and the predominantly African Dioscoreaceae. Many more families have some members which are woody climbers but others which are shrubs, trees or herbs. In the tropics the most important families with the largest numbers of climbers are the Apocynaceae, the Bignoniaceae and the Aristolochiaceae (particularly in the Americas), the Convolvulaceae and the Oleaceae. In Africa the most important families are the Celastraceae, Connaraceae and the Hippocrateaceae. The pea family (Leguminosae) contributes some huge forest lianes. Some of these (for example, species of *Mucuna*, and *Strongylodon macrobotrys*) have superb flowers, as does the large family, Acanthaceae. In general the richest habitat for climbers of all families is secondary or disturbed forest, where they spring up like weeds in the increased light. Overall, the greatest number of species is probably in the Americas, closely followed by Asia. South-east Asia is particularly rich in climbing members of the palm family. These are described in chapter 5.

Quite a few climbers have important economic uses. The African species of *Dioscorea* (yams) yield edible root tubers. Some of these are cultivated; others are relied upon only in times of famine. Many of the South American species of *Passiflora* yield edible fruits (passion fruits). The roots of some species of *Smilax* (particularly *S. longifolia* and *S. officinalis*) yield the drink sarsaparilla. Some of the jasmines are used in the perfume trade and *Jasminum sambac* is used to flavour jasmine teas. The climbing palms yield 'cane' for rattan furniture. Several species have given chemists the blueprints for very important drugs, *Strophanthus* for cardiac drugs and *Dioscorea* for the various types of contraceptive pill, sex hormones and steroids.

The methods by which vines climb provides an interesting insight into how plants adapt themselves to exploit their environment. This fascinated Charles Darwin, who first published *The Movements and Habits of Climbing Plants* in 1865. There are about six basic methods. The simplest is twining or spiralling of the stems. This usually happens either in a clockwise or anti-clockwise direction. It is very rare for different species in any one genus to twine differently. One instance is in *Dioscorea*, where the characteristic is used to divide the African species into two groups. Most climbers twine anti-clockwise and the shoot tips make circular movements, called nutation, until they contact a support to ascend. In the Palm House the largest group of twining climbers are *Dioscorea*, mainly in the south wing, and *Aristolochia* in the centre transept. In leaf twiners, sensitive leaf stalks twine around an attachment point although the stems themselves do not twine.

Primitive climbers merely scramble over other vegetation, developing shoots at right angles to the main stem to prevent them slipping. Others, such as *Allamanda* and *Solandra* in the centre transept, develop long cane-like stems which arch over any available support. However, most vines have developed specific structures to help them climb. Some possess recurved hooks on the stems which grapple onto other vegetation. Examples in the south wing of the house are *Bougainvillea*, whose thorns are adaptations of axillary buds, and *Quisqualis indica*, the Rangoon creeper, whose thorns are formed from the remnants of leaf stalks of shed foliage. Hooks can also be formed from prickles and stipules. Root climbers such as species of *Marcgravia* form adventitious roots from the stems, which grow into the bark of a host tree, some cementing their attachment by secreting resins. Tendril climbers have developed holdfasts. In the Bignoniaceae it is common for the terminal leaflet of three to be aborted into a tripartite, hooked tendril. Examples of this adaptation in the centre transept are visible on *Clytostoma*, *Macfadyena* and *Pyrostegia*. In passion flowers (Passifloraceae) the tendrils are formed from modified flower stalks. Many genera have tendrils coiled like a spring. This makes possible considerable movement by the main stem (caused for example by wind or by the collapse of the host support) before the tendril breaks. The spiralling also shortens the tendril and draws the climber closer to its support. In the Cucurbitaceae the spiral reverses in the middle, thus shortening it even further. These examples show that plants will evolve modifications to assist their ascent and in this they show a remarkable economy of plant tissue. Sometimes several modifications are combined, tendrils with hooked stems in *Smilax*, for example. In climbing palms very thorny stems are combined with recurved hooks on structures formed either from the leaf midrib or aborted inflorescences. Examples can be seen in the centre transept and north wing.

Allamanda cathartica is a scandent climber with fine vanilla-scented flowers borne from late spring to early autumn. In the wild it occurs in mangrove swamps in the Americas.

Kew has always had a good collection of tropical climbers and at present around 100 species are planted in the Palm House. The establishment of beds around the pillars in the centre transept was one of the first accomplishments of the first Curator of Kew, John Smith. Since then climbers have been grown in brick boxes built around two-thirds of the low-level vent boxes adjacent to the main arches of the building, a rather *ad hoc* arrangement made because it was necessary to get some rooting depth for these vigorous plants. Since the 1980s restoration the climbers around the perimeter of the building can have unobstructed root runs in the beds and we anticipate very vigorous growth. Stainless steel stranded hawser wire has been fixed to carry their weight up to the second purlin bar of the building and up the central columns. At the apse ends, planter boxes have been designed and here we have planted climbers which prefer seasonal drought and need it to flower well. This we can provide better where the roots are isolated from the beds. Other climbers have been planted to grow up other woody plants and also around the six aspirated screen stands in the building which sense temperatures and humidity. As in nature, climbing plants make use of whatever support is available. They are nature's opportunists.

Climbers of the Americas

Allamanda cathartica (Apocynaceae), the golden trumpet flower, comes from the moist and seasonally dry areas of Central America and north-eastern South America, including areas of mangrove swamp. It produces cane-like growths with whorled and then paired leaves which terminate in clusters of pure yellow trumpets with a pervasive fragrance of vanilla. Flowering is continuous between June and September. In the larger-flowered and vigorous 'Hendersonii' the flower colour is deeper and the buds are brownish. These are some of the most floriferous climbers, provided they have rich, moist soil and good light.

Anemopaegma chamberlaynii (Bignoniaceae) is a yellow-flowered vine from Brazil. The central of the normal three leaflets is modified into a tendril. The flowers consist of a tube 6 cm long with five flared petals. Flowering is intermittent. The species *A. carrerense* from Trinidad and Tobago, Guyana and Venezuela is very similar but less well known in cultivation.

Antigonon leptopus, the coral vine, is a pretty Mexican relative of the common-or-garden Russian vine in the Polygonaceae. It is slender-stemmed but vigorous, with heart-shaped leaves. In good light it covers itself with profuse racemes of coral-pink flowers, though the flower colour varies when the plant is grown from seed. The inflorescences end in hooked tendrils to assist in climbing and the plant forms root tubers. This plant is widely grown throughout northern South America, South Africa, Hawaii (where it is called the Honolulu creeper) and Florida, where it is almost a weed.

Aristolochia is a genus of around 350 species forming its own family (Aristolochiaceae), and the Palm House has a fine collection of the tropical species of South America. They are strange plants, all pollinated by insects attracted to the foul smell of the flowers and, in most species, imprisoned therein until the flowers' aging releases them. None of them actually devours insects but the bizarrely shaped flowers, normally tubular and hooded, are adapted as temporary traps. All species need abundant moisture to maintain the turgor of the rather fleshy flowers and all contain rank-smelling essential oils throughout their root and shoot tissue. They produce capsule fruits, subterranean tubers and some species have attractive corky outgrowths on the old wood. All prefer a dry resting period but will produce flowers without one. They always flower on the young growth. Their common name of birthwort refers to the foetus-like shape of their flowers and their supposed medicinal value in easing the pains of childbirth. Most species have purple, brown, green or maroon flowers, often highly speckled, but it is the variety of sculptural shapes which is the main ornamental feature of the genus. All species come from Brazil unless otherwise noted.

A. elegans, the calico flower, has neat, elegant flowers with a small pouch and a vertically held face of a maroon-brown colour, showing clearly the yellow tube down to the stigma. This species seeds freely at Kew.

A. gigantea is the giant of the genus, with a huge flower up to 20 cm long but with no tail. If it has a scent it is only detectable by insects. This extraordinary plant has been grown at Kew since at least 1910.

A. grandiflora, the pelican flower from Mexico, Panama and the West Indies, has a flower as large as *A. gigantea* but with a long twisted tail. It is extremely rank-smelling.

A. × kewensis is a hybrid between *A. labiata* and *A. macroura*. The flowers are pale green, veined purple-brown and resemble *A. labiata* in odour and general shape, but lack the crest of this parent.

A. labiata (*A. brasiliensis*), the rooster flower, has heart-shaped, apple-green leaves. The rank-smelling flowers have an inflated flask which narrows into a hairy, maroon lip from which hangs a large brown-veined flap like a cockerel's crest. It is one of the showiest species.

A. leuconeura (*A. veraguensis*) from Panama is a rampant species with coppery-green rugose leaves with yellow veins. The flowers are maroon and red but rather small.

The birthworts (Aristolochia *spp.) are a large group of mainly twining climbers from the Americas. The Palm House has a good collection of these bizarre plants. The rooster flower,* Aristolochia labiata, *is a showy species but it is fly-pollinated and therefore rank-smelling.*

A. ridicula has a horizontal tubular flower 9 cm long with a hairy and glandular tip. As in some other insectivorous plants, flies attracted by its smell are drawn down the tube by a 'window' of pale tissue at the base falsely promising escape. The species is self-sterile and must attract pollinators for cross-pollination.

A. trilobata from tropical South America and the West Indies only grows to 2.5 metres. Its leaves are unusual for the genus, being trilobed with yellow veins. The flowers, like classic Dutchman's pipes, have the upper lip extended into a tail, which can reach 30 cm long.

Banisteriopsis caapi (Malpighiaceae) is a vigorous climber which yields banisterine, a hallucinogenic alkaloid used by Indians in Brazil, Peru and Ecuador in various tribal ceremonies. The leaves are veined red. Deep pink flowers are borne in long, axillary umbels and the fruits are winged.

Bignonia capreolata (Bignoniaceae) is called the cross vine after the quartered arrangement of its tissue. It is native to rich, moist, woodland habitats of the south-eastern United States, where it will grow to 17 metres or more. The showy flowers are red and yellow.

Clytostoma (Bignoniaceae) is a genus of eight species from South America. They climb by a simple tendril centred between each pair of leaves and have pale purple flowers veined purple and with yellow-white throats. The fruits are very prickly. These are plants of freshwater swamps which prefer a cooler, drier period in the winter. Drying out appears to trigger flowering. We hold *C. binatum* and *C. callistegioides*.

The genus **Dioscorea** (Dioscoreaceae) is the source of several drugs and also the root tubers called yams. (See pp. 73–74.) *D. alata*, the winged or white yam, originated in South-east Asia, but several selected forms are now cultivated, principally in West Africa. It grows to 15 metres and produces quadrangular, winged stems. It is useful in that it tolerates poor soil but still produces huge tubers. These are detoxified and rendered palatable by boiling or baking. It yields more than any other cultivated yam, up to 20 to 30 tonnes per hectare.

D. macrostachya from Mexico is one of the species used to yield various sapogenins, particularly diosgenin, which in the 1970s formed the source of 95 per cent of steroidal drugs prescribed in the United States. Diosgenin is therefore the base of most of the world's contraceptive pills, sex hormones, cortisones and other anti-inflammatory drugs. Production from this species and others (including *D. composita*) was very important for the Mexican economy until other sources were found and, later, when the drugs became artificially synthesised. However, the world would not have had these drugs if the chemical blueprint had not been found in these wild plants.

Ipomoea indica (*I. acuminata*) (Convolvulaceae), the blue dawn flower or perennial morning glory, is a pantropically distributed climber which originated in the West Indies and continental tropical America. It produces a dense mass of twining stems and trilobed leaves, with clear sky-blue flowers fading to purplish blue during the same day. This is a wayside plant in the tropics, needing bright light to flower.

Macfadyena (Bignoniaceae) comes from tropical America. It has the typical climbing mechanism of the family, a central tripartite tendril between two leaflets. We hold *M. dentata* and *M. uncata*. The former flowers more freely, producing light yellow bells in racemes. In the wild both species frequent streamsides and freshwater swamps. Rather similar in habit and flower is the Brazilian bignoniaceous climber *Mansoa difficulis*.

Mascagnia septentrionalis (Malpighiaceae) is a twiner from Central and South America which has been introduced to Florida. It has yellow flowers with fringed petals of a crepe-like texture and winged fruits typical of the Malpighiaceae.

Aristolochia grandiflora from Central America and the West Indies has very sculptured flowers. The twisted shape of many of the species is supposed to resemble the shape of a foetus, hence the name 'birthwort'.

The genus **Merremia** (Convolvulaceae) comes from tropical America and Africa but has now been introduced throughout the tropics of the world. It is closely related to *Ipomoea*. The species grow in deep, moist soil, flourishing best at the margins of rainforest where they get full sun. *M. dissecta*, the moonflower, is a twiner with five- to seven-lobed leaves and white bell-shaped flowers stained red within. They open in sun at midday and remain open a short time.

M. tuberosa, the gold morning glory, is a tuberous plant with palmate leaves and yellow funnel-shaped flowers reaching 6 cm across. In this species the capsular fruits become lignified and dry, the sepals opening to form a structure like a wooden rose. An alternative common name is wood rose and the fruits are often used in dried arrangements. This ornamental species is important horticulturally in Sri Lanka, Puerto Rico, Hawaii and Hong Kong.

The genus **Passiflora** (Passifloraceae) forms a very large and important group of climbers, about 350 species of which come from the New World. Comparatively few are known in cultivation. Some fine species come from upland areas in South America and need temperate conditions. There are probably many tropical species still to be discovered.

The name passion flower derives from the Passion of Christ on the Cross and originated during the invasion of South America by the Catholic Spanish in the seventeenth century. According to the 'doctrine of signatures' the resemblance of a plant (or part of a plant) to a part of the body indicated its purpose as a remedy for any ailment thereof. (q.v. *Aristolochia*). The flower, which seemed to them to commemorate the Crucifixion, was thought to lend blessing to the conversion of the local populations to Christianity. The five sepals and petals represent the ten apostles at the Cross, the corona the crown of thorns, the five stamens the five wounds of Christ, the central column the scourging post, the three styles the three nails and the tendrils of the plant the cords binding Christ to the Cross. No other plant can ever have been endowed with such a powerful symbolism, except perhaps the mandrake, which was reputed to kill anyone who lifted the root. We grow at least five species in the centre transept.

P. coccinea from Venezuela, Bolivia, Peru, Brazil and the Guianas has simple, softly hairy, scalloped leaves, unusual in the genus. The flowers are a magnificent scarlet and reach 7–10 cm across. They are followed by fruits which are striped and marked in green and orange. This species hates pot culture and will only flower well when planted out. It has such horticultural value that it was given an Award of Merit by the Royal Horticultural Society in 1972.

Aristolochia elegans *has richly coloured flowers with a vertically held face. Like most aristolochias it comes from Brazil.*

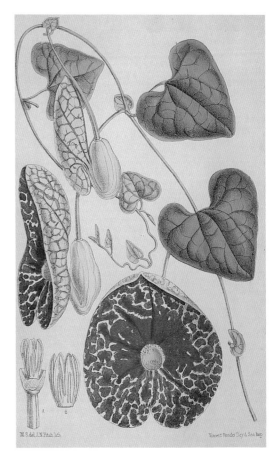

P. coriacea, the bat leaf vine, is found from Mexico down to Peru. It has curiously angled leaves, almost oblong and of a bluish green mottled with silver. The flowers are mainly pale green and rather insignificant.

P. edulis, the purple granadilla, is probably a Brazilian species, widely cultivated in Australia, Sri Lanka, the southern United States and elsewhere as a source of fresh passion fruit. Passion fruit juice is mainly produced from the yellow-fruited form *P. edulis* var. *flavicarpa* and is a notable industry in Hawaii and in Australia. The flowers of the species are like a smaller edition of the semi-hardy *P. caerulea*, which is often grown outdoors in this country. The leaves are trilobed.

P. quadrangularis is commonly called the giant granadilla. It occurs throughout tropical America but is also cultivated in India and Indonesia. It is one of the most vigorous species, with four-angled stems and smooth, pale green, ovate leaves. The large flowers are pendent and pinkish-purple with wavy corona filaments banded white and purple, which hang down like tentacles from a jellyfish. This must rank as the showiest of all the purple species. The fruits look like small, smooth-skinned marrows and can grow up to 30 cm long. They are very slow in ripening and are then edible, though uninteresting compared to those of *P. edulis*.

P. nitida resembles the giant granadilla in its ovate leaves but is nowhere near as vigorous. The flowers are white with a red and blue corona.

Pseudogynoxys is a genus of 16 species from tropical South America in the family Compositae, a family not overly endowed with genera which climb. We hold *P. chenopodioides* (*Senecio confusus*), the Mexican flame vine, which produces profuse heads of brilliant orange scented daisies even as a young plant. Its natural range extends from Mexico to Colombia.

Pyrostegia venusta, the flame vine or firecracker flower, is a vigorous Brazilian climber in the family Bignoniaceae. It bears dense panicles of brilliant orange flowers at the tips of branches or on short side shoots, provided it has a cooler, drier period at some stage in the year to initiate flower buds.

Smilax utilis (Smilacaceae) is the source of sarsaparilla, which is used as a tonic, for treating rheumatism and as a constituent of 'root beer', and is made from the rhizomatous roots. The tendrils are formed from modified leaf sheaths and the stems are prickly. Male and female flowers are borne on separate plants.

Solandra grandiflora, the silver cup or chalice vine, comes from the West Indies, Venezuela and Brazil. It is a member of the potato family, the Solanaceae. It clambers to about 6 metres producing leathery, elliptic leaves on cane-like growth, and chalice-like, yellowish flowers marked purple inside and up to 20 cm long. The flowers have the texture of chamois leather and age to a deeper yellow. This vine is seen all over the tropics and subtropics. It flowers best in full sun and with a period of winter rest, when it is kept drier.

Stigmaphyllon ciliatum (Malpighiaceae), the golden vine, is a slender Brazilian twiner with very showy yellow flowers in dense corymbs. Both the heart-shaped leaves and the flowers are attractively fringed. It needs rich soil in full sun. It is cultivated in Trinidad, South Africa and in Malaysia, as well as in tropical America.

African climbers

Members of the genus **Bougainvillea** are woody climbers originally from the subtropics of South America, but their hybrids and cultivars are now cultivated all over the tropics, where they are responsible for introducing more colour than any other genus. They do particularly well in parts of Africa with a pronounced dry season. Extensive hybridisation took place early this century in Kenya and in Natal, as well as in the West Indies, Queensland and northern India. Bougainvilleas have small white flowers, their display of colour coming from the showy papery bracts which surround them. They climb by means of recurved hooks in the axils of the leaves. The Palm House once had a large collection, a good proportion of the 60 or so cultivars which now exist. We now grow a greater variety of climbers (mostly true species) and fewer cultivars. However, some are planted in the south apse end, where they benefit from the best light available in the house. They are given a dry resting period in winter to initiate flower buds.

Clerodendrum is a large genus of around 400 species in the Verbenaceae. Several of the shrubs are cultivated in the Palm House and two are splendid flowering climbers, both from West Africa. They are notable for their long exserted stamens and showy persistent calyces. Both are pruned after flowering.

C. splendens is a twiner with rounded, dark green leaves and terminal heads of brilliant scarlet flowers borne intermittently throughout the summer. These are followed by purplish-red calyces. This species flowers best with a dry season.

C. thomsonae (*C. thomsonae* var. *balfourii*) the bleeding heart vine, is a twiner with ovate, puckered leaves. The flowers are borne terminally and on side shoots and consist of a pure white inflated calyx surrounding a blood-red corolla. The calyces persist and become flushed with purple after the corollas have dropped. Blue fruits and brilliant orange seed are sometimes set. This is a spectacular climber, flowering non-stop from April to September. It was introduced into cultivation in 1861 and is sometimes available as a conservatory plant. There is a form with variegated leaves. *C. thomsonae* and *C. splendens* have produced a hybrid, *C.* × *speciosum* and, unusually for a hybrid, this is less striking than its parents.

C. schweinfurthii, also from tropical West Africa, is a large, lax shrub which is frequently trained as a climber. It has downy shoots and softly hairy pale green leaves. Large panicles of pure white flowers arise from the old growth in late spring and summer, so this species is lightly pruned to preserve the flowering wood. Its green fruits ripen to black.

The genus *Dioscorea* (Dioscoreaceae) is a huge genus of around 600 species closely related to the lily family. They are collectively known as the yams. Many species yield steroid drugs, while the African species are either a staple food crop or, in the case of less palatable varieties, a fall-back in times of famine. Because of their storage qualities they were used to provision slavers' ships. Production is heaviest in West Africa and may exceed 20 tonnes per hectare. All species twine and produce more or less heart-shaped leaves. The yam is the edible root tuber, which is boiled, pounded into a dough called fufu, mixed with a sauce and eaten with fish or meat. The most economically important species are *D. rotundata*, *D. cayenensis*, *D. alata* and *D. dumetorum*, but all are declining in importance relative to cassava because their staking and harvesting is labour-intensive and the yearly increase is only a multiple of three or five upon what is planted. Formerly all propagation of these crops was done from tuber sets, as we use seed potatoes. Considerable research has been done by the National Root Crops Centre at Umudike, Nigeria, on developing methods of excision so that less material has to be used. The International Institute of Tropical Agriculture is working on improving yields, resistance to pests and disease, storability and nutritional levels, as well as methods of rooting vegetative growth, developing a stock of seed which will breed true, growing the crop without staking and harvesting the crops mechanically. The aim is to increase the profitability of the crop so that it is available to more people and is less of a luxury item. Yams contain more protein than cassava and also vitamin C which is not destroyed in cooking and so have the potential to improve local diets. Most species are dormant in the winter months and their foliage in the Palm House is cut down. Though uninteresting in flower these represent an important gene pool at Kew. We satisfy more requests for live material for chemical testing from this genus than any other in the Palm House.

D. bulbifera, the potato yam or air potato, grows to 6 metres and produces aerial bulbils in the axils of the leaves with much-reduced tuber growth at the root. There are many races of this species, some highly toxic. Some races are used as a famine food and they have important local medicinal uses. The species also occurs wild in Asia.

D. dumetorum, the bitter yam, only grows to 3 metres. Most forms of it are highly toxic because they contain dihydrodioscorine, which paralyses the nervous system. The tubers have to be steeped in running water for five days before the poisons are leached out and it can be used as a famine food.

D. minutiflora reaches 10 metres and has spiny stems, an unusual feature in yams. It forms rather woody tubers, used as famine food.

D. praehensilis, the bush yam from West Africa, is a vigorous form reaching 20 metres with a huge tuber which projects above soil level. The young shoots are cooked and eaten like asparagus and the tuber is a famine food.

Hibiscus schizopetalus is an East African shrub with arching growth which can be trained as a climber, allowing its pendent flowers to be seen to best effect.

D. preussii grows to 30 metres. Its tubers are very deeply buried and take 15 days of leaching before they are palatable.

D. rotundata, the white Guinea yam, is an old West African cultivar with highly palatable white flesh. It is drought-tolerant and an important crop in Nigeria, where there are many different cultivated forms.

D. sansibarensis produces both a massive tuber and bulbils in the leaf axils. It has particularly handsome, deeply quilted foliage which contains glands bearing nitrifying bacteria to assist its growth. All parts of the plant are toxic and it is used as an animal and fish poison to stun hunted prey.

Hibiscus schizopetalus (Malvaceae) is the only scandent member of this popular genus of tropical and subtropical species, most of which are showy shrubs or small trees. It develops arching, cane-like growth which is best trained to a support. The red flowers have the prominent style seen in all hibiscus but the petals are very divided and completely reflexed, giving them the appearance of decorative Chinese lanterns. The flower stalks are also very long so the flowers hang well clear of the foliage. This species comes from tropical East Africa.

The genus **Jasminum** (jasmines), of the Oleaceae family, are a large group of 200–300 sun-loving species, mostly climbers and nearly all Asian in origin. However, tropical Africa sports several species. Most have white flowers and climb by twining. Their best feature is their fragrance.

74

J. dichotomum has leaves in whorls of three. The flowers are small, scented, white and extremely profuse, in inflorescences of up to 60 individual florets. They develop from pink buds and are borne in terminal clusters throughout the year.

J. sambac, the Arabian jasmine, comes from Arabia and India and has also been adopted as the national flower of the Philippines. It is the flowers of this species which are used to perfume jasmine tea and for the extraction of essential oils for perfume. It forms either a bushy shrub or a semi-climber, with arching canes reaching 2 or 3 metres. The leaves are dark green and rather puckered, unlike any other jasmine, and in cultivated forms the flowers are double, gardenia-like and extremely fragrant, though not long-lived. In habitat it prefers full sun and a dryish soil. In India the flowers are considered sacred to Vishnu and here and also in Hawaii they are used to make floral garlands.

Pararistolochia promissa (Aristolochiaceae) is one of 16 species from West Africa, the equivalent in Africa to the genus *Aristolochia* in the Americas. In foliage it resembles many species of *Aristolochia*, with glaucous leaves, but the flowers are yellow and form spectacular inflorescences up to 45 cm long.

Quisqualis is a genus of about 17 species, around half of which are tropical African. It is in the family Combretaceae. All species come from river and forest margins in rainforest.

Q. indica, the Rangoon creeper, is cultivated in tropical and South Africa and throughout Indo-Malaysia. When young it acts as a shrub and then sends out twining shoots. As it ages it develops lignified hooks from the petioles of fallen leaves, with which it grapples towards the forest canopy. The flowers are very fragrant, notably so in the evening. Each inflorescence may bear 20 or so flowers which open successively and change colour as they age, from white to pink to deep rose-pink over a 48-hour period. The effect is charming. The flexuous stems are used in basketry and for fashioning fish traps. The ripe seeds are toxic but the plant has some local medicinal uses in Africa.

Q. mussaendiflora (*Q. falcata* var. *mussaendiflora*) is a climber of secondary forest, where it grows to 5 or 7 metres, but it is not at all common in cultivation. The small flowers are white, from green to pink buds, but a fine display is provided by the surrounding scarlet floral bracts. The heads are reputed to last well when cut. At Kew this flowers from April until November provided it is kept rather dry in winter with the old growth pruned out. The specific name commemorates the genus *Mussaenda* (Rubiaceae), a fine group of shrubs with spectacular floral bracts.

Saba comorensis, the African rubber vine, is a strong woody climber in the Apocynaceae, found throughout tropical Africa. It produces twining reddish purple stems and jasmine-like white flowers which are flushed yellow in the throat. The yellow fruits are edible.

Strophanthus is a mainly African genus with flowers bearing elongated 'tails'. Some species have been used as the source of cardiac drugs. This is S. preussii, *a source of arrow poison.*

Strophanthus (Apocynaceae) is a genus of about 30 species mostly from West Africa, with great horticultural merit and of historic importance as the source of important drugs. Nearly all species are variable in form, acting first as a shrub and then becoming a climber. All prefer seasonal drought, during which they may drop their leaves, and then flower as the wet season commences. The petals of most species are elongated into highly ornamental 'tails'.

S. intermedius reaches 4 metres as a shrub or 20 metres as a climber and is drought-deciduous. The flowers are deep purple and orange within and reach 15 cm long. From each petal extends a horizontal tail 4 cm long. The roots and leaves of this species are used locally to treat rheumatism.

S. preussii reaches 12 metres as a climber and it normally remains evergreen. The dramatic and fragrant flowers are cream, flushed orange and dotted purple. The purple petaloid tails droop down to reach a full 30 cm in length. The latex of this species is used for arrow poison in Zaire, and fibres from the stems are used to make rope and fishing-line.

S. sarmentosus has fragrant white flowers flushed pink within, with drooping petaloid tails 6 cm long. Its habitat is savannah thicket, where it is normally deciduous and may flower before the leaves appear. Its seeds were used in the 1950s to yield the anti-arthritic drug cortisone, which is nowadays synthesised artificially. The seeds of various other African species have been used to yield the toxic glycosides strophanthin and ouabain. These have been used as cardiac drugs along with digitalin, though the interest in them now is mainly historic. Like so many of the Apocynaceae the genus contains active chemicals which can be toxic or beneficial to humankind depending on how they are exploited.

Climbers of Asia and Australasia

Argyreia splendens (Convolvulaceae) is one of 25 Indian species of the 90 or so in the genus. It comes from Assam, where it forms a vigorous twining vine with heart-shaped leaves densely felted underneath by very fine silver hairs. This is also particularly marked on the young growth and is very attractive. If in full sun, the vine will produce lilac, trumpet-shaped flowers, rather smaller than one would expect in the morning glory family, but a fine complement to the leaves.

Bauhinia vahlii (Leguminosae) is the closest we get in the Palm House to a vigorous forest liane. In the wild in the sub-Himalayan area of India its trunk may become up to 2 metres in girth and it is considered an annoying pest by forestry officers. Like all species of *Bauhinia* it produces two-lobed leaves, which give it the descriptive common name of camel's foot climber. The leaves are used as plates by local people (and sometimes as bow-ties by wayward Kew students). This vine is a tendril climber with brown tomentum on its branches. It rarely produces its yellowish-white flowers at Kew.

Chonemorpha fragrans (*C. macrophylla*) is a large woody twining climber from India, Burma, Sri Lanka, Malaysia, South China and the Philippines. It is in the family Apocynaceae and, in common with many other genera in this family, the bark and leaves contain poisonous alkaloids. Its redeeming horticultural feature is its floral display. Very fragrant white flowers up to 10 cm across and with a yellow throat are carried on branched inflorescences. The fruits are slim pods reaching 45 cm long and bear abundant fertile seed. The leaves are large and ovate and these and all parts of the plant produce white latex if they are damaged. This species has been valued in cultivation since the end of the nineteenth century.

Faradaya splendida (Verbenaceae) is one of a genus of 17 species and comes from New Guinea, Borneo and Queensland. It grows either as a shrub or a twining woody climber, with large ovate leaves. The greenish-white flowers appear in large panicles in the axils of the leaves and are pleasantly scented, smelling of carnations. The floor of the Queensland rainforest is sometimes littered with the fleshy white fruits of this species, each the size of a hen's egg.

The genus **Jasminum** is widespread in South-east Asia where it is valued for its fine display of flowers, which are mostly white and highly scented. Five species are grown in the north wing. All of them are twiners.

J. didymum is a relatively weak grower attaining 2–5 metres. It comes from dry brushwood forests in the Pacific area.

J. kedahense from the Malay peninsula is a vigorous climber with terminal clusters of fragrant white flowers in groups of 7–15. This is a large-flowered species, the corolla reaching 5 cm across.

J. maingayi from Penang and peninsular Malaysia is a beautiful but entirely scentless species. It has attractive dark green, glossy leaves and pure white flowers with very pointed petals.

J. sinense is a Chinese species with small, ovate leaves covered with a soft down. The flowers are profuse and scented.

The genus **Strongylodon** (Leguminosae) consists of vigorous twining lianes, about 20 species in all. There are two centres of diversity in the genus, Madagascar and the Philippines. From the Philippines comes the jade vine, *S. macrobotrys*, one of the most famous climbing plants at Kew and notable for its luminous jade-green flowers, a colour almost impossible to capture on film. In the wild the vine comes from montane forest but it must be tolerant of a wide range of temperatures, for it flowers as well in steamy Singapore as it does on Penang Hill and in the cool highland tea estates of peninsular Malaysia. I have even seen it in full flower under the shade of pines in temperate Madeira. The plant produces trifoliate leaves. The young growth emerges pale purple then becomes creamy white and then green. The pendent inflorescences are often over 60 cm long in cultivation, with over 100 flowers in groups of two to four along the raceme. In the wild, racemes nearly 3 metres long have been reported. Our plant flowered profusely just before the 1980s restoration and cuttings were preserved for replanting. The north wing also houses *S. lucida*, a red-flowered species from Christmas Island. Unfortunately the flowers are slender and less impressive than its Philippine cousin. Kew is interested in increasing the number of this genus in horticultural circulation, particularly those of Madagascar, where yellow-flowered species are known to exist.

Strophanthus divaricatus (Apocynaceae), the cow's horn fruit, is an Asian species of this mainly African genus. (See p. 76.) It comes from south-east China and Vietnam, where it grows to 4 or 5 metres as a shrub but far more as a climber. The flowers are yellow, spotted with red inside and each petal is elongated into a horizontal or pendent 'tail' about 9 cm long and usually twisted. The two-pronged woody fruits give the plant its common name. This is a good (though poisonous) ornamental and was first introduced into Britain in 1816.

Tecomanthe venusta (Bignoniaceae) is one of about 20 species of twining woody lianes mainly from New Guinea. The leaves are pinnate with five to seven leaflets and the bell-like flowers are borne on the old, leafless wood in the leaf axils. It is the nearest that a climber gets to the cauliflorous habit of flowering. (See pp. 27–28.) The flowers are maroon and yellow inside and are carried in clusters of 20 to 25. It is not common in cultivation.

Tetrastigma, the chestnut vines (Vitaceae), are a large group of about 90 species of vigorous, woody, tendril-clinging lianes from South-east Asia. They have fleshy, palmate leaves and are very demanding of water.

T. voinierianum from Vietnam has leaves with three to five lobes up to 30 cm across and brown-haired underneath. It occasionally produces greenish flowers dotted with red. These are borne on the old wood and are followed by edible, acid-tasting grapes. This species is sometimes seen as a pot plant in Britain, generally trained on a moss pole. *T. obovatum* is tolerant of rather lower temperatures, as it comes from the eastern Himalayas and southern China. It has more rounded leaflets but makes an equally lush foliage plant.

Thunbergia in the Acanthaceae is a large genus of about 150 species, some shrubs but mostly vigorous twining climbers, most of which are extremely free-flowering. They are an Old World genus and of these we display four Asian species in the north wing. All of them prefer a cool, dry resting period in winter and *T. mysorensis* is unlikely to flower without it. They all sucker freely from the rootstock.

T. coccinea comes from montane regions of northern India and northern Indonesia, where it grows to 25 metres in secondary forest on wet, alluvial soils. It has rather narrow leaves and profuse pendent racemes of red flowers marked yellow inside. Each floret is comparatively small but the racemes can reach 20–60 cm long overall.

T. grandiflora, the Bengal clockvine, is a very variable vine in flower and foliage. Some forms have hairy leaves. All forms always produce dense foliage and pendent racemes of white or pale blue flowers up to 7.5 cm across and with five flaring petals surrounded by bracts. They broadly resemble those of *T. laurifolia* but with shorter racemes.

The genus Tecomanthe *is a group of woody rainforest lianes, most of them native to New Guinea. This is* T. venusta.

T. laurifolia has leaves which are sometimes rounded at the base (like laurel) and long racemes of blue flowers which appear almost all year round. The form grown at Kew was given an Award of Merit by the Royal Horticultural Society in 1971 because of its constant floral display, under the cultivar name 'Augusta's Blue'. This form never sets seed. A form grown in Hong Kong is reported to produce racemes up to 1.8 metres long and this sets fertile seed.

T. mysorensis comes from southern India. It produces three-nerved leaves and long pendent racemes on the current year's growth. The flowers are generally rich yellow, marked brownish-red on each petal and on each of the flower bracts. The length of raceme in flower is generally about 20 cm. This is a fine ornamental commonly grown on pergolas in the drier tropics.

8 Yields of the rainforest: fruits, crops, medicines

TROPICAL FRUITS

THE PUBLIC IS BECOMING more and more aware of the variety of tropical fruits available, now that they are appearing alongside apples and pears in supermarkets and on market stalls. Before the building of the Palm House the introduction of exotic fruits and their successful cultivation was often a sign of social prestige. In about 1677 an anonymous artist painted a gardener, supposedly John Rose, the royal gardener, presenting the first pineapple cultivated in England to Charles II. Pineapple-shaped finials became popular ornaments on the gateposts and boundary walls of the estates of the English aristocracy. A new design of building, the glass-fronted 'orangery', was developed in the eighteenth century to overwinter subtropical citrus fruits; Kew's Orangery was designed by William Chambers in 1761. Today the common availability of tropical fruit is associated with the culinary demands of our multicultural society and improvements in freighted air transport and refrigeration as well as the familiarity of a wider section of the public with these products through their holidays abroad. British culinary taste is rapidly becoming more varied and adventurous. In many cases tropical fruits are now cultivated in areas well away from their countries of origin, for reasons to do with soil, labour availability, the absence of native pests and diseases and the demands of world trade patterns. Sometimes cultivation and production have become pantropical. In the Palm House these crops are mostly planted in the section which displays the flora of the country where they originated, if space allows.

Fruits of the Americas

In the centre transept are planted a good variety of fruits, including the familiar banana, which has always been a feature of this house and attracted an enormous number of visitors in the Victorian era. *Musa* species originated in the Old World but the cultivars bred from them are now cultivated worldwide. Several true species are planted in the north wing but the cultivar collection is grown in a special bed of well manured soil in the centre of the building, as in Victorian times. This provides them with maximum light and the absence of root competition which they need. Other fruits planted here are the cherimoya, soursop, bullock's heart, custard apple, breadnut, pawpaw, seagrape, anchovy pear, mammee apple and the more familiar avocado pear.

The various fruits of the genus **Annona** (Annonaceae) are still not very well known in Britain, perhaps because they do not travel well. However, several of them, particularly the cherimoya, are now cultivated in Europe.

A. cherimola, the cherimoya, is a semi-deciduous tree which grows to 5–9 metres and originated in the valleys of the Andes in Ecuador, Bolivia and Colombia. Its fruits are green, heart-shaped, marked by regular thumbprint-like depressions and can weigh up to 2 kg. These are eaten as dessert fruits and have a white flesh with a flavour of pineapple and banana. It is probably the most delicious of all the species but is the least tropical in its requirements, fruiting best at 17–20°C. It has been cultivated since the early seventeenth century in the highlands of many South American countries and was introduced into Spain in 1757, Jamaica in 1785, Hawaii in 1790 and reached India and Ceylon by 1880. The trees bear fruit at four or five years old and do so only when carefully hand pollinated (sometimes from trees of the related *A. senegalensis*). Yields average 25–80 fruits per year (Colombia). In the 1950s, *A. cherimola* was planted to replace diseased orange trees in Granada, Spain, and the crop is now common between there and the Mediterranean coast. In Jamaica the small, green, fragrant flowers are used to flavour snuff.

As a fruit the cherimoya is best served cut open so that the flesh can be spooned out, or it can be used to make sherbet or ice-cream. When squeezed the juice can be mixed with water and lemon to make a delicious soft drink.

A. montana is the least edible of the species and its fruit is generally considered only as a survival or famine food. However, its wood is useful as fuel and it is used as rootstock material for other species, particularly for cultivation in wet soil conditions. It is found wild in Peru, Brazil and the West Indies and is cultivated in the Philippines.

A. muricata, the soursop, is the most tropical of all the species and produces the largest fruit. It is an evergreen tree growing to 7 metres and produces heart- or kidney-shaped fruit covered with fleshy spines. Good fruits weigh over 2 kg and contain a white, cottony and very aromatic flesh with a flavour of pineapple and mango. This was one of the first fruits introduced from America to the Old World and is now cultivated all over the lowland tropics, producing about 12–24 fruits per tree each year in rich soil.

As a ripe fruit it is eaten fresh and added to fruit salads. Its pulp is often chilled and served as a drink or made into custard, sherbet or ice-cream. Immature fruits are cooked as a vegetable in Indonesia.

A. reticulata, the bullock's heart, is a semi-deciduous species growing to 7–8 metres and yielding heart-shaped fruits usually under 1 kg in weight. Its fruit has been described as 'mawkishly sweet' and is considered inferior to that of most of the other species. However, it crops in late winter and spring when other more desirable species are out of season and it also bears heavily, with mature trees carrying 34–45 kg of fruit per tree annually. This species is native to the West Indies but was naturalised and cultivated in Peru and Brazil very early. It was introduced to tropical Africa in the seventeenth century and is now also cultivated in Malaysia, the Philippines, the Bahamas, Bermuda and southern Florida. It needs similar cultivation conditions to the soursop, that is, deep, rich soil with good moisture and drainage. The fruit is commonly eaten fresh or juiced for drinks.

A. squamosa, the custard apple, is also known as the sweetsop or sugar apple. It is a semi-deciduous tree reaching 5–7 metres and produces small, yellow-green fruits only 5–9 cm across with fleshy spines. This is the most widely cultivated species. It was probably spread by the Spanish from South America to the Philippines and by the Portuguese to southern India before 1590. It was grown in Indonesia by the early seventeenth century and is now grown in China, Australia (Queensland), the West Indies, Hawaii, Polynesia and tropical Africa as well as Egypt and southern Israel. Its main area of commercial production is in India and it is the most important fruit crop in Brazil. It is very shallow rooted and it prefers dryish soil and perfect drainage. As a fruit it is eaten fresh, the seeds being removed in the mouth. It can also be pressed to produce juice which is added to ice-cream or used to flavour milk.

In addition to their uses as fruit crops, the various species have a wide range of other local uses. The seeds are poisonous and are used as insecticides or as emetics in local medicine and as fish poisons. The bark of several species is used in tanning and the seeds and leaves are crushed to form a louse-killer for both humans and domesticated animals. The juice, crushed leaves, flowers, roots and pounded immature fruits (particularly of the soursop and bullock's heart) have a wide range of local (unproven) medicinal uses for everything from urethritis, leprosy and dysentery to catarrh and eczema. The seed of the sugar apple is used in soap manufacture, the leaves in perfumery and the trunk to produce cordage fibre.

Brosimum alicastrum (Moraceae), the breadnut, is a dense-crowned tree which reaches 33 metres in its native Yucatan (Mexico) and the West Indies. It produces leathery, ovate leaves and flowers in globose heads followed by yellow spherical fruits 2.5 cm across. These contain one seed each, which can be boiled or roasted as a human food. All parts of the tree are important for animal fodder.

Carica papaya (Caricaceae) is known as pawpaw or papaya. It originated in the Americas although it is now cultivated worldwide. It produces a single, undivided stem up to 8 metres tall crowned by a head of palmate leaves up to 60 cm across. The fruits are fleshy berries produced in a cluster just under the crown and reach 7–30 cm long. They are smooth-skinned, green and ripen to yellow or orange. The flesh is also yellow or orange (rarely pink) and has an aromatic flavour rather like mango but with the smooth texture of a peach. It contains 10 per cent sugars and is a rich source of vitamin A, with some vitamin B and vitamin C. These plants are very fast-growing and require a very rich, well drained soil. They are also short-lived, starting to bear at 9–14 months and declining after three to five years. Most forms are dioecious and in orchard cultivation one male tree is planted for every 25–100 fruit-bearers. They are pollinated nocturnally by moths. Hermaphrodite cultivars do exist and these are very important in large-scale production, particularly in Hawaii. Expected yields are 30–150 fruits per plant per year, giving about 40 tonnes per hectare. All parts of the plant contain a milky sap which bears the pepsin-like enzymes papain and chymopapain, which is why the fruit is often recommended as a treatment for

Left: the custard apple,
Annona squamosa,
produces soft, sweet fruits
which can be eaten fresh or
added to ice-cream. They
sometimes find their way to
British supermarkets, as
does the related cherimoya.

Right: the pawpaw, or
papaya, Carica papaya,
comes from the Americas.
The yellow-orange fruit is
delicious in chilled fruit
salads. Plants fruit regularly
in the Palm House.

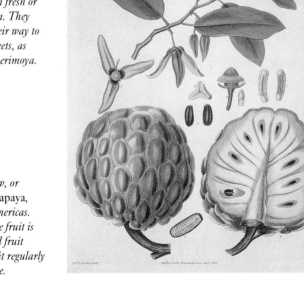

Bananas forming in ranks behind the male flower on a plantation on the Caribbean island of St Lucia. They are the most important export crop in the island's economy.

indigestion. These enzymes are commercially important in tenderising meat and in the canned meat and leather-tanning industries. For enzyme production the latex is tapped from unripe fruits, mainly in Tanzania and in Sri Lanka, primarily for the biggest meat-eating market in the world, the United States.

The ripe fruit is mainly eaten locally as it does not transport very well. It is eaten fresh for breakfast and in fruit salads or can be crystallised or tinned. Pulped fruit is used to make soft drinks, jams and ice-cream flavourings. Unripe fruit is sometimes cooked as a substitute for marrow and the young leaves can be eaten as a spinach.

Coccoloba uvifera (Polygonaceae), the seagrape, is a small tropical American tree or shrub of sandy sea-shores, rarely exceeding 6 metres and sometimes planted and clipped as a hedge. It produces rounded, olive-green leaves with red veins and very attractive, bronze, glossy new growth. The flowering stalk is a raceme up to 30 cm long, borne at the tips of stems and with white flowers. The green fruits ripen to purple and resemble bunches of grapes. They make a particularly good jelly.

Grias cauliflora, the anchovy pear, is a native of the West Indies. It is in the brazil nut family, the Lecythidaceae, and bears cauliflorous flowers, that is, flowers which grow directly out of the stem. It grows 10–17 metres tall in damp thickets and produces lance-shaped leaves up to a metre long in a tuft at the top of the stem. This is a common feature in tropical trees. The flowers are large, pale yellow and extremely fragrant. Writing in *Curtis's Botanical Magazine* in 1867, Dr Hooker reported that the anchovy pear had flowered several times at Kew in the 1860s and called it 'one of the most striking and easily managed of all those stately, palm-like dicotyledonous trees that are so greatly admired, and are essential for the decoration of every stove'. The fruit he compared to that of the mammee-apple (see below) and he described it as 'a large, brown, fleshy drupe . . . which was, according to Sloane, pickled and eaten by the Spaniards in lieu of mangoes, and was sent as a great rarity to Spain'.

Mammea americana (Guttiferae), the mammee-apple or mamey tree, is native to the West Indies, Central America and northern South America. It has been cultivated under glass in England since 1735 and is grown also in the Old World tropics. A medium-sized tree growing to 15 metres, the mammee produces ovate to elliptic leaves and fragrant white flowers. The fruits are berries – yellow, globular and up to 15 cm across. They are often produced in two crops a year and ripen over several months. Trees propagated vegetatively from high-yielding forms may produce 300–400 fruits per tree annually.

The fresh fruit of good forms is picked, deseeded and eaten fresh or in fruit salads or blended with sugar and made into a frozen sherbet. Bitter fruits are steeped in water and then cooked with sugar into a jam or stewed with sugar and lemon or lime juice. They also make good tarts and pies when seasoned with cinnamon and ginger. Mammee syrup is mixed with lemon juice to make a lemonade. In Brazil a wine is made from unripe fruit and a fermented toddy from the sap of the tree. Cuba exports the canned fruit.

The seed and gum of this tree is also insecticidal; it is one-fifth as active as pyrethrum. It is applied as a dust in order to poison by contact and is reported to be effective against a wide variety of insects, including cockroaches, ants, termites, mosquitoes, jiggers, fleas and sheep ticks.

The cultivars of ***Musa*** which produce our edible bananas are grouped in one bed in the centre transept. They are really jungle weeds of disturbed habitats, fast-growing and gross-feeding. Bananas are giant evergreen perennial herbs 2–9 metres tall, their trunks (pseudostems) being formed by overlapping leaf sheaths. Each shoot springs from a rhizome and flowers, fruits and then dies as it is replaced by a sucker. The growing point eventually becomes an inflorescence, which grows up the middle of the pseudostem and then emerges among the leaves. Some species produce erect inflorescences with violet-bracted flowers. These are insect-pollinated. Most of the cultivated edible bananas produce pendulous inflorescences with basal female flowers on a long axis which terminates in a maroon-bracted male bud which (to the Victorians) must have looked rather like a bell pull. Bats are the normal pollinators of maroon-bracted plants, but are not needed in the cultivars which set fruit parthenocarpically, that is without pollination. The fruits are berries and have been selected for parthenocarpy and female sterility to give the maximum quantity of fruit pulp, most wild forms being very thin-skinned and full of very hard seeds. The fruit clusters are termed 'hands' and each fruit a 'finger'. A fruiting head may contain 24–250 fruits and weigh 14–40 kg.

All cultivated bananas have been derived from the diploids *M. acuminata* and *M. balbisiana*. Many are triploid hybrids, a condition which ensures their sterility and seedlessness and thus their palatability. It also increases their vigour, growth rate and fruit size as well as their hardiness, disease resistance and the flavour of the fruit. Two or three hundred named cultivars have been produced, mainly from mutations from hybrids and all these must be propagated vegetatively. About half the world's bananas are edible raw and about half are plantains, that is, clones with a starchier and drier flesh which are more suited to frying and baking or the production of plantain flour.

It is thought that bananas were taken to Madagascar from Malaysia around 400 AD and from there to the African mainland. They were known to the Arabs and figure in the Koran as the 'tree of paradise'. In the early fifteenth century the Portuguese took them from Africa to the Canary Islands. Hispaniola was the recipient of plants in 1516 and this foothold in the New World was followed by a rapid spread. The precise date of introduction to Britain is not known. The first illustration of the fruit was published in John Gerard's *Herbal* of 1633 and was drawn from fruit imported from the Bermudas. Joseph Paxton, gardener to the 6th Duke of Devonshire, claimed that the plant had been grown in England in the 1730s. In 1829 Paxton obtained a dwarf plant which he named *M. cavendishii* after the family name of his employer. This is a clone, not a true species, and we now call it 'Dwarf Cavendish'. It is an important clone in international trade and is probably Chinese in origin. Bananas were cultivated in Britain in the hothouses of the wealthy throughout the latter half of the nineteenth century, in hotbeds of fermenting bark from tanneries. A weighty stem from the Palm House was presented to Queen Victoria at the gates of Kew and the amusing story of this and the subsequent demotion of the unfortunate gardener concerned is described on p. 14. Meanwhile the American United Fruit Company was attempting to fulfil the demand for bananas in the United States from 1870 onwards by bulk orders from Central America. The resulting influence on the economies and power struggles within these countries has given us the phrase 'banana republics'. Current world production (1987) is 39,354,000 tonnes (excluding plantains), of which Asia produces over a third, South America (mainly Ecuador and Brazil) a quarter, Africa under an eighth and the erstwhile banana republics of Central America only a sixth. Other banana products include banana wine, which has been made in the West Indies since the 1650s, and banana beer. Uses for the leaves include roofing and food packaging. Bananas are also planted as a shade crop for young coffee and cocoa trees. Several species yield cordage fibre from their stems. The most commercially important is *M. textilis* from the Philippines, commonly called Manila hemp. Several species with purple-flushed or marked leaves are used as ornamentals. They were particularly favoured by the Victorians.

Bananas are the most important of all the tropical fruits in terms of world production, and Kew can claim to have had an important part to play in the spread of their cultivation around the world and in the quarantining of varieties to prevent the spread of disease (particularly leaf spot and Panama disease). Many new varieties were shipped around the world in Wardian cases in Victorian times and later from the quarantine houses at Kew built in 1927 and 1951. The main area of breeding has been the West Indies, particularly Trinidad and Jamaica.

M. 'Dwarf Cavendish' was introduced to Britain from southern China via Mauritius in 1829 and was grown at Berryhill by a Mr Barclay before finding its way to Chatsworth and Mr Paxton, who flowered it in 1836. It only grows 1.8 metres tall and produces very glaucous leaves on short petioles. The fingers are 10–12 cm long, thin-skinned and very sweet and are produced at lower temperatures than in other clones. John Williams transported plants in a Wardian case from Chatsworth to the Navigator Islands and from there the clone found its way to Fiji and Tonga in 1848. Due to its compact size (which made it more wind-resistant) it established well, became a major item in the economy and reduced famine. It reached the Canary Islands probably direct from Indo-China in 1820 and is now the basis of the banana trade in the Canaries, and also in Brazil and Israel.

The jackfruit, Artocarpus heterophyllus *(see p. 88), produces huge fruits up to 18 kg in weight, which are supported directly on the main branches. The flesh is rich and banana-like. A taste of durian, breadfruit and jackfruit is a must for visitors to the Asian tropics.*

M. ensete (now correctly *Ensete ventricosum*), the giant Abyssinian banana, is a very vigorous species but the fruit is not edible. It is subtropical and is no longer grown in the Palm House, but it was grown in 1860 and flowered then and again in 1878 when it formed a spectacular feature. (See p. 14.)

M. 'Lacatan' is a triploid hybrid and became one of the most important commercial cultivars due to its resistance to Panama disease.

M. 'Lady's Finger' (sometimes called small fig) is a small-fruited, thin-skinned commercial cultivar producing fruits only 10 cm long but with a mild, buttery flavour.

M. 'Hapa'i' is a plantain clone producing bananas up to 30 cm long suitable for cooking. It will easily reach 7 metres. This is an old Hawaiian clone which is endangered.

M. ornata (*M. rosacea*) does not produce edible fruits but is valued for its attractive leaves, which are flushed purple underneath and borne on long, slender petioles. It reaches 2–2.4 metres. This and other ornamental bananas were popular with the Victorians, who used them in the summer months in bedding schemes with a subtropical theme. It was introduced into Europe from Mauritius in 1805. There are records of it flowering at Kew in October 1881 and June 1890.

M. 'Robusta' is an important commercial clone similar to *M.* 'Lacatan' but shorter at 3–4 metres and less prone to wind damage.

The starfruit, Averrhoa carambola (see p. 88), receives its name from the star-shaped cross-section of the fruit. Malaysia produces the finest crop, crisp yet juicy, and refreshingly aromatic.

The ripe fruits of edible bananas are particularly easy to digest. They can also be dried to produce banana figs and ground into a powder for incorporation into confectionery. Ripe fruits can also be baked with honey and lemon as a dessert. Common as they are in shops nowadays, it is only during this century that bananas have been imported in any quantity into the United Kingdom.

Persea americana (Lauraceae), the avocado pear, is a native of Central America. An evergreen tree growing to 20 metres (or less where trees are budded), it is rather shallow rooted and produces its elliptic leaves in flushes. Fragrant yellow flowers are produced in axillary panicles. The fruit, now well known all over the world, is a large fleshy berry, 7–20 cm long and yellowish-green with a butter-like flesh. However, there are many races of this species, including a highland Mexican race which is small and thin-skinned, a highland Guatemalan race with warty skin and a large lowland Central American form with smooth very hard rind. Many cultivars have also been developed, producing fruit not only different in size and thickness of skin but also in oil content and tolerance of cold. Avocados begin bearing at 3–4 years from budding, though they often bear biennially like mangoes. The fruit has an extraordinary composition, with 1–4 per cent protein, which is high for a fruit, and 3–30 per cent oil. The oil is similar to olive oil and is very digestible. It is produced more freely than in any other fruit. Avocados have the highest energy value of any fruit, tropical or temperate. The fruit was introduced to Europe in 1601 and rather late into Asia, where cultivation developed only in the nineteenth century. The main areas of commercial production nowadays are California, Cuba, Florida, Argentina, Brazil, South Africa, Israel, Hawaii and Australia.

Like bananas, avocados have mainly become popular this century. They are served as halved fruit with vinaigrette or other dressings, as a seasoned pulp (guacamole), in salads or ice-creams and milk shakes. Avocado oil is also used in cosmetics.

Fruits of tropical Asia

Of the distinctive fruits of this region, two (the starfruit and the mango) are now common in the West. Other fruits planted in the north wing are far rarer out of their native regions. These include the jackfruit, breadfruit and mangosteen. Many are distinctly seasonal and eaten by local peoples in large quantities because they cannot be stored.

Artocarpus altilis (*A. communis*) (Moraceae), the breadfruit, was the cargo carried by Captain Bligh on his fateful trip on the *Bounty*, the subsequent mutiny making the breadfruit a household name. (See p. 15.) In its native Polynesia it is an extremely handsome evergreen tree reaching 20 metres and producing a broad head of dark green, very lobed foliage. The fruit is a syncarp formed from the entire inflorescence, round and 10–30 cm across with a yellow-green rind. Inside, the seedless pale yellow pulp contains 20 per cent carbohydrate and 1.3 per cent protein, a composition more like a loaf than a fruit! The trees are slow to propagate vegetatively from root suckers or root cuttings, which accounted for Bligh's prolonged stay in Tahiti while the young plants were growing. They will bear at 3–6 years and can carry up to 700 fruits when mature but will only do so in very tropical conditions.

In Polynesia and the West Indies the fruits are boiled, baked, roasted or fried. Seeded forms exist, where the seeds alone are eaten, roasted like chestnuts.

A. heterophyllus, the jackfruit, is closely related to the breadfruit and produces the largest of any cultivated fruit, at up to 60 cm long. They can weigh up to 18 kg. The tree is less handsome than the breadfruit though just as sizeable. It bears the fruit cauliflorously, either on the trunk or on large limbs which can sustain its weight. They are pale green and studded all over with fleshy spines. Inside, the aromatic, banana-like flesh is held in sections around the seeds. It is eaten fresh, dried, preserved in syrup or made into a blancmange and it can be frozen. It is rather an acquired taste, and very rich, with 23.4 per cent carbohydrate. The seeds can be roasted. To eat jackfruit is one of the culinary experiences of a visit to the tropics.

Averrhoa carambola (Oxalidaceae), the carambola or starfruit, is an evergreen tree from India, Malaysia and southern China, growing to 5–10 metres. It has pinnate leaves which close at night in so-called 'sleep movements'. The small rose and purple flowers are borne on older wood and are followed by bright yellow fruits 10 cm long and with five-angled ribs which produce the star-like cross-section of the fruit. The flesh is crisp yet juicy with an aromatic flavour of quince. The trees are normally grafted onto seedling stock and will yield 45–135 kg of fruit a year if planted in full sun and well fertilised. Malaysia produces the juiciest fruits all the year round but the crop is more seasonal in India.

The fresh fruit is sliced as an attractive garnish in fruit salads or cooked in tarts and curries. In India it is made into preserves. China and Taiwan can it in syrup for export. In Malaysia it is stewed with cloves and sugar as a dessert. The flowers are eaten in salads in Java, the leaves are a good substitute for sorrel and the fruit can be juiced.

Garcinia mangostana (Guttiferae), the mangosteen, is mainly cultivated in Indonesia and Malaysia and it is now being imported into Western supermarkets. Like the breadfruit and jackfruit it is extremely tropical in its requirements and produces a sizeable tree. It is slow-growing and rarely fruits before 10–15 years old. Many people would rate it as the most delicious of any fruit. The fruits are round, purple and hard-rinded, yielding white segments tasting of very ripe plums. No pollination is required and a good tree will yield 200–500 fruits a year.

Mangifera indica (Anarcardiaceae), the mango, is an Asian tree now cultivated throughout the tropics. This 'king of all fruits' is as common there as the apple is in temperate countries. The tree is evergreen, long-lived, often huge at up to 30 metres across and produces its lance-shaped leaves in flushes of young pink growth. The panicles of pinkish-white flowers are followed by the green, yellow or reddish fruits 2.5–30 cm long, so juicy they are 'best eaten in the bath'. The flavour of mangoes has been described as a cross between apricot and pineapple. Good forms are stringless and are propagated by budding. The tree is of ancient cultivation and important in Hindu culture. It spread throughout Asia before the time of Christ, to Africa in the tenth century AD and to Brazil by the eighteenth century. Good forms were cultivated in the Palm House in the 1860s and the first inarch-grafted mango was introduced from India to Jamaica, via Kew, in 1869. The fruits have a high sugar content (10–20 per cent) and are an important source of vitamins A, B and C. The main producer is India, which has the seasonal drought required to get good flowers and fruit. Britain imports quantities air-freighted from Kenya.

The ripe fruits are eaten raw or juiced and can be used for squashes, jams and preserves. Unripe fruits can be used in chutneys.

TROPICAL CROP PLANTS

Besides yielding delicious fruits, the tropics give us a wide range of natural products – from fibres to dyes, from timbers to spices, from beverages to perfumes and from root crops to building materials. Some of these, including mahogany, rubber and cotton, have been, or still are, the mainstay of several countries' economies. Others, particularly coffee and cocoa and several of the spices, have profoundly influenced our diets.

Crops of the Americas

Bixa orellana (Bixaceae), the lipstick tree or annatto, is one of our most important natural food colourants and one which everyone is likely to consume every day. It is a tropical American shrub or small tree growing to a maximum of 5 metres and with heart-shaped leaves. The showy pink and white flowers are followed by prickly red fruits. The orange seed pulp is crushed in water, dried and made into cakes of a reddish-yellow dye which is widely used in colouring cheese and butter, margarine and some edible oils. In the EEC permitted colouring list it is numbered E160(b). It has no known harmful effects. The plant is also used as a quick-growing ornamental and as a hedge and is the source of all American Indian warpaints.

Carludovica palmata (Cyclanthaceae) is the source of fibre for panama hats. The production of these from this understorey palmlike plant is described on p. 120.

Gossypium is the genus in the Malvaceae which yields our cottons, the most important of the world's vegetable fibres. There are about 30 species, some annual and some perennial, now distributed throughout the world in the subtropics as well as the tropics, with some races more suited to the dry subtropics. All of them need bright sunlight. All species have palmate leaves and attractive serrated calyces, yellow, white or purplish flowers and capsular fruits (bolls). These contain the fluffy cotton lint surrounding the seeds. The cotton which would have been familiar to the slaves of the old American South is the high-quality tetraploid *G. barbadense*, the shrubby sea island cotton from Peru via the West Indies. Planted in the centre transept is one of the many cultivated forms of cotton, *G. punctatum* 'Hopi'. The annual Levant cotton, *G. herbaceum*, is planted in the south wing. It is diploid like other Old World cottons.

Cotton is harvested mainly by hand and then machined (ginned) to remove the lint, which is classed according to its length or 'staple' and then spun. Medium-staple cotton is mainly produced in the United States and yields 75 per cent of world production. The chief world producers of all types of cotton are the Soviet Union, China and the USA, followed by India. Cotton seed is pressed for its 16–24 per cent oil content, which is used in the manufacture of margarine and industrial oils. Pressed seed cake is used as cattle food.

Rubber, Hevea brasiliensis, *is a heat-demanding Amazonian tree. Young plants were shipped from Kew to Malaya in Wardian cases to start the Asian rubber industry. A consignment was reconstructed to commemorate this at the 1987 Chelsea Flower Show.*

The cultivation of cotton, mainly from *G. barbadense*, was already well under way in the Americas at the time of Columbus. However, in Europe, wool and hemp were the most important fibres until the industrialisation of cotton production in the nineteenth century by ginning. The disruption of the American Civil War and then the ravages of the boll weevil led to the spread of so-called upland cotton, based on cultivars of *G. hirsutum*. These are now the most important types in modern production. The by-product known as cotton wool is made from the fuzz left when the lint has been removed in ginning.

Hevea brasiliensis (Euphorbiaceae) is the source of 99 per cent of natural commercial rubber, which is produced by tapping the latex of the stem. An Amazonian rainforest tree by origin, this was introduced to Malaya via Kew in 1877 and from the turn of the century formed the backbone of the Malayan economy, a position which it retains to this day. Kew's role in this remarkable story is described on p. 16.

The tree is a very fast-growing species, easily reaching 20 metres and with digitate leaves on long petioles which are produced in purplish flushes, as in many tropical trees. It is extremely sensitive to cold. In its native Amazon it was used by local Indians to produce footwear and for waterproofing fabrics. This is chronicled by Columbus in the accounts of his second voyage of 1493–6. Rubber was first brought to London and sold as a curiosity in the 1770s. The first rubber tubing was made in 1791. In 1823 Macintosh developed a way of coating raincoats to make waterproofs, thereafter known as mackintoshes, garments looked on with much amazement, as were the first umbrellas. Unfortunately the solution of rubber in naphtha was not stable and became tacky except in a narrow temperature range. It was not until the latex was heated with sulphur (vulcanisation) that rubber really took off as a mouldable material, and this single industrial process has had a profound

Cocoa is produced from the tropical American understorey tree Theobroma cacao. *Half of the world's production now comes from Ghana and the Ivory Coast, where the beans are extracted from the pods and exported for the manufacture of milk chocolate.*

effect on our daily quality of life. Vulcanised rubber has been used in the production of barrier contraceptives from the early birth-control movement to today. In 1888 Dunlop's invention of the pneumatic tyre laid the foundations for motor transport and 70 per cent of all rubber consumption is now associated with automobile production. Huge amounts of rubber are used in waterproofing clothing, and it was this use (for the uniforms of troops in the American Civil War) which led to demand first outstripping supply in 1865. In the Second World War the fall of Malaya to the Japanese stimulated the search for rubber from other plant sources and particularly for synthetic rubbers. These finally overtook natural rubber in 1961, but although this and plastics are now used extensively, natural rubber is still a major industry. In 1987 world production was 4,574,000 tonnes. Of this Malaysia produced the greatest share at 1,580,000 tonnes, followed by Thailand. The only other significant producers are in Africa, in particular Liberia and Nigeria. Latin America, the original home of the rubber tree, now produces only 1 per cent, although it is the home of many related *Hevea* species which could be a marketable source of disease-resistant stock. The current threats to the Amazonian rainforest are endangering this genetic resource.

In Malaysia, rubber is produced from plantations of 240–450 trees per hectare grown either by large landowners or smallholders. The time-honoured method of excision tapping involves paring the bark in a sloping cut just to, but not into, the growing cambial tissue. This is done daily, before or soon after dawn and involves some skill. A spout placed at the base of the cut drains the latex into a glass or pottery cup, from which it is collected daily. Tapping usually starts when the trees are 5–7 years old. Double tapping involves two cuts and usually reduces the life of the plantation. Slaughter-tapping is draining the tree to exhaustion prior to replanting. Seedling trees may produce 4–270 kg of dry rubber per hectare but the best budded clones, as developed by the Rubber Institute of Malaya, may yield over 900 kg.

The traditional method of processing is the production of smoked sheet rubber. This involves diluting the latex with water, straining it, coagulating it with acetic or formic acid and then skimming it. When it has coagulated into a curd, it is rolled into sheets, dried in a smoke house for several days at 50°C and then graded and baled. Other methods have been developed to make it more competitive with synthetic rubber. These involve centrifuging the latex to concentrate it for export as a liquid, or production in crumb form.

Other plants which have been commercially planted in plantations for rubber production include the well-known rubber plant (*Ficus elastica*) and the related *Castilla elastica* (both in Moraceae), *Manihot glaziovii* (Euphorbiaceae) and *Funtumia elastica* (Apocynaceae). *Funtumia* is planted in the south wing and *Castilla* in the centre transept.

Manilkara zapota (Sapotaceae), the sapodilla, is a tropical American tree from which latex is tapped to produce chewing-gum. A slow-growing, evergreen tree, eventually reaching 17–25 metres, it produces small white flowers and brown fruits which are edible when ripe. They taste of pears and brown sugar. These are eaten as a dessert fruit and are locally called sapodilla plums or nisperos. Production is increased by hand pollination. The tapping of the trees for 'chicle' is an ancient art, gum having been widely used by the Aztecs. Today most production is from wild trees in south-east Mexico, Guatemala and Belize. The trunks are tapped every two to three years and the latex is boiled to produce gum which is mainly exported to the United States. A productive tree will yield 50–180 kg of latex annually after it is ten years old. Several heavy-yielding cultivars have been developed.

Myroxylon balsamum (*M. pereirae*) (Leguminosae), the balsam of Tolu, is a huge South American tree eventually attaining 33 metres and with a trunk of at least 1 metre in diameter. It is tapped to produce balsam, which is used as a fixative in perfumes, ointments and cough syrups. The main centre of production is Salvador but it is exported via Peru. Other trees important in the perfume industry include the Asian *Cananga odorata*, the ylang ylang tree, which is planted in the north wing. (See pp. 98–99.)

Ochroma pyramidale (*O. lagopus*) (Bombacaceae), is the tropical American tree which gives us balsa wood. An extremely fast-growing tree of lowland secondary forest, it is almost classed as a weed because of its short life. It will grow to 21 metres in seven years or so and is mature at 12 to 15 years. Balsa means raft and commemorates the use the Indians had for its wood, which is the softest and most perishable of all commercial timbers and is lighter than cork. It is possibly the most rapid-growing tree known to humankind. Its wood is used wherever buoyancy and lightness are required, in liferafts, fishing floats, splints and in packing materials. Most of the world's production comes from Ecuador.

Pimenta dioica (Myrtaceae), the culinary allspice or pimento, is a native of Central America and the West Indies. A small, evergreen tree growing to 7–10 metres, it produces cream flowers with the numerous stamens characteristic of the family. The fruit is a berry, 5 or 6 mm across, which is picked green and dried in the sun for seven to ten days to produce the spice. First introduced to Europe in 1601, it was named allspice because it gave the flavours of cinnamon, nutmeg, and clove all in one go. It is used in pickles and in curing meats. An oil extracted from the leaves and the dry fruit is used in perfumery. The main producer of allspice is Jamaica, where it is grown in plantations of budded stock of female trees, a few males being planted as pollinators. Trees bear from six years onwards and can yield up to 2 kg in a good year. Wild trees are also harvested but are far less productive.

Swietenia mahagoni (Meliaceae) is the true Spanish mahogany tree of tropical America. An evergreen tree growing to 25 metres, it has attractive pinnate leaves up to 30 cm long, small white flowers and green, woody fruits. It produces basal buttresses even as a young tree. This species and the related *S. macrophylla* produce the finest wood in the world for cabinet-making and are prized for their dark red colour and the working properties and finish of the timber. The search for mahogany in the seventeenth century led to the foundation of several mahogany colonies in Central America, including British Honduras, now the independent state of Belize. The species is now almost completely logged out in the West Indies and is seriously overexploited in the Amazon, where it is being 'mined' rather than treated as a resource to be managed. The so-called African mahoganies (*Khaya* and *Entandrophragma* species) are close to *Swietenia* and are sometimes used as substitutes for it. They did not become important in trade with Britain until the 1870s. *Khaya anthotheca* and *K. nyasica* are planted in the south wing.

Theobroma cacao (Sterculiaceae), the cocoa tree, was called the 'food of the Gods' by Linnaeus, to commemorate the Mexican Indian belief that the crop was a divine gift. Cocoa is an understorey tree growing to a maximum of 8 metres and with large papery leaves which are pendent and, in some clones, flushed pink when young. The tiny cauliflorous flowers are borne on the old wood and the fruits are furrowed pods. They ripen to green, yellow, red or purple (depending on the cultivar) and usually bear 20–60 seeds per pod. The cocoa 'beans' are extracted from the pod by cracking it open and they are then fermented for six or seven days to remove astringency, prevent them germinating and to develop the

The dye called henna is produced from the dried leaves of the subtropical shrub Lawsonia inermis. *In the wild in North Africa and Arabia this flowers profusely. Its common name is the mignonette tree.*

flavour of chocolate. Around 30 pods are needed to produce 1 kg of dry cocoa. After fermentation the beans are sun-dried and then polished mechanically or by treading, much as the French tread grapes, a procedure known locally as 'dancing the cocoa'.

Cocoa is an extremely tropical crop, surpassing the coconut in sensitivity to cold. It is only cultivated within 15° of the Equator and at low elevations, usually under 300 metres above sea-level. It needs constant moisture, a rich well-drained soil, and shade. It is often interplanted with rubber, oil palm, coconuts or pawpaw, or under bananas. There are many different clones of cocoa (propagated by cuttings or by patch budding) which have different qualities and command different prices on the world market. Trinidad cocoas, for example, are valued for the manufacture of astringent dark chocolate. Bushes will produce 215–3240 kg per hectare, depending on the clone.

Cocoa has an interesting history. It was taken from its native Andes to Europe by Columbus. The Spanish first prepared it by roasting the beans with vanilla and sugar. It became popular in the seventeenth century as a warming beverage in the cool temperate countries, especially Italy, France, Holland, Germany and Britain. It was expensive and only consumed by the wealthy, chocolate-houses becoming as much a feature of London society as coffee-houses and gentlemen's clubs. In 1828 the Dutch discovered how to remove the cocoa fat from the bean to produce a powder which could be ground with sugar to make chocolate. Nearly 50 years later, in 1876, the Swiss boosted their long association with chocolate manufacture by first making milk chocolate, using dried or powdered milk. In 1879 'Amelonado' clones, the finest for producing milk chocolate, were introduced into Ghana from Fernando Po, and Ghana thereafter became the leading producer. In 1987 world production of all cocoas stood at 2,002,000 tonnes. Of this, 780,000 tonnes were produced by the Ivory Coast and Ghana. New World production (in Brazil and Ecuador) was 672,000 tonnes. The by-product of cocoa called cocoa butter is used in making white chocolate and in cosmetic creams. Nearly all cocoa consumption is in temperate countries, a fact easily appreciated by anyone who has tried to eat chocolate in hot, tropical conditions! Kew has held an important role in the quarantining of cocoa germplasm between areas of cultivation in Africa and the New World.

Coffee, Coffea *species, produces fine scented flowers and fruits which ripen from green to orange. When fully ripe the bright red fruits are picked to yield the coffee beans.*

Crops of Africa

Blighia sapida (Sapindaceae), the akee, was named after Captain Bligh of the *Bounty*. Native to West Africa, it was introduced into Jamaica in the late eighteenth century and became naturalised. It is a large tree with pinnate leaves and small, greenish-white, fragrant flowers. The crop is the fruit, which must be eaten with extreme care. They consist of red capsules which split open to reveal black seeds surrounded by a white fleshy aril. The arils are edible but only when ripe. Unripe arils and the seeds themselves are highly poisonous, the active agents being hypoglycine A and B.

Coffea is the genus in the Rubiaceae which yields our commercial coffees. The most important species, producing 75 per cent of the world's crop, is the upland species, *C. arabica*, Arabian coffee. This originated in Ethiopia and was first cultivated in the Yemen in the eleventh century AD. The first news of the plant in Europe arrived in 1576 and coffee-houses became widespread in the third quarter of the seventeenth century.

C. arabica is an evergreen shrub reaching 5 metres and requiring shade, as does cocoa. It has very dark green, glossy leaves, pure white fragrant flowers and brilliant crimson berries called 'cherries', each containing two seeds or coffee 'beans'. The sight and scent of a plantation in full flower is not easily forgotten. The beans ripen over 8–12 months and are harvested, processed to remove the pulp and sun-dried. This produces green coffee, which must be roasted to release the water-soluble flavours and aromas before the drink can be prepared. Expected yields are 500–4000 kg per hectare. There are many cultivars, including the famous Jamaican 'Blue Mountain'.

C. canephora (*C. robusta*), Congo or robusta coffee, comes from Zaire and is a more vigorous tree, easily reaching 10 metres. It grows at lower altitudes than *C. arabica*, preferring areas at 300–600 metres above sea-level, and produces heavily in wetter climates, but gives a lower quality crop. It is the dominant species in Brazilian plantations and is primarily used in the manufacture of instant coffees. As with many tropical crops, Kew has had a role in the spread of germplasm worldwide. *C. canephora* was introduced to Singapore and to Trinidad via Kew in 1898.

Coffee is usually grown in plantations under shade trees, as is cocoa, and the plants are raised from seed selected from good mother trees. They are tolerant of wider temperature ranges than cocoas and are cultivated 28° north and south of the Equator. Coffee was first cultivated on plantations in Brazil in the mid-eighteenth century and Brazil is the biggest producer, with 2,112,000 tonnes (1987). World production at that date was 6,145,000 tonnes of green coffee, with Africa contributing 1,294,000.

Cola nitida (Sterculiaceae), the cola nut, is one of the species originally used in the world's cola drinks. It is native to the rainforest of West and Central Africa but is now cultivated in plantations in Africa, the Caribbean, South America and eastern Asia. An evergreen tree growing 6–15 metres tall, it is related to the cocoa tree and bears small, yellowish-purple flowers on the older wood. These are followed by star-shaped fruits consisting of several pods. Each pod holds five to nine large seeds which contain 2 per cent caffeine and 0.05 per cent of the active ingredient also found in cocoa, theobromine. Each tree will yield up to 16 kg of seed a year and the plantations are very long-lived. Besides their historic use in cola drinks, local people in Africa and South America chew the nuts to release the stimulants in a similar practice to betel-chewing in Asia. (See p. 45.)

Funtumia elastica (Apocynaceae) is the most important of Africa's rubber-producing trees. It is an enormous tree growing to 30 metres or more. However, its yield is only one-twentieth of that of good clones of *Hevea brasiliensis* in Malaysia.

Ipomoea batatas (Convolvulaceae) gives the world the sweet potato, a crop now grown all over the globe. It has a long tradition of cultivation in pre-Columbian times in Central and South America and the Caribbean, and has been grown in Polynesia and New Zealand since the fourteenth century.

Columbus took it to Spain in 1492 where it later became confused with the true potato, which was probably named through a corruption of the species name 'batatas'. *I. batatas* is either a prostrate or an ascending herb with scandent, succulent shoots. The edible parts are mainly the underground tubers, which contain up to 2 per cent protein, 27 per cent carbohydrate and 3–6 per cent sugars. The yellow- and orange-fleshed cultivars are the sweetest and are also a rich source of vitamin A. Unfortunately they do not keep well. Sweet potatoes are an important crop in Africa, competing with cassava and yams. Africa now grows more than any other producer apart from China. The leaves are variable in shape and colour between cultivars but all are useful for forage or as a source of fresh greens. Above an altitude of 2200 metres the crop is only grown for forage. In the Palm House we grow sweet potatoes as ground-cover plants. Flowers are produced in the tropics but these rarely occur in temperate zones under glass.

Sweet potatoes are mainly propagated by stem cuttings and grown as annuals on ridges or mounds of well manured soil. The crop is harvested as required and cannot be stored. Expected yields are around 17 tonnes per hectare unless the crop is infected with virus. The tubers are usually eaten boiled or baked, being particularly delicious with butter and cinnamon. When dried they can also be ground into a flour or fermented into an alcoholic drink.

Lawsonia inermis (Lythraceae) is the so-called mignonette tree which produces the henna of commerce. It comes from the drier, sunny, subtropical areas of North Africa and Arabia, where it produces a shrub to 2 metres tall with small, elliptic leaves 2–5 cm long. The fast orange dye known as henna is produced by drying the leaves and grinding them. The dust is then applied to the skin or hair mixed with lime juice, or as a constituent of commercially prepared shampoos and hair dyes. The fragrant white and rose flowers are produced in panicles at the branch tips and are used in perfumes. The plant responds well to the pruning involved in repeated cropping and plantations are not allowed to flower.

Tamarindus indica (Leguminosae), the tamarind tree, is a tree of semi-arid areas of Africa and India but is included here because it is also grown in areas of monsoonal rainforest on well drained soils. It is semi-evergreen and grows to 20 metres with a spreading, rounded crown of pinnate foliage, making it useful as a shade tree. The flowers are gold with red veins and prominent stamens and are borne in long racemes. They are followed by sausage-like pods up to 14 cm long, constricted around the seeds and covered with a brown scurf. Inside is an edible fruit pulp consisting of around 70 per cent carbohydrate (mostly in the form of sugar) and 3 per cent protein. The pulp is brown and acid in taste due to the presence of 10 per cent tartaric acid. It is eaten in curries, preserves, jams and sweetmeats and can be made into a drink or sherbet. When dried or tinned it is exported and is used in the West in meat sauces and chutneys. The seeds are also edible when roasted or boiled and they can be ground into a flour.

This tree is now distributed throughout the tropics. It was possibly introduced in early times from Africa or Madagascar to India and its fruit has a long history of use in Hindu medicine.

Many tropical trees have highly perfumed flowers. The perfume known as ylang ylang is produced from the green flowers of Cananga odorata, *an Asian relative of the custard apple.*

Crops of Asia

Cananga odorata (Annonaceae) is the ylang ylang of the perfume trade. A native of Malaysia, it is an attractive evergreen tree up to 25 metres tall in the wild, with gracefully drooping branches and foliage similar to the fruit-bearing *Annona* species of the Americas. The flowers are yellowish-green with strap-shaped petals and are borne in clusters on the old wood and profusely in the leaf axils of the pendent branches. They are extremely fragrant, with a perfume that carries in warm, humid air, particularly in the evening. The black, olive-like fruits are also attractive.

It is cultivated in plantations, where the leading shoot is taken out when the trees are 3 metres high to ease the harvesting of the flowers. Harvesting is done before dawn and the crop is distilled to produce ylang ylang oil which is used in high-class perfumes. Subsequent distillations produce cananga oil which is used to perfume soaps and other products. Production is now concentrated in Java, the Philippines and Nigeria. The tree has been introduced into many tropical countries as an ornamental. It is sometimes planted in the courtyards of Buddhist temples and the flowers are often seen on sale in Asia as offerings, along with those of frangipani.

Corchorus olitorius (Tiliaceae) is the source of much of the world's jute fibre. The plant is an annual with a single stem which grows rapidly to 4 metres in one season and bears rather nettle-like leaves. The small flowers are followed by long, thin seed capsules. Jute is often cultivated in association with rice in the Ganges delta and up into the foothills of the Himalayas. It is a labour-intensive crop, hand planted like rice using seed-raised plants. The stems are harvested, bundled and retted in water to separate the fibres from the rest of the plant tissue. It is then dried and spun before manufacture into sacking, cable-covering, wallpaper, backing for linoleum, and a host of other products, including common twine. Jute was first introduced to England in 1828 and has grown in importance as a fibre with the development of spinning processes. It has recently been successfully introduced as a smallholder's crop in the Amazon basin.

Curcuma longa (*C. domestica*) (Zingiberaceae), yields our culinary turmeric and is widely cultivated in Indo-Malaysia. An understorey herb, this plant produces leafy stems up to 1 metre in height from basal rhizomes. The white and yellow flowers appear on a separate basal stalk of rose-coloured bracts. However, the species will only flower if it has a dry period of dormancy, as in the monsoonal teak forest where it grows wild. The rhizomes have orange flesh and it is these which are used, dried and powdered, as a curry spice and also for colouring rice. The dye can be used to colour cloth, but the colour is not permanent.

Diospyros ebenum (Ebenaceae) from Sri Lanka and southern India is one of the species which produces our commercial ebony timber. An evergreen tree reaching 26 metres it grows slowly in dry forest rather than true rainforest. It is in high demand for the very black heartwood it produces, which is worked for decorative purposes where strength is not required. It takes a high, lustrous polish and is principally used in turnery and for inlay work.

Elettaria cardamomum (Zingiberaceae) is the forest-floor herb from southern India and Sri Lanka which yields the culinary spice cardamom. This plant forms a dense clump of leafy shoots to 60 cm tall which spring from spreading rhizomes. The yellow and red hooded flowers are borne just at ground level and are followed by ellipsoid, longitudinally ridged pods which form the spice that plays such a large part in Indian cuisine. The plant is attractive in foliage and would make a fine houseplant if more readily available from the nursery trade. The leaves give off a spicy aroma when bruised.

Gigantochloa (Gramineae) is one of several genera of giant bamboo which are important for building materials in the Far East. Giant bamboos are the fastest-growing plants on earth and can achieve growth of 30–75 cm *per day* in optimum conditions. In the Palm House they are cut when about a metre or so above balcony level. If left they are capable of breaking glass and growing 2–8 metres beyond the top lantern! They grow from rhizomes and produce erect culms with lateral, leafy growth. Both species of *Gigantochloa* come from Java. *G. apus* has particularly durable culms and is preferred to *G. verticillata*, although the latter grows taller, to 25 metres. The culms are used whole for building houses, rafts, bridges and for scaffolding. When split they are used for basketry of all kinds and for veneers. In China and in India bamboo pulp is used for paper-making. Particularly good pulp is produced by another giant species, *Bambusa vulgaris*, which is of unknown origin. It is common in Central America and the West Indies, where the culms are used as banana props.

Musa textilis (Musaceae), Manila hemp, is the species of banana used to produce hemp fibre in the Philippines, an industry which has only come to prominence this century. This species produces inedible, bat-pollinated fruits and is prized for the very fibrous quality of the outer sheaths of the pseudostems. These are removed by hand, or by machine on larger estates, and dried prior to grading. Manila hemp is resistant to salt- and fresh water and is used in the United States, Japan and the United Kingdom for the manufacture of marine cables and fishing nets, towropes and mining cordage. Lesser-quality fibre is used in paper-making and to make tear-resistant teabags. Other fibre plants planted in the Palm House include jute (*Corchorus olitorius*, see previous page) and kenaf, (*Hibiscus cannabinus*, see p. 112).

Piper nigrum (Piperaceae) gives us black and white pepper. The plant is a vine which can grow 10–15 metres high, normally rooting into the bark of host trees in the wild. It has a heart-shaped leaf and tiny flowers on a spike. When cross-pollinated the spikes develop small round green fruits. These are harvested and dried to produce black pepper. White pepper is obtained from ripe, red fruits which are fermented to remove the skin and reveal the smooth peppercorns. The characteristic flavour of pepper comes from several oils and alkaloids. Pepper originated in Assam and Burma but is now cultivated all over the moist tropics in all three continents, usually trained on frames for ease of harvesting.

Saccharum officinarum (Gramineae) is the tropical, reed-like grass which produces over half the world's sugar. Thought to have originated in New Guinea, it was spread by Arab traders to the Mediterranean region in the eighth century AD. The Spanish and Portuguese were responsible for introducing it to the New World but it remained a luxury until this century.

Sugar cane is a rhizomatous grass growing 5 metres high or more and containing a sugary sap. It is cut by hand about 12 months after planting and yields around 22 tonnes per hectare in good soil. Production involves crushing the cane mechanically and filtering the juice, before heating it to produce crystallised brown sugar. Molasses is removed by centrifuging and further refining produces white sugar. The molasses is a valuable by-product used for making rum. With burning over and refertilisation, the field will produce a further four to eight crops before replanting becomes necessary. In the 1980s Brazil became the world's heaviest producer, followed by India and Cuba.

Zingiber officinale (Zingiberaceae) yields the spice ginger. A forest-floor plant originally from India or the Pacific Islands, it produces a pale brown branching rhizome which sends up shoots to 1 metre high. These bear narrow, pointed leaves. Separate stems send up club-like, bracted inflorescences with small yellow and purple flowers which are nearly always sterile. The characteristic taste of ginger comes from a mixture of oils, alkaloids and resins. It is of very ancient cultivation and was spread around the Old World by Arab traders. The principal producers are now China, Indo-Malaysia and the West Indies; Hong Kong being the main producer of cooked ginger in crystallised or syrup form. Ginger has a good range of medicinal virtues and is the dominant spice used in Chinese cookery.

The crop demands rich soil and if well grown yields 10–25 tonnes per hectare after ten months of growth. Green ginger yields up to 30 per cent of its weight as dry ground ginger.

MEDICINAL PLANTS OF THE TROPICS

The richness and diversity of the tropical floras have led to them being called the world's medicine chest. The Worldwide Fund for Nature (WWF) has estimated that over a quarter of prescriptions currently dispensed in the United States contain a principal ingredient derived from a plant. There is a huge wealth of compounds both discovered and still undiscovered in the tropics, some of them known only to native populations. In Amazonia, for example, only 1 per cent of the flora has been screened for medicinal use. As these forests are progressively destroyed so is this resource. As native populations decline through imported disease and younger people are tempted to more westernised life in the cities, so the transmission of this knowledge between the generations breaks down. We may never know what we have destroyed.

Many of the plants in the Palm House have medicinal uses even though they may be grown for other reasons, such as their fruits. A good example is the *Annona* collection, described on pp. 80–82. Other plants have made particular contributions to the history of mainstream medicine from Victorian times to the present day. The following paragraphs point out the most important of these.

In the Victorian period, a plant valued for the insecticidal properties of its bark was *Quassia amara* (Simaroubaceae), or Quassia wood, which contains the alkaloid quassin. This shrub has fine scarlet flowers and is planted in the central transept.

In the late 1940s and 1950s the genus *Strophanthus* (Apocynaceae) was used to develop drugs to strengthen and regulate the heartbeat and as a source of the anti-arthritic drug cortisone. Several of these species are planted in the south wing. In the same family is *Cerbera manghas*, a small, white-flowered evergreen tree of coastal areas from Madagascar and Australasia. This is also a source of cardiac glycosides. It is planted in the north wing.

In the 1960s various species of yam (*Dioscorea*), mainly from Mexico, were discovered to contain the glycoside saponin. This yields various steroids of which the most important is diosgenin. Nearly all steroidal drugs were derived from this in the 1970s, including oral contraceptives and other sex hormones. Although most of these are now synthesised, the world would not have had 'the pill' without the compounds first isolated from these plants.

The giant bamboos are the fastest-growing plants on earth and are a particularly important source of building materials in the Far East. Several species, including Bambusa vulgaris, *shown here, are also used to make paper.*

The plant kingdom provides both the medicine chest and medical research library for humankind. The various alkaloids isolated from the Madagascar periwinkle, Catharanthus roseus, *are used as an effective treatment for leukaemia in children.*

One of the most ornamental small shrubs in the south wing is *Catharanthus roseus*, once known as *Vinca rosea*, the Madagascar periwinkle (Apocynaceae), which is often obtainable nowadays as a pot plant. It is a small shrub, rarely more than 60 cm tall, with pale green leaves and five-petalled flowers of a rich carmine pink, white on the reverse. There are several naturally occurring forms of this plant: 'Albus' is pure white with very large flowers, while 'Ocellata' is white with a red central ring. This plant was introduced to Britain from Madagascar and is now cultivated and naturalised all over the tropics. Extracts from it have long been used to treat diabetes in Jamaica, but the story of the real discovery of its value began in Indianapolis, Indiana, where organic research chemists of the Eli Lilly Company began investigating the many alkaloids in this species. They prepared a wide range of pure crystalline compounds but knew little about their pharmacology. By chance another research department in the company had a strain of leukaemic mice. The compounds were tried on them and produced a significant drop in the number of circulating leukaemic cells. A small-scale clinical trial followed and produced the same result. Nowadays the alkaloids vincristine and vinblastine are used to treat various leukaemias in children and adults and have been largely responsible for the drop in the death-rate from nine out of ten to three or four out of ten. They are also highly successful in the treatment of lymphomas, Hodgkin's disease and other malignancies of the blood. Vincristine was first used on children in Britain in 1960 by Professor W Jacobson of Cambridge University, who had obtained it from the head of medical research at Eli Lilly during an attachment to the Harvard Medical School.

In the 1980s considerable interest has developed in a large ornamental leguminous tree from the rainforests of Queensland and New South Wales in Australia and also from Vanuatu, called *Castanospermum australe*. This appears to offer hope for AIDS sufferers. The active ingredient, castanospermine, was isolated by a young American research student (studying with Professor E A Bell) at King's College London in 1981. It belonged to a newly discovered type of plant chemical known as 'sugar-mimic' alkaloids, so-called because they resemble simple sugars in size and shape. The sugar-mimics had not been found sooner because they did not react positively in the tests traditionally carried out by chemists when testing plants for alkaloids.

Castanospermine was tested for activity against influenza and other viruses in 1983 without success. In 1987, biochemists at Kew's Jodrell Laboratory, in collaboration with virologists at St Mary's Hospital, Paddington, London, tested a number of compounds which they had isolated against the AIDS virus, HIV. Three sugar-mimic alkaloids, castanospermine, deoxynojirimycin (from mulberry) and DMDP (from several tropical legumes) all inhibited HIV at concentrations which were not harmful to cells. They did this by causing changes in the sequence of sugars in the sugar chains attached to the surface protein of the virus. The virus was then unable to infect new cells.

The concentration of alkaloid required to stop the virus was high, about 1000 times higher than that of the anti-AIDS drug AZT. By chemically modifying both castanospermine and deoxynojirimycin, chemists have produced compounds which are effective at far lower concentrations, with a reduced risk of unwanted side-effects. At least one of these compounds is now under clinical trials in the United States. Since they act in quite a different way from AZT, they have given doctors another way of attacking the virus. Preliminary studies have indicated that mixtures of sugar-mimics and AZT may be more effective than either compound alone.

Castanospermum is not known as a medicinal plant. Ten years ago no one knew about castanospermine and no one had heard of AIDS. This highlights the potential value of the chemicals of all our wild plants. Although a rainforest tree, *Castanospermum australe* is capable of withstanding lower temperatures than the Palm House provides and is currently planted in the Australian House.

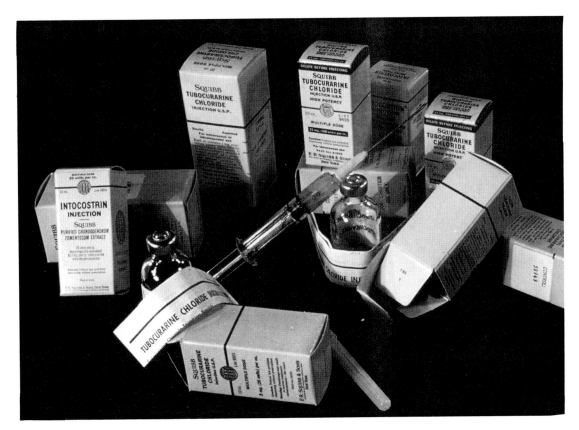

Many prescription drugs contain a principal ingredient derived from a tropical plant. Curare, obtained from Strychnos toxifera, *is widely used by South American Indians as an arrow poison. Their knowledge has led to the development of curative medicines based on the active ingredients strychnine and brucine.*

9 Flowers of the rainforest

THE PALM HOUSE CONTAINS a broad selection of flowering trees and shrubs, some of them true rainforest plants and others from the sunnier forest edges. From the subtropics comes an even wider selection of exotic blooms. We anticipate good floral displays after the house is planted following the 1980s restoration, particularly from the light-demanding shrubs such as *Ixora* and *Hibiscus*. Once the foliage canopy closes all plants will be competing for light and the true flowers of the rainforest will predominate.

This chapter is intended to identify and describe some of the most notable and attractive species, many of which have a tradition of cultivation in the house since Victorian times.

Acalypha hispida (Euphorbiaceae), the chenille plant, is a shrub normally reaching 1 or 2 metres but up to 4 metres in the tropics. Male and female flowers are borne on separate plants. The female of the species produces pendulous catkin-like inflorescences up to 45 cm long and with a dense mat of crimson styles. The origin of the plant is uncertain. Dr Hooker described how it had been collected for the firm of Sander 'no doubt in a wild state' in the Bismarck Archipelago of New Guinea in 1896. At that date it had only just been introduced to Europe, though it was well known in India and Malaya, and is now cultivated all over the tropics. Historically this plant has always been a feature of the Palm House and Dr Hooker praised it fulsomely:

Acalypha hispida cannot fail to become an exceptionally popular stove plant, not only because of its great beauty and striking habit, but from its flowering literally all the year round. The largest plant now at Kew, procured from Messrs Sander in 1898, has been in fine condition ever since, having now upwards of fifty flowering spikes, and others still to expand.[69]

There is a very similar hybrid, known only in cultivation, with long pale green catkins. This is *Acalypha* × *camphauseniana* 'Compacta'. Most other acalyphas are grown for their attractively variegated foliage and have insignificant flowers.

Amherstia nobilis (Leguminosae) is a truly noble tree from Burma and rivals the beauty of the South American genus *Brownea* (see below). An evergreen tree growing to 9–18 metres, it produces pinnate leaves which, like those of many rainforest plants, hang in brownish-pink clusters when young. The flowers are bright red, marked with yellow, up to 7 or 8 cm long and borne well-spaced in a pendent raceme. The seeds are held in scimitar-shaped pods.

This extraordinary tree was named by Wallich as a compliment to the Countess Amherst and her daughter Lady Sarah, both of whom were keen patrons of botany in India. Wallich found the tree in 1826 in the province of Martaban:

There were two individuals of this tree here: the largest, about forty feet high, with a girth, at three feet above the base, of six feet, stood close to the cave . . . They were profusely ornamented with pendulous racemes of large vermilion-coloured blossoms, forming superb objects, unequalled in the Flora of the East Indies . . . The ground was strewed, even at a distance, with its blossoms, which are carried daily as offerings to the images in the adjoining caves.[70]

Wallich obtained the plant for the Calcutta Garden, where it was layered and young plants sent to

Female plants of Acalypha hispida *bear striking red catkin-like inflorescences and are a feature of the Palm House in the summer. The species was introduced to Europe in the 1890s, probably from New Guinea.*

Europe. It was originally imported into Britain for the Duke of Devonshire at Chatsworth, but was first flowered by a Mrs Lawrence in her stove house at Ealing Park, Middlesex, in April 1849. This remarkable feat was achieved by growing the plant in a bed of fermenting tannery bark to raise the root zone temperature to 32°C and surrounding it with canvas to improve shade and humidity. Nowadays the same effect is given by the use of soil-warming cables and thermal screening. The first raceme was presented to Queen Victoria and the second was painted for *Curtis's Botanical Magazine*. When the plant became too big it was presented to Kew but unfortunately did not survive. Since then the species has been grown in the Aroid House and also in the Palm House, where it flowered in the 1970s and 1980s.

The genus **Barringtonia** (Lecythidaceae) contains about 39 species from coastal areas of the Old World tropics. These trees produce oblanceolate leaves and dramatic inflorescences, some pendent to 60 cm or more, with white or yellowish flowers along the raceme, each one centred with a bush of numerous stamens and red styles. We hold *B. asiatica*, collected from Queensland, and *B. racemosa* from Trivandrum in southern India.

The genus **Brownea** (Leguminosae) is a group of about 25 species of evergreen trees from the Central and South American rainforests called 'roses of Venezuela'. The nomenclature of the group is quite confused despite much work done at Kew early this century by the botanist Sprague. All of the species bear large, pinnate leaves opening brown from drooping, elongated bracts and greening and becoming more horizontal as they harden, a not unusual feature in rainforest trees. The showy flowers are red, closely bunched in nodding heads with prominent stamens, and borne either on the tips of branches or directly out of the old wood.

The hybrid browneas at Kew were received after the death of Dr W Crawford of County Cork, 'whose gardens', wrote Dr Hooker in January 1889 in his annual report, 'are celebrated for the number of fine plants that have flowered there for the first time.' The accession book for 1889 held at Kew records that on 21 October were received large plants of *Brownea grandiceps* × *macrophylla*, *B. coccinea* × *latifolia* and *B. macrophylla*. *B. grandiceps* had first flowered in Europe in 1855 and was noted for the size of its flowers. Dr Crawford crossed it with *B. macrophylla* to produce a hybrid which had flowers which lasted much longer than either of its parents. The hybrid was named *B.* × *crawfordii* and this plant grew and flowered profusely until it was lifted and moved to the Temporary Palm House in September 1984, before the 1980s restoration. It lived for a year and then succumbed to the shock, flowering once as a swansong before it died. An air layer from this plant was struck successfully by George Anderson, the Foreman of the Palm House in the 1950s. It now forms a plant of good shape and has been replanted in the restored house.

B. coccinea × *latifolia* is a hybrid which reproduces the rich scarlet flower colour of *B. coccinea*. Kew has raised plants from cuttings and the original plant donated by Crawford was successfully lifted from the Palm House by the Supervisor, Sue MacDonald, in 1983, and has been replanted in the restored house. Flowers from this specimen were exhibited at the Royal Horticultural Society on 19 April 1983 and gained an Award of Merit. It flowers regularly several times a year and forms a vivid reminder of how horticultural hybridisation has improved a fine rainforest plant.

Caesalpinia pulcherrima is also a legume which flowers freely in the Palm House. A shrub or small tree growing to 6 metres, it is grown worldwide in the monsoonal tropics. It has finely divided bipinnate foliage and scarlet flowers edged with yellow which are very showy. It can be trimmed or even coppiced and in Barbados is sometimes planted as a hedge and given the common name of Barbados flower-fence. Many selected forms of this plant exist, with flowers ranging from yellow, orange and scarlet to pink. It has been cultivated in Britain at least since 1691, when Sir Hans Sloane grew it at his Chelsea garden.

Clerodendrum is a large genus of about 400 tropical and subtropical species in the vervain family, Verbenaceae. Several species are very floriferous climbers (see p. 73) but there is also a good representation of shrubs.

C. myricoides, the so-called Oxford and Cambridge bush, comes from tropical Africa and South Africa. A dense shrub to 2 metres tall, it bears spoon-shaped leaves and light lavender-blue flowers with violet tips and long, curling stamens. Dr Hooker called it 'a small stove shrub, which has long been in cultivation in the Palm-House at Kew, flowering annually in spring.'[71]

C. nutans is probably the showiest of the shrubby clerodendrums. Originally from India and Burma, it is now a highly prized ornamental shrub in Malaysia and has been grown in Britain since at least 1830. A branched shrub to 1.2 metres tall, it bears very dark green, glossy leaves and pendent inflorescences of pure white flowers up to 35 cm long. These are borne at the branch tips and make a fine contrast to the foliage.

C. ugandense from Kenya resembles *C. myricoides* but has larger, more deeply coloured flowers. It has been cultivated at Kew since 1906.

Couroupita guianensis, the cannonball tree, comes from Guiana and is in the same family as the brazil nut (Lecythidaceae). It forms a tall tree with lanceolate leaves. These redden and fall several times a year but new ones are produced within the week, a not uncommon feature in tropical trees but which has led to many a gardener at Kew being told off for 'letting it dry out'. It needs a rich, moist soil in sun and now it has been replanted in the restored Palm House, we hope to flower it. The flowering of this species is a quite extraordinary development of cauliflory. The flowers develop on long, leafless flowering branches which grow directly out of the old, woody stem and may become up to a metre long. The condition is called idiocladanthy. The bat-pollinated flowers themselves are showy and sweet-smelling, being red and yellow with numerous stamens. The common name, cannonball tree, refers to the round woody fruits, up to 20 cm across, which release their seeds through a kind of lid. This plant is now a feature of tropical gardens all round the world. It will flower in Florida and there is a particularly fine avenue in the Singapore Botanic Garden.

Deherainia smaragdina (Theophrastaceae) is a Mexican shrub, a favourite among children visiting the Palm House because of its gloriously malodorous green flowers (presumably adapted to attracting pollination by flies or bats), usually pointed out to them as an educational feature. The plant was named by Decaisnes after M Pierre-Paul Deherain, a naturalist of the Museum of the Jardin des Plantes in Paris. It is a much branched shrub with leaves crowded at the ends of the twigs, much like those of *Theophrasta* and *Clavija*, shrubs to which it is related and which can also be seen in the centre transept. The flowers are 3–4 cm across, borne singly in the leaf axils and are very dark green, paling towards the edge, with black throats. Dr Hooker reported that 'Our plant flowered in the Palm House of Kew in May [1878], when quite small.'[72] He made no mention at all of their odd perfume!

Caesalpinia pulcherrima *is a floriferous tree of the legume family and is distributed throughout the monsoonal tropics.*

Gmelina hystrix (Verbenaceae), the hedgehog shrub, is a scandent shrub from the Philippines; when grown in drier conditions it develops spines, accounting for the common name. Its flowers are borne terminally and consist of yellow bells up to 8 cm long surrounded by purple bracts with red veins. In the nineteenth century this was grown at Kew in the Waterlily House, where Dr Hooker described it in 1894 as 'trained against the glass roof where it has the habit of a *Bougainvillea*, and flowers freely.'

Goethea strictiflora (Malvaceae) is a small Brazilian shrub of very erect growth and ovate, toothed leaves. In this species the flowers are tiny but surrounded by quite showy, pointed crimson bracts arranged in a bell shape. They are borne on the old wood, another example of cauliflory.

The genus **Hibiscus** is well known to the visitor to sunnier parts of the tropics and subtropics, mainly from cultivars of *H. rosa-sinensis*, which are widely planted as ornamentals along with bougainvillea, jacaranda and oleander. With over 300 species the genus is the largest in the Malvaceae and is most closely related to the cottons (*Gossypium*). All have more or less campanulate flowers with prominent, sometimes dramatic, styles and stamens. The flower colour is generally very vivid. The Palm House has an extensive collection but they have always been difficult to maintain well in pots due to their rapid growth. We hope they will flower well when they are planted out in beds and especially before the canopy of foliage develops and cuts out much of the light they love. The following are a selection of the species and cultivars.

H. × *archeri* is a cross between *H. rosa-sinensis* and *H. schizopetalus*, combining the rich red flower colour from the former parent with the attractively reflexed petals from the latter. It flowers nearly all year round.

110

Hibiscus *are commonly planted in the sunnier parts of the tropics and subtropics, where they freely produce their ephemeral flowers. There are many cultivars. This is* H. rosa-sinensis *'Variegata'.*

H. brackenridgei var. *mokuleiana* is a Hawaiian species native to the island of Oahu and is threatened in the wild. It forms a small tree to 5 metres with toothed leaves up to 10 cm across and bears large yellow flowers.

H. calyphyllus comes from South Africa and also Madagascar, the Mascarenes and tropical Africa. An undershrub rarely growing more than 2 metres, it bears long-stalked leaves and large yellow flowers with a reddish-purple throat.

H. cannabinus or kenaf is a tropical African species which is cultivated in India, Asia and subtropical Australia for its stem fibre. An erect plant, it bears slightly prickly and glandular five- to seven-lobed leaves, and yellow flowers centred purple. As a fibre plant it is normally grown as an annual from seed.

H. cisplatinus from Uruguay forms a shrub only 1–2 metres tall and has bright rose flowers fading to pale rose-violet.

H. clayi is an endangered species endemic to Hawaii. It forms an erect twiggy shrub up to 3 metres with elliptic leaves, rather unusual for *Hibiscus*, and red flowers at the tips of the twigs.

H. columnaris is a species from Mauritius and Réunion, vulnerable in the wild like so many species on these islands. It has leaves which are rounded to heart-shaped, borne on long petioles, and yellow flowers with a dark eye.

H. diversifolius is a prickly species distributed from tropical East Africa to the Pacific. It grows to 2 metres and produces very large flowers up to 15 cm across, yellow to purple with a blackish-red centre.

H. lavateroides (*H. marmoratus*) from Mexico was introduced to Europe in 1854. It is unusual for its white flowers, 6–7 cm across, which are heavily mottled with bright rose-pink.

H. rockii is one of the rarest of the endemic yellow-flowered *Hibiscus* of Hawaii, extinct or nearly so in the wild and surviving only in cultivation. It has dark green leaves which are rounded to three-lobed. The flowers are up to 10 cm across and have a dark brown basal eye.

H. rosa-sinensis is the species, probably native to China or the East Indies, which has yielded so many floriferous cultivars. It has long been in cultivation in the West, William Curtis in *The Botanical Magazine* of 1791 reporting that: 'With us it is kept in the stove, where it thrives and flowers readily during most of the summer; the single blossoms last but a short time, yet their superiority arising from the curious and beautiful structure of the interior parts of the flower, compensates for the shortness of their duration.'[73] Current breeding programmes have been directed at increasing the life of each flower and many of the cultivars available nowadays in the pot plant trade are much improved in this respect. The cultivars listed here are all single-, rather than double-flowered: 'Cooperi' – scarlet flowers and foliage mottled with white, pink and crimson; 'Feathercock' – ruffled yellow flowers with a blood-red eye; 'Lae Orange' – huge, bright orange flowers, very freely produced; 'Miss Kitty' – clear yellow flowers; 'Orange Beauty' – orange flowers with a blood-red eye; 'The President' – large pink flowers; and 'Variegata' – red flowers and foliage heavily marbled with white.

H. rostellatus from tropical Africa is a prickly shrub reaching 1.2 metres. It has five-lobed cordate leaves and pink flowers.

H. scottii is a threatened species from Socotra which grows to 3 metres and produces hairy, rather lobed leaves. The butter-yellow flowers are 9 cm across, marked carmine at the base and have a blood-red stigma. This fine plant was described and named in 1879 and introduced to Britain in 1899.

H. storckii is an extremely free-flowering species endemic to Fiji. It exists in several forms. One is pink-flowered and another is deep cream. Both have a deep maroon eye.

H. tiliaceus, or mahoe, is distributed worldwide in the coastal tropics and is common in mangrove swamps. It forms a shrub 3–4 metres high and produces cordate, matt green leaves and abundant yellow flowers with a mauve eye which turn orange and then red as they age and shrivel. The variety *immaculatus* has lemon-yellow, unmarked flowers. In Polynesia, fibre from the inner bark layers is used as cordage.

There are two other genera closely related to *Hibiscus* grown in the Palm House. One is *Lebronnecia kokioides*, a threatened monotypic genus from the Marquesas Islands north-east of Tahiti in the Pacific. The other is the pantropical portia tree, *Thespesia acutiloba*, similar in form and habitat to *Hibiscus tiliaceus*.

Ixora (Rubiaceae) is a genus which produces nearly as much floral colour in the tropics as does *Hibiscus*. Although each flower is small they are arranged in dense, rounded corymbs. Like *Hibiscus* they are cultivated in full sun and often planted as hedges which are clipped after flowering.

I. chinensis comes from southern China and Malaysia and produces orange-red flowers. There are forms with yellow or with white flowers.

I. coccinea comes from India and grows 1–4 metres tall, producing salmon-red flowers. This species was introduced to Britain in 1690 unsuccessfully (according to William Aiton, the first Head Gardener at Kew) and then reintroduced in the 1770s. William Curtis gave a description of its common name: 'Its clusters of flowers, seen from afar, are so brilliant as to resemble a burning coal, especially in a dark wood, whence its name of Flamma Sylvarum' (flame of the woods).[74] The species has been crossed with others to produce many named cultivars, including the lilac-pink 'Herrara's Pink' and the scarlet 'Super King'. Very compact cultivars rarely growing more than 60 cm and with tiny leaves are becoming common in bedding schemes and the pot plant trade in the Far East.

I. williamsii is a large-leaved, rather lax-growing species with large terminal heads of brilliant scarlet flowers. Like all the other species it lasts reasonably well when cut for floral display.

Kigelia africana (Bignoniaceae), the sausage tree, is native to tropical Africa, where it occurs in a wide range of habitats from rainforest to dry woodland. It grows to 20 metres or more with a spreading crown from which hang lax panicles up to a metre long of maroon flowers veined yellow. These are adapted to bat pollination. The flowers are followed by long, sausage-like fruits, a tree in full bearing producing a dramatic feature. In central Africa the tree is venerated and sometimes planted along roads to provide shade.

The cannonball tree,
Couroupita guianensis
(see p. 109), is a relative of
the brazil nut with a curious
habit of flowering. The buds
appear on long, woody
growths which later bear the
cannonball-like fruits. The
Palm House plant is 30
years old and has yet to
flower.

The genus **Leea** (Leeaceae) is a genus of understorey shrubs from the Old World tropics, mostly with pinnate leaves and highly attractive corymbose or cymose flowers.

L. guineensis is a rather lax shrub from tropical Africa, Asia and Polynesia which grows to 2.5 metres and is very variable in habit. It has bipinnate leaves and yellow or red flowers in flat cymes.

Monodora (Annonaceae) is an African genus whose fine orchid-like flowers give them the name of orchid trees. The flowers are an example of cauliflory. They are borne on the naked branches during spring while the trees are briefly deciduous. The seeds contain an aromatic oil with the flavour of mild nutmeg and are used as a substitute for it in food and in medicine. The trees are sometimes called African nutmegs. They occur in evergreen rainforest, or secondary, regenerating forests on deep, moist soils.

M. myristica (*M. grandiflora*) comes from west tropical Africa where it grows to 6 metres. The yellow, pendulous flowers are spotted with red and have crisped outer petals about 8–10 cm long. This fine ornamental has a long association with the Palm House:

M. grandiflora has been long cultivated at Kew, having probably being [*sic*] sent by Mr Mann about the year 1860. It has attained in the Palm House a height of fifteen feet, where it flowers in spring. Mr Watson informs me that it loses its leaves in autumn, and forms new ones in spring of a glossy rose purple when young, turning to a glossy green when mature.[75]

The African orchid tree, Monodora myristica, has been grown at Kew since 1860 and regularly produces its exotic flowers. The seed is used as a substitute for nutmeg.

M. tenuifolia is a taller species reaching 17 metres. The flowers are white and yellow with crimson spots and 10 cm across overall. This species coppices well and produces a tough, white, durable wood.

Newbouldia laevis (Bignoniaceae) is a monotypic genus native to tropical West Africa, where it occurs in woodland or deciduous forest subject to seasonal drought. The plant is a small tree growing to 7 metres (rarely 20) and produces very vertical branches. Large terminal inflorescences of showy purple flowers are produced at branch tips before branching occurs. The tree is sacred to some tribes and has extensive medicinal uses. It is frequently planted as a boundary tree, often from large cuttings which establish easily as a so-called live fence.

Pachira aquatica (Bombacaceae) is known as the Guinea or Malabar chestnut. It probably originated in Mexico in riverine habitats subject to periodic flooding. It is now grown as an ornamental in Central and South America, Africa and Asia and also cultivated for its edible young leaves and seeds. The species is a rapid-growing tree of 5–23 metres, buttressing at the base and producing tiers of growth in the 'pagoda branching' so typical of rainforest trees. The leaves are digitate with five to nine segments. The flowers are very ornamental and consist of a mass of pendent reddish-brown stamens surrounded by leathery, yellowish petals. Each flower can reach 35 cm long overall. The fruits are globular or oval, up to 30 cm long and contain wedge-shaped seeds which can be eaten raw or roasted, tasting like sweet chestnuts. When ground they also form a good substitute for cocoa. This tree has always

The Guinea chestnut, Pachira aquatica, *has many of the features of rainforest trees, including fast growth, buttressing of the trunk and a tiered habit of branching called 'pagoda growth'. Its flowers are very showy.*

flowered well in the Palm House, often producing a good display at balcony level. A species of *Pachira* was one of the first plants to go into Turner and Burton's new Palm House. John Smith, the first Curator, reported that this plant 'quickly attained the height of twenty-five feet, and, according to its present rate of growth, will soon double that height.'[76]

Pleiocarpa mutica (Apocynaceae) is a native of the Cameroons which has been grown at Kew since at least 1902. It is an undergrowth shrub growing to 1.8 metres or, rarely, a tree to 8 metres. It is much valued for its highly fragrant white flowers, which are borne in clusters in the axils of the leaves or directly on the old wood. The flowers are highly attractive against the black bark. If it was not so extremely slow-growing it would make a good candidate for the pot plant industry.

The genus ***Plumeria*** or frangipani is another very fragrant member of the family Apocynaceae. These shrubs or small trees are probably native to South America but are widely planted as ornamentals throughout the drier tropics and subtropics. In India they are usually planted around temples. They were named after Charles Plumier, a French ecclesiastic and traveller to the West Indies and the common

116

name derives from *franchipane*, the French word for the poisonous coagulated milk which is yielded by the cut stems. The trees have rather succulent branches and elliptic leaves, which usually fall at some point in the year. The flowers are variable in colour but always saucer-shaped and centred with a yellow eye. They often appear on the naked branches. There are several forms of the species *P. rubra*, including var. *lutea*, which has yellow flowers flushed rose underneath; var. *acutifolia*, which is white; and var. *tricolor*, which is white edged with rose. These plants were very highly valued by the Victorians:

Those who have a good stove and sufficient height should not fail to cultivate this beautiful tropical-looking plant. The foliage is large and handsome; the flowers copious, each three inches in diameter, and so deliciously fragrant that a very large house is scented throughout by a very few of the expanded flowers, and this scent is retained by the corolla for some time after it has fallen from the tree.[77]

Spathodea campanulata (Bignoniaceae), the African tulip tree, from West Africa, is a large tree with pinnate leaves and terminal corymbs of rich orange-red, hooded flowers in showy groups of eight to ten. A plant of it grew in the Great Stove House at Kew and had reached over 9 metres when the house was demolished in 1861 following the removal of its plants to the Palm House. Various specimens of this quick-growing tree have been planted in the Palm House since then.

Tabernaemontana divaricata (*Ervatamia coronaria*) (Apocynaceae) is known as the paper gardenia. A dense evergreen shrub growing to 2 metres, it produces waxy, pure white, strongly scented flowers up to 5 cm across. These are beautifully set off by the dark green foliage. This plant has good potential as a pot plant.

Thunbergia erecta (Acanthaceae) is a floriferous shrub from Sierra Leone but is now cultivated throughout the tropics. It forms a bush 1 or 2 metres high with small, lance-shaped leaves and solitary, axillary purple flowers with yellow throats. It has been cultivated in Britain since at least 1856. There is also a pure white form.

Turnera ulmifolia (Turneraceae) is a small West Indian shrublet which has been grown as a stove plant at Kew since the 1840s. It forms a rounded, soft-stemmed bush to 60 cm, with small, serrated leaves. The yellow, five-petalled flowers with dark centres are very showy but very light-demanding. They close on cloudy afternoons. The plants require frequent renewal by seed or cuttings.

10 Plants of the forest floor

THE FOREST FLOOR REPRESENTS a very distinct layer within the rainforest. Characterised by low light levels and a constant high humidity undisturbed by breezes, it lends itself to two types of plant. First, there are the young seedlings of woody plants and climbers, some of which will succeed in the competition to ascend into the canopy. Many of them have juvenile leaves differing markedly from those of mature plants, adapted to the low light of this phase of their existence. Secondly, there are woody plants (particularly palms) and herbaceous plants, which are totally adapted to the low light and exploit this niche in the structure of the forest without entering into the competition going on above.

Sometimes, particularly where the canopy above is closed, there is so little light that the ground flora is almost non-existent. This is a familiar story in temperate forests where light is obviously the crucial factor in determining species on the ground. Oak forests, for example, permit dappled light and a good mixture of herbs, whereas beech, with its heavy shade and dense mat of shallow roots, often has little below it. In the tropics the ground cover is developed in clearings, on the forest margins, by paths and streambanks and on slopes where the tree cover is less dense. Under the full canopy are represented shade-enduring and shade-loving species, but these are always sparse in comparison to the huge volume and variety of woody species above. Throughout the tropics the ground flora consists of highly specialised plants evolved from a very limited range of families. The Rubiaceae is the most common family, and ferns (especially of the Polypodiaceae) are relatively common, as are members of the Zingiberaceae, Costaceae, Araceae, Begoniaceae and Melastomataceae. Grasses are sparsely represented, whereas they are common in drier tropical communities. Such as do occur are broad-leaved and scarcely recognisable to the layman. The different continents show pronounced differences in the distribution of notable genera, *Heliconia* for example, being almost entirely American, and *Alpinia* entirely South-east Asian. In addition, the Malaysian and South-east Asian rainforests are very rich in herbs overall when compared to those of America and Africa. By contrast the ground flora of the Australian rainforest is very sparse indeed.

The structure of these forest-floor plants is obviously adapted to the constantly damp conditions. Many have brittle, sappy stems which last for many years. Where they form rhizomes, bulbs, tubers or corms, this is an adaptation to help them spread rather than, as in temperate regions, to assist them in overwintering warm and safe below ground. If the plant does die back, as do the Australian *Curcuma* species or the African *Cyanastrum*, for example, it is because they come from monsoonal forest with a pronounced dry season. Most plants have thin and soft leaves with a greater range of form than the plants of the woody layers. Many have quite large leaves adapted to maximise photosynthesis; few have drip tips. Some species have velvety leaves and some (particularly some *Selaginella* and *Begonia* species) have a very metallic blue-green sheen; the precise function of this is unclear but it is certainly an ornamental feature. Several species have flowers which appear at ground level, for example *Orchidantha*, *Cyanastrum*, *Elettaria* and *Aspidistra*, which may be an adaptation to pollination by ground-living creatures. Many of the Zingiberaceae (gingers) bear flowers on club-like heads arising on stalks near the ground while the leaves are borne on separate structures. Some understorey herbs bear variegated leaves, a feature which is very rare in the woody members of the rainforest flora. Many of the houseplants commonly seen nowadays are chosen because of their suitability for low light indoors and several of these are variegated forest-floor species.

In the Palm House these plants demonstrate a layer in the rainforest flora, but the richness of the flora in this house is in the woody plants. A fuller planting of herbaceous ground flora can be found in the Princess of Wales Conservatory.

The Americas

The forest floor of the American rainforest is relatively rich in comparison with that of Africa but less so than that of South-east Asia. Several important genera are only distributed in the New World and are well represented in the Palm House. These include the banana-like *Heliconia* (Heliconiaceae) and genera of the primitive family related to the palms, the Cyclanthaceae. The house also shows a good variety of *Costus* (Costaceae) and of several iridaceous plants and tropical grasses, as well as particularly beautiful white-flowered bulbous plants of the Amaryllidaceae, *Hymenocallis* and *Eucharis*, both of which are scented. The understorey is very rich in palms as well, particularly species of the genus *Chamaedorea*. These are described in chapter 5.

Plants of the family Cyclanthaceae are frequently mistaken for fan palms because of their palmate leaves borne on long stems. They are monocotyledonous plants closely related to the palms and especially to the aroids for, like them, they bear flowers in spadices. Their centre of diversity is in the Amazon basin, particularly western Colombia, and they formed an important collection in the nineteenth-century Palm

The spider lilies come from the humid forest margins and stream beds of American tropical rainforests. They are highly perfumed. This is a hybrid, Hymenocallis × macrostephana.

House. They are not common in botanic gardens nowadays. The most well researched member of the group is **Carludovica palmata**, the Panama hat plant, which is mostly cultivated in plantations in the hot coastal plain of Ecuador. Like all members of the Cyclanthaceae, it likes wet, shady humid conditions in fertile soils. Its tissue contains air canals which enable it to survive in swamps. *C. palmata* can grow to 4–5 metres with fan leaves on 1–4-metre stalks arising from rhizomes. The flowers are borne in a basal spadix and are followed by orange berries with a mucus-covered seed coat. The flowers are probably pollinated by weevils and the seeds are distributed by rain. The young leaves of this plant are harvested in bud, boiled, sun-dried and then bleached with sulphur fumes to make toquilla straw which is used to manufacture panama hats, six leaves being used per hat. It was the second most important industry in Ecuador prior to the 1950s and primarily involved women but since then it has been hit by competition from the Philippines and Japan. Four million hats were still being made each year in Ecuador in the 1970s. The straw is also used to make mats, baskets and cigar cases, and is a useful material for thatching. The plant is a highly ornamental species also cultivated in the West Indies. *C. drudei* from southern Mexico, Costa Rica and Panama is less vigorous at 1.5–2.5 metres.

Several other members of this family are displayed in the centre transept.

Asplundia insignis has deeply folded fan leaves and white flowers in a basal spadix.

Cyclanthus bipartitus from Central America, northern South America, Trinidad and the Lesser Antilles is a rhizomatous plant with dark green, lance-shaped leaves up to 1.2 metres long on lengthy petioles. It is a variable species bearing pure yellow or white and red spathes with pendent spadices up to 20 cm long and scented of cinnamon or vanilla. In north-east Peru it is used in making perfume. This is a plant of lowland swamps, needing deep shade. It is often cultivated as an ornamental.

Ludovia lancifolia is widely distributed throughout South America. It grows as a terrestrial herb or sometimes as a root-climber on fallen logs. This species produces a leaf blade up to 1.1 metres long on a short petiole, and basal spathes with pure white ephemeral staminodes looking like strings of spaghetti. It is a lowland plant found by streamsides below 1000 metres.

The centre transept houses several bulbous plants in the family Amaryllidaceae. These include **Crinum americanum**, the American swamp lily, which is an aquatic bulbous species from the Florida Everglades, where it grows in association with the swamp cypress (*Taxodium distichum*) and, as in the Palm House, with the Everglades palm, *Acoelorraphe wrightii*. It produces a small rosette of evergreen strap-like leaves from a basally swollen stem, and white flowers. Its seeds are distributed by water but it will survive in non-aquatic habitats provided the soil is fertile and moist. It needs full sun. Its Australian relative, *C. pedunculatum*, from the coasts of Queensland, is grown in the north wing.

Eucharis hartwegiana (*Caliphruria hartwegiana*) from Colombia bears fleshy heart-shaped leaves on short stalks, and white flowers. Closely related is *E. amazonica*, the Amazon lily, whose fine white flowers have stamens attached to the central corona cup. They are sometimes available commercially as a cut flower.

Hymenocallis, also in the Amaryllidaceae, is a tropical American genus from humid forest margins and stream beds. They are collectively known as the spider lilies. All species bear evergreen, strap-shaped leaves arising from subterranean bulbs. Long stalks rising to 75 cm carry umbelliform heads of very fragrant white flowers. The petals are thin and spidery but connected at the base into a staminal cup. We hold *H.* × *macrostephana* (which is probably a hybrid between *H. speciosa* and *H. narcissiflora*) and *H. expansa*. Both need abundant water and fertile soil, and resent root disturbance. These are some of the most ornamental plants in the house, and flower best with some sun.

The genus **Costus** (Costaceae) contains about 70 species, 40 of which occur in the Americas, most of the others being African in origin. This is a group of fleshy-leaved, occasionally hairy perennials producing cane-like growth from basal rhizomes. They are sometimes deciduous. They grow in wet, shady conditions in primary or secondary lowland forest in association with Musaceae, Zingiberaceae and Cyclanthaceae. Many *Costus* are given local names as 'gingers' although this name is more appropriately applied to the chiefly Indo-Malaysian Zingiberaceae. The aerial parts of *Costus* are not aromatic, and their leaves are arranged in an open spiral, not in two rows as in the true gingers. The flowers are usually produced in fleshy inflorescences at the tips of the stems, which may bend down under the weight of the enlarged fruit. Seeds held in mucilage may then germinate so that the plant is effectively distributing live seedlings around itself. These plants are pollinated by bees and birds, particularly hummingbirds. The juice of several species is used as an (unproven) local remedy against a huge variety of ills, ranging from gonorrhoea to coughs.

C. glaucus is a broad-leaved species from Costa Rica with very handsome glaucous green foliage.

C. guanaiensis var. *macrostrobilus* from north-west South America and Panama produces canes up to 2 metres tall with huge hairy leaves up to 30 cm long. The inflorescence bears pink, green-tipped bracts and from these emerge white flowers tinged pink and yellow.

C. pulverulentus from Mexico and central and western South America is a very variable species growing from 0.5 to 2.5 metres tall, usually with hairy leaves. The flowers are red and yellow with long stamens.

C. scaber is widespread in tropical America including the West Indies. It produces reddish canes and red buds with yellowish-orange corollas.

C. spiralis from the eastern parts of tropical South America is a narrow-leaved species 1–3.5 metres in height bearing salmon-pink flowers. The variety *spiralis* has hairless leaves and tolerates more drought.

C. villosissimus from north-western South America, Panama and parts of the West Indies is a particularly showy species with fine yellow flowers. The leaves are hairy and borne on stems up to 4 metres tall.

C. woodsonii is a relatively short species from Panama, Costa Rica and Nicaragua, never growing more than 2 metres, with hairless leaves and red and yellow flowers.

A rare genus in the Costaceae is *Monocostus uniflorus* from eastern Peru, which is a dwarf plant at 20–60 cm tall and bears yellow flowers at its base, unlike any other *Costus*.

The genus **Heliconia** in the Heliconiaceae is an almost entirely tropical American group closely related to the bananas (Musaceae) in both habit and ecology, often occuring naturally in marshes, in forest clearings and at forest margins. As a group they are the counterpart in the Americas of *Musa* in Asia.

Over the decades there has been much taxonomic disagreement over them and they have been variously placed in their own family, in Strelitziaceae and in Musaceae. They mostly produce large, banana-like leaves on long stalks and bear flowers in the axils of large, highly coloured, boat-shaped bracts which are very long-lasting when cut. The inflorescences are either erect or pendulous and the fruits are usually blue. This group has become very popular in tropical collections and there is a growing cut flower industry in the West Indies. They are difficult to flower as pot plants and we hope to flower them better planted out in the Palm House with the bananas themselves. They usually flower best in some sun.

H. caribaea is a very ornamental species with 8–15 deep blood-red bracts on an inflorescence up to 50 cm long. It grows 2–3 metres tall and does best in full sun.

H. imbricata from Central America attains 3 metres and produces an erect inflorescence with very broad red bracts.

H. psittacorum, the parrot flower, is distributed throughout tropical America. It is one of the shortest species, at 60–90 cm, with narrow lance-shaped leaves only 6 cm across. The bright orange and red inflorescence is held well clear of the foliage and produces yellow flowers tipped with black. This species has always flowered very freely in the Palm House.

Plants of the genus Heliconia *are banana-like in habit and come from the margins of American rainforests.* H. chartacea, *seen here, has pendent blooms, but the genus shows a wide variety in inflorescence form.*

H. wagneriana is a West Indian species growing to around 2 metres. It produces an erect panicle of light red bracts edged with green which can be as long as 45 cm. The flowers are white.

The genus **Neomarica** (Iridaceae) contains 15 species of iris-like plants from the shade of the forest floor in tropical America, primarily in Brazil. These ornamental plants bear short-lived, transient, easily damaged flowers on erect stems. They need high humidity and propagate themselves by producing plantlets towards the tops of the flowering stems, which bend and root into the leaf litter. Most species produce brilliant orange seeds. The genus deserves to be better known in horticulture. *N. caerulea*, the apostle plant, has leaves 6 or 7 cm across and produces a clump 60 cm high. The flowers are borne successively in groups and are a perfect sky-blue, marked yellow and brown on the central standard petals. In more open forest this plant develops a far more glaucous leaf. *N. gracilis*, *N. lutea* and *N. vittata* are all much smaller, with narrower leaves and yellow flowers about 4 cm across, variously marked blue and brown on the standard petals.

The centre transept also contains a rainforest grass from Brazil which exhibits the broad leaves typical of Gramineae from the heavily shaded forest floor. It is herbaceous, and un-grass-like in habit, being related to the bamboos. Taxonomists call it a bambusoid grass:

Olyra ciliatifolia is a loosely tufted species growing 0.5–1.2 metres high with cane-like stems. It is pretty in flower and not very invasive. In Brazil it comes from the semi-shade of disturbed forest or the edges of forest paths. Another species of this genus from Africa and South America, *Olyra latifolia*, is planted in the south wing.

Several species of
Heliconia *flower in the*
Palm House and
H. psittacorum, *the parrot*
flower, blooms regularly.
They all make excellent cut
flowers.

Xiphidium caeruleum (Haemodoraceae) is a West Indian monocotyledonous plant which produces a low rosette of strap-like leaves up to 30 cm tall with gracefully curved tips. Tall, dense racemes of white flowers arise from what can become a very dense clump of foliage.

Africa

The forest floor of the continental African rainforest is less rich in species than the equivalent stratum in the Americas or Asia. However, tropical West Africa has a good representation, particularly of Rubiaceae and Cyperaceae and we hope to build up our collections in these families. The present plantings are mainly of the families Apocynaceae, Anthericaceae, Cyanastraceae, Gramineae and Melastomataceae. In addition, Madagascar and the Mascarenes are comparatively rich in palms of the forest floor, as described in chapter 5.

Chlorophytum is a group of liliaceous plants now classified in Anthericaceae. There are nearly 300 species, mostly in tropical Africa, and they come from a wide range of habitats, including the savannahs of East Africa. *C. comosum*, the well-known spider plant, comes from semi-arid areas of South Africa. Several species, however, come from the moist forest floor of West African rainforest and their far broader leaves show adaptation to this shady environment.

C. macrophyllum is common along path edges in Ghana and throughout Central Africa. It occasionally grows on fallen debris. Its glossy pale green lanceolate leaves form a clump to 75 cm high. White flowers are borne in slender racemes rising well above the leaves.

The Palm House has always housed a large collection of the genus ***Clivia*** (Amaryllidaceae), species of which were extremely popular in Victorian times. These bulbous plants with strap-like leaves are all subtropical and come from semi-arid areas in South Africa, where they are known as kaffir lilies. Since they are not rainforest plants we have not planted them out. They are kept on the south end grating along with the South African *Encephalartos* as part of a display commemorating the Victorian use of the house. Clivias are particularly well adapted to clay pot culture, where their roots are restricted. *Clivia miniata*, with its orange-red flowers, is well known as a houseplant. Less commonly seen is the yellow form, *C. miniata* var. *citrina*, and *C. nobilis*, which has drooping, narrowly funnel-shaped flowers, salmon in colour, tipped green.

The genus ***Costus*** (Costaceae) has 25 species in tropical Africa and the group is represented in the south wing by *C. lucanusianus* from West and Central Africa. This species has white flowers with crimson and orange markings.

Cyanastrum contains six species of tuberous rooted herbs in the family Cyanastraceae. *C. cordifolium* is a widespread and common species in Central African rainforests, where it forms dense patches to 30 cm high. The glossy leaves are heart-shaped and the small blue flowers appear below them at ground level, where they must be pollinated by ground-living creatures.

C. hostifolium is a species of tropical East Africa from shady places at the forest edge or in clearings. It appears to be adapted to seasonal drought and many become deciduous prior to dormancy. This species produces ovate to lance-shaped leaves and aerial flowers on a stem 35 cm long. They are white with yellow anthers.

124

C. johnstonii comes from a similar habitat to *C. hostifolium* but at slightly higher altitudes. The flowers are blue with yellow anthers.

Dissotis rotundifolia (Melastomataceae) is a procumbent herb found throughout tropical Africa. It produces long stems which root at the nodes, ovate leaves and fine magenta-purple flowers. This is a plant for moist habitats from a large family of tropical and subtropical species, many of which are fine ornamentals.

The south wing also houses several species of the grass family, Gramineae. These include *Olyra latifolia*, a bamboo-like grass, and a species of *Megastachya* from coastal forest in Madagascar which forms mats, and *Oplismenus compositus* 'Variegatus', the variegated form of basket grass, which forms attractive ground cover with its white and green lanceolate leaves occasionally tinged pink.

South-east Asia and Australasia

The extreme richness of the South-east Asian forest floor is shown in the north wing, where a wide variety of herbs and understorey palms are planted. The palms are fully described in chapter 5. In the herbaceous ground flora the main families represented are the Urticaceae, Musaceae, Commelinaceae and Costaceae, but the largest number of species belong to the ginger family.

Of the Australian forest floor little is presented because little exists, this stratum of the forest being quite sparse. **Pollia crispata** (Commelinaceae) comes from northern Queensland, where it produces its nodding inflorescences of small blue flowers at the margins of the rainforest.

From Vietnam comes the aluminium plant, **Pilea cadierei** (Urticaceae), well known in the pot plant trade, with its rather succulent stems and quilted leaves made silvery by the raising of the epidermis on the leaf surface. **Procris pedunculata** is another member of the Urticaceae but rare in the wild in New Caledonia where it grows as a ground herb or epiphyte, its succulent stems and leaves extending up to 2 metres.

Costus (Costaceae) is mainly an American genus but there are five species in South-east Asia, and one other genus, **Tapeinochilos**, in the same family. *T. ananassae* comes from Malaysia and Queensland, Australia where it is known as the giant spiral ginger. This spectacular plant grows to 2.5 metres with costus-like shoots bearing spirally arranged leaves. The inflorescences arise from the rootstock and consist of heads of crimson bracts 10 cm across bearing yellow flowers.

The genus **Musa** (Musaceae), the bananas, are giant rainforest herbs which become an important element in secondary forest. They are mainly Old World in origin and we hold several species in the north wing. The cultivated edible species are grown all over the tropics for their fruit and fibre. These are planted as a collection in the centre transept and described in chapter 8.

M. velutina, the velvet banana from Assam, grows less than 4 metres tall and produces highly ornamental (though inedible) fruit which is pinkish-red and covered with a velvet fur. The flowers have a bright yellow calyx and are surrounded by red bracts. It was introduced into cultivation as an ornamental plant in 1875.

A species closely related to the bananas is **Orchidantha maxillarioides**, the orchid flower, in the family Lowiaceae. This is a stemless rainforest herb from Malaysia growing to 30 cm. Below clumps of lanceolate leaves appear violet flowers borne very close to the soil. They are three-petalled with an orchid-like appearance.

Of the true gingers (Zingiberaceae) the genera represented in the north wing are *Alpinia, Amomum, Boesenbergia, Brachychilum, Curcuma, Globba, Hedychium* and *Zingiber*. They are all rhizomatous herbs with spicily scented foliage and some have economic uses as well as fine flowers. The rhizomes are organs of vegetative propagation and are adapted to continuous growth. Some produce bulbils or mucilaginous fruits in which the seed can germinate. In this they are similar to the Costaceae of Africa and the Americas.

The genus **Alpinia** is a group of about 250 Asian, Australian and Polynesian plants of the forest margin. Many produce excellent cut flowers and bloom intermittently throughout the year. They produce tall, cane-like stems with lance-shaped leaves.

A. caerulea comes from the edges of rainforest and brushwood forests in coastal areas in Queensland and New South Wales. Its arching canes reach 1.8 metres and terminate in spikes of white and blue flowers.

The Indonesian species Brachychilum horsfieldii *produces the leathery leaves typical of understorey herbs of the ginger family. The seed pods and seeds are very ornamental.*

A. malaccensis from north-eastern India is a vigorous species growing to 3 metres. It produces erect panicles of flowers up to 35 cm long. The flowers are white with a yellow and red variegated lip or labellum.

A. mutica from India and Malaysia reaches 1.3–2 metres. The flowers are white with an orange and red lip, followed by attractive orange seed capsules.

Amomum is a genus of about 150 Old World species. *A. aculeatum* comes from New Guinea, where it grows to 2.4 metres and produces a basal inflorescence of green and white flowers followed by spiny green fruits.

Boesenbergia rotundata (*B. pandurata*), Chinese keys, from Indonesia is a dwarf herb with pink flowers. It is widely grown in India, Sri Lanka, Malaysia and Vietnam as a spice and medicinal plant. The rhizome is used as a flavouring for food.

Brachychilum horsfieldii from the islands of Indonesia is a short herb reaching about 30–40 cm and producing slender, lance-shaped leaves of a very glossy green. The flowers are greenish-white but the ornamental feature of this species is the fleshy seed capsules, which split open to reveal crimson seeds.

The genus **Curcuma** is an economically important genus of five species from Indo-Malaysia and China. They are all species of seasonally dry forests and need drying off to allow a resting season. The rhizomes produce leafy stems and a club-like terminal inflorescence, usually on a separate basal shoot. These are often spectacularly coloured and become mucilaginous as they age, the seeds germinating as the head dies down.

C. aeruginosa from Burma produces shoots to 1 metre high. The basal inflorescence grows to 50 cm and bears deep crimson flowers with a pale yellow lip. The rhizome is bluish inside and is used medicinally.

C. australasica from Queensland, New Guinea and the Pacific Islands produces pleated leaves and fine heads of light pink bracts with yellow flowers. In Australia it grows in association with *Eucalyptus* and *Cycas media* in brushwood forests subject to seasonal burning. The plants flower profusely in the wet season in January and February and then become dormant for the rest of the year. The rhizomes of *C. longa* (*C. domestica*) are known as turmeric and are widely cultivated in Indo-Malaysia as a spice and food colourant and also as a dye for cloth. (See p. 99.)

C. zedoaria (*C. xanthorrhiza*), from South-east Asia, produces leaves with an attractive purple variegation, and basal inflorescences 20 cm long. The flowers are pale red with a yellow lip. The large, bitter-tasting rhizomes are used in cooking and in local medicine.

Globba is a genus of about 70 slender herbs from Asia, most of which spread by bulbils produced viviparously on the flower stem.

G. cernua from the floor of montane rainforest in Malaysia produces slender stalks to 45 cm and lance-shaped leaves. Tiny, butter-yellow flowers arise from an arching inflorescence and produce small plantlets very prolifically.

G. strigulosa is a more vigorous species from Guizhou Province in China, reaching 1.2 metres.

Hedychium has about 40 species mostly from subtropical Indo-Malaysia and south-western China, and, in particular, from the temperate forests of the Himalayas. A few tropical species are spectacularly scented and are highly prized as ornamentals. All have terminal inflorescences of long-tubed flowers with prominent stamens.

H. coronarium, the butterfly lily or white ginger, is much cultivated in Indo-Malaysia and worldwide for its extremely fragrant white flowers marked yellow on the lip. The heads are used for making floral garlands in Hawaii. It grows to 2 metres and needs moist, rich soil.

H. ellipticum, from India and Thailand, grows to 1.6 metres. The flowering spikes reach 10 cm long and bear yellowish-white flowers with purple stamens.

The genus Zingiber *contains our culinary root ginger but this species rarely flowers. Z. spectabile, however, produces the largest basal inflorescences of all the Malaysian gingers and does so annually in the Palm House.*

H. flavescens (*H. flavum*), the yellow ginger, comes from the Himalayas, where it grows to 1.5 metres and produces heads of clear yellow flowers marked orange on the lip and with cream stamens. It is highly fragrant and prized in Hawaii for making floral leis.

H. stenopetalum is a white-flowered ginger tolerant of lower temperatures in montane rainforest. It has a wide distribution in India, Burma, Thailand, Laos and North Vietnam.

The genus **Zingiber** contains around 100 species from eastern Asia, Indo-Malaysia and northern Australia and includes the culinary root ginger, *Z. officinale*. (See p. 101.) Many species bear inflorescences basally on shoots separate from the leaf-bearing shoots. Each flower is fragile and short-lived, and they open in succession from large, bracted, club-like inflorescences over many weeks. The bracts hold water and become mucilaginous as they die, encouraging the seed to germinate within. In the following two species the inflorescences are extremely showy.

Z. spectabile comes from Malaysia, where its leafy stems rise to 2 metres. The basal inflorescences are the largest of all the Malaysian species, at 30 cm tall by 7 cm wide, and are a mahogany colour. The flowers are deep maroon and yellow. This species flowers well annually in the Palm House and always excites interest.

Z. zerumbet, the bitter ginger, comes from India but is widely cultivated in South-east Asia for medicinal rather than culinary use. This species is shorter than *Z. spectabile* at 1–2 metres, with purplish leaves which are hairy beneath. The inflorescence ripens from green to a showy red and the flowers are white or creamy yellow.

Closely related to the zingibers is **Elettaria cardamomum** from southern India and Sri Lanka, which produces the culinary spice cardamon. (See pp. 99–100.) In many ways this plant summarises the characteristics of the gingers. It is rhizomatous with scented leaves and basal flowers and it yields a good crop for human benefit.

Restoration and renovation

FACTS AND FIGURES ON THE PALM HOUSE

Built: 1844–1848
Height: 65 ft (19.8 metres)
Length: 360 ft (109.7 metres)
Area: 2600 sq. yards (2173.8 sq. metres)
Restored: 1955–1957. Main contractor: Higgs and Hill
Restored: 1985–1988 by the Property Services Agency (PSA). Main contractor: Balfour Beatty Building

There are 16,000 panes of toughened glass, 10 miles (16 km) of stainless steel glazing bar and over 5500 re-erected iron components in the restored house. Approximately 1000 plants were removed in 1984 and replanted in 1989.

11 Iron glasshouses: the historical background

Chris Jones

THE MOST SIGNIFICANT FEATURES of the Palm House at Kew are that it is built of iron and that its outline is curved. It thus represents a milestone in the history of engineering during the Victorian 'Age of Iron', particularly in the application of the material to glazed structures for the growing of plants.

In the late seventeenth and eighteenth centuries the largest glasshouses were orangeries. These were built from masonry and used for the cultivation of citrus fruits and the 'evergreens' for winter display from which 'greenhouses' take their name. They were used only to serve as frost protection in the winter; each summer the plants would be moved out into the open. Glass formed an increasingly large percentage of their total area: about half the front wall would have been glazed in orangeries built between 1676 and 1748, and more than three-quarters in ones built between then and 1850. The Orangery at Kew, designed by William Chambers in 1761, is a typical example. This is no longer used for growing plants, for structural reasons, but a working example of a formal orangery can still be seen at the Palace of Versailles where citrus, tender evergreens and palms in massive tubs are moved out onto a courtyard display area every April.

At the beginning of the nineteenth century there were significant advances in the materials used in glasshouse design and at the same time more and more complex plant collections were being formed, especially since the introduction of palms. Iron began to be used as a structural material on a scale not known before. The first major structure to be built in cast iron was Ironbridge, which spanned 100 ft (30.5 metres) over the River Severn. The use of iron as a major structural material in this bridge had been urged by 'Iron-mad' John Wilkinson, who had already used it for a wide range of purposes, even to the extent of making his own coffin out of the material (although he died too plump to use it). The outline of the bridge mirrored closely the shape of contemporary masonry bridges and some of the connections between the iron members were a direct copy from timberwork. It may be that this was because the architect, Thomas Pritchard, had been a time-shared joiner. Whatever the reason, timber jointing methods were used to good effect henceforth in iron structures. The Palm House, for example, contains some very tight dovetail joints.

Subsequent bridge designers were inspired by natural phenomena. Thomas Paine, later to be the author of *The Rights of Man*, thought that the spider's web would provide a more effective shape than that chosen for Ironbridge. One major advantage of his design was that he foresaw, correctly, that a bridge could be built from a series of very small but identical prefabricated components. Unfortunately his ideas were never put into practice.

There were some setbacks in the use of iron and a bridge designed by John Nash in 1795 collapsed soon after construction. However, it was not long before iron became the major building material for bridges and canal aqueducts designed by engineers such as Telford and Rennie. Strangely for those times, iron was often chosen not because of cost but for the speed of erection compared with masonry structures.

Ironbridge, completed in 1779 with a 100 ft (30.5 metre) span over the River Severn in Shropshire, was the first major structure in Britain made in iron.

Another reason for the structural use of cast iron was to reduce the danger of fire in industrial buildings. By the end of the nineteenth century an enormous number of mill buildings had been put up. These multi-storey structures had thick brick walls and heavy timber flooring, and although large timber members tended to char and were therefore in themselves fairly fireproof, the combustible material stored in the cotton mills could feed the flames and were a direct cause of the disastrous gutting of the Albion Mill in Blackfriars, London. This fire gave the impetus to the use of cast iron in buildings as it was thought it would be more fire-resistant than timber. The first such building was erected by Bolton & Watt in 1801 for cotton-spinners in Manchester, and it was not long before iron industrial structures of this type became common. The beams supporting the floor were of cast iron in an inverted T-shape, and the columns were generally circular tubes with flattened ends to support the beams. Perhaps the most ambitious T-shaped beams were used by Smirke in the British Museum in 1824. These beams were up to 3 ft (0.9 metres) deep and spanned 41 ft (12.5 metres).

Architects were quick to appreciate the possibilities of iron in the construction of glasshouses, and their influence led to the design of many extremely light and elegant structures not to be equalled (and never superseded) until the middle of the Railway Age. The first iron glasshouse was recorded in Germany in 1770, but possibly the first surviving house in Britain (*c*.1800) is at Chiselhampton. This is also one of the first structures to have a glazed roof. Whereas this roof is straight, the roof of the Italianate Conservatory at Ramsgate (1805) is elliptical. Its glazing bars are copper, typically for the period, and the main iron ribs which support the house are also sheathed in copper, possibly as protection against corrosion.

A look at four glasshouses of the late 1820s shows that a wide variety of styles and methods of using iron in glasshouses was developing at this time. The Aroid House at Kew was designed in 1825 by John

Nash, and was originally constructed in the grounds of Buckingham Palace. It was moved to Kew in 1836 and was redesigned and then used as the 'Palm House' to hold newly introduced species until the current Palm House was built. The details are reminiscent of early orangeries, with heavy stone walls punctuated by limited areas of glazing. The roof is supported by a fairly crude cast-iron truss, which is really only a flat plate of thick cast iron containing some holes, and the glazing bars are timber.

What perhaps proved to be the ultimate orangery was designed by Charles Fowler at Syon, Middlesex, for the 3rd Duke of Northumberland in 1827. Here the vertical glazing comprises fairly conventional timber sash-windows, albeit with copper glazing bars, but the central dome and main doors are of cast iron. The recent restoration has emphasised the lightness of construction.

The Great Conservatory at Syon, Middlesex, was built by Charles Fowler in 1827 for the 3rd Duke of Northumberland and has been recently restored. The central dome and main doors are of cast iron and the glazing bars are made of copper.

The Camellia House at Wollaton Hall, Nottingham, resembles an orangery from the front. Internally iron has been used to its best advantage, particularly in the use of numerous small parts which can be bolted together. This was the forerunner of the 'kit of parts' whereby mass-produced houses were constructed all over Britain, and indeed exported to the rest of the world.

The novelty of the Palm House at Kew, however, is not only that it is made from iron but also that it is curved. Sir Gordon Mackenzie had suggested in 1815 that the form of glass roofs best calculated for the admission of the sun's rays 'is a hemispherical figure' which 'has already given rise to many beautiful curvilinear structures.' Loudon, who wrote prolifically on gardening matters, gave a great impetus to the practical development of this theory by inventing the rolled wrought-iron glazing bar, which could be made into a curvilinear shape. He was not, however, a business man, and made over his patent to the firm of W & D Bailey, who became responsible for many very attractive structures, probably including the houses at Bicton (Budleigh Salterton, Devon) and Dalehead (Cumbria). Of these, Bicton was the most daring in its lightness of form. However, not everybody was convinced of the efficiency of curvilinear structures. A Frenchman called Delchevalier wrote in 1867 that they were quick to warm up but cooled rapidly. Loudon himself also mentions many prejudices against roofs with iron bars, including their cost and the breakage of glass arising from corrosion. He experimented in his garden at Bayswater with other shapes, notably the ridge and furrow developed by Paxton in the Great Conservatory at Chatsworth, Derbyshire, where the roof was angled to face east and west, thus catching more sun in the early morning and afternoon.

The shape of the Palm House is heir to the theories of Mackenzie and the glazing bar of Loudon as patented by the firm of Bailey, but it was the skilled Irish ironfounder, Richard Turner, who first applied wrought iron to the structure of such a large glasshouse. A masterpiece in iron and glass, it is particularly important today because there are no other large, curved iron glasshouses left to us.

The Palm House at Bicton, Budleigh Salterton, Devon, was probably designed by the firm W & D Bailey. Their patented wrought-iron glazing bar was later applied by Turner in the Palm House at Kew.

IRON PRODUCTION

Wrought iron and cast iron are very different materials. Wrought iron is tough and fibrous whereas cast iron, although able to withstand compressive loads, is comparatively brittle. A glance at each under the microscope (see below) helps to show why: cast iron contains a high proportion of carbon, which is distributed amongst the iron in the form of flakes of graphite, rather like a scattered packet of crisps. Wrought (or worked) iron, on the other hand, is almost pure iron and can undergo severe deformation before failure occurs.

The men who produced iron through the centuries combined strength, stamina, science and artistry unmatched by any other craft, except perhaps that of glass-making. Cast iron was probably an accidental discovery, found when iron had been left too long in the fire at a temperature of around 1500°C.

The different structures of cast and wrought iron can be seen under the microscope. The flakes of carbon scattered in cast iron (left) make it too brittle to work into curved structures like the main arches of the Palm House, although it will take compression, as in the columns. Wrought iron (right) is far more malleable.

Combining with the carbon from the fire, it would run off into the nearest hollow; later, these hollows would be made into a bed of sand and became known as 'pigs' and 'sows', hence the name 'pig iron'. However, for many years the primary aim remained the production of wrought iron.

Although the ores were often of poor quality compared with those of, say, Sweden, England was fortunate to have deposits of iron ore in almost every county, as well as extensive forests to make the charcoal required to power the furnaces. 'British' iron was supplied to the Roman fleet and army nearly 2000 years ago, but perhaps the most famous smiths prior to the Victorians were the Vikings, who produced iron needles, and arrowheads and swords and knives with steel cutting-edges. Examples of these can be seen at the Jorvik Museum in York.

The basic trade of blacksmith became even more sophisticated in medieval times, and specialists such as bladesmiths, armourers, arrowsmiths, cutlers and even spurriers appeared. Probably the armourer was the most skilled, producing coats of chain-mail made from 'knitting' thousands of links into patterns. Some excellent blacksmiths' work also survives in the form of intricately decorated church doors. In an early use of mass-production techniques, dies were often cast from steel or hardened iron to reproduce vine scrolls and flowers in the wrought iron, as in St George's Chapel at Windsor (c.1244). Unfortunately blacksmiths tended to copy wooden carvings and as it was quickly realised that timber could be obtained more cheaply, decorative ironwork became unfashionable between 1450 and 1650.

Only limited structural use was made of iron during this period, however. Wrought-iron tie bars were first used (in Westminster Abbey) around 1230 although they did not serve any practical purpose. In 1334, at St Stephen's Chapel, a 'Walter the Smith' was recorded making 12 cramps called 'tiraunz' for strengthening the stones of tracery work, each 2 ft (0.6 metres) long and 2 in (5 cm) square.

Early iron was manufactured by heating a mixture of iron ore and charcoal on a fire in a shallow pit. Subsequently the pit was provided with a forced draught from manually operated bellows. After reheating and forging in the blacksmith's shop to remove impurities, the product was very similar to nineteenth-century wrought iron. The introduction of the blast furnace from Belgium around 1400 together with the use of the water-powered hammer increased the scale of production dramatically from a matter of pounds to a ton each day. This leap in efficiency coincided with much experimental work to arrive at the most effective materials for shot and cannon. Cast-iron cannon balls quickly replaced the stone ones which were originally used. Early cannons had been cast from bronze or tin but copper was expensive, had to be imported and supplies were vulnerable to blockade in time of war. Probably the most famous and earliest wrought-iron cannon of all is Mons Meg, manufactured at Mons (in Hainault, Belgium) in 1449 and now to be seen at Edinburgh Castle. This huge beast is 4.04 metres long, with a bore of 0.49 metres. Two monarchs, Henry VII and Henry VIII, were responsible for the development of the technology to produce cast-iron cannon with the aid of the new blast furnace, presumably because these could be manufactured more quickly and more cheaply than wrought iron.

More mundane uses of cast iron were for equipment for the hearth such as fire dogs and screens, and simple rolling and slitting mills which had been used to cut thin strips of precious metal for jewellery were modified to produce iron rods and flats. The chief restriction to further efficiency in production was the use of charcoal as a fuel, since it was soft and could not be used to make a large quantity of iron. Moreover, the extensive clearance of forests to provide both charcoal and ships for the King's Navy

A ball of wrought iron is 'raced' to the hammer for working, to avoid contamination by the air.

A 'cherry red' wrought-iron bar is squeezed into shape in a rolling-mill.

pushed the centres of iron-making into remote places further and further into the woods, making it more expensive. The scale of this deforestation can be gauged by an estimate from the Weald Research Institute that 50 acres (20.25 hectares) of coppice could be turned into charcoal to make 4 tons of iron. The purchase by the British Board of Ordnance of some 40,000 tons of cannon between 1700 and 1760 was therefore the equivalent of ½ million acres (202,350 hectares) of woodland, a striking parallel to the destruction of modern tropical rainforest for short-term gain in our own times. The shortage of charcoal became so acute that many furnaces were forced to close down. As home-produced iron was so expensive Britain imported nearly 20,000 tons of wrought iron annually over the period of the eighteenth century. This figure was to drop significantly to 1700 tons by 1817 after the development of coke as a fuel.

Various people have been given credit for the replacement of charcoal by coke, but it is generally thought that Abraham Darby developed the idea and made it work in 1709. Based at Coalbrookdale in Shropshire, he found that the local coal was ideal for coking and then firing the furnaces. (The site of his foundries is now covered by the Ironbridge Museum complex, which is well worth a visit.) It was not until the 1750s that the second Abraham Darby produced coke-blast pig iron that was competitive in price with charcoal blast. According to Darby's descendants, he spent three days and three nights at the furnace before achieving his goal, after which he was carried home asleep.

It was, however, many years before coke was used throughout the country, as there were significant disadvantages to its use. In particular, the cast iron produced was of low strength, and the wrought iron was brittle. To overcome this, Henry Cort patented the first workable puddling furnace in 1784, using what was known as the 'dry' process (as opposed to the 'wet' process which came later), which involved the stirring or puddling of the red-hot iron until the carbon combined with the air and was purified. The furnace had a sand bottom, which was wasteful and therefore expensive, since some of the iron mixed with the sand to form slag, but the iron remaining was of high quality, so much so that the process was still in use at the Low Moor Ironworks in 1957 for the production of 'Best Yorkshire' iron. In 1784 Henry Cort also made a significant development in the rolling of wrought iron: he patented the idea of grooving the rolls, so that various shapes such as rods could be produced.

Cast iron production was improved further by William Wilkinson in the 1790s. He developed the use of remelting furnaces known as cupulas or 'hells'. It was found that they worked best with a mixture of different kinds of pig iron and scrap to help the mixture run. Joseph Hall developed the puddling process further in about 1816 by providing a cast-iron tray at the bottom of the furnace onto which oxidised compounds of iron (cinders or millscale) were laid. The carbon from the stirred iron combined with these compounds to form carbon monoxide which burned with characteristic blue flames known as 'puddlers' candles'. It was very hard and hot work since the puddlers had to keep stirring and at the same time ensure that the iron was kept to the exact high temperature (based on the colour of the iron) needed to prevent a brittle product. The iron was produced in balls, each weighing about 1 hundredweight, or as much as a man could handle. A spoilt ball was called a 'shadrack' and at least one firm charged its puddlers for shadracks at the rate of one penny each if they produced more than ten in a week. A quotation from the *Ironworkers' Journal* of April 1872 gives some indication of the life of a puddler: 'Few men of fifty are seen at the infernal task, it burns them up long before that date; scorched, roasted, dazed into blindness, and dried into fever by the furnace, the puddler gets enormous pay as long as he can stand it, and then is oxidised like the carbon and other ingredients which had to be eliminated.'

From the puddling furnace the ball of iron was 'raced' to the hammer as quickly as possible to avoid contamination from the air. Normally two balls were hammered or 'shingled' together to expel the slag remaining in the iron. For larger billets, up to five balls could be introduced but it was difficult to remove the slag from the middle of the mass, which might therefore double the cost.

After hammering, the iron was rolled. The rolling-mill was still fairly basic and looked rather like a larger version of a laundry mangle, except that instead of water being squeezed from the clothes, the iron was gradually squeezed into shape. The rolls were powered by steam but the rolling was done manually. For the small sections, one man (the bolter-down) would lift a bar heated to cherry-red (1400°C) and introduce it into the rolls. A second man (the catcher) would pick it up and send it back. Five or six rollings would be needed before the iron was shaped. Here again speed was essential, to ensure that the work was done before the temperature dropped. In this way a short billet would be squeezed into a shape some 30 ft (9 metres) long. Alternate rolling and hammering squeezed out the slag and purified the iron, making it more ductile, but of course each stage increased the cost. The iron was sold after rolling as 'Puddled Bar' and then after further rollings as 'Merchant' or 'Crown Quality', 'Best Bar', 'Best Best Bar' and finally 'Best Best Best Bar'. Each stage added about £1 per ton to the value (around £30 per tonne at 1980s prices).

By 1831 it became possible to roll angle, tee and rail sections, but the size of rolled section was inhibited by the size of the billet that could be produced from the water hammer. The invention of the steam hammer in 1839 enabled Kennedy Vernon to patent their deck beam section in 1844. This was nearly the first symmetrical I-section except that one of the flanges was flat and the other slightly bulbous. The first truly symmetrical I-section, similar to the 'Rolled Steel Joist' (RSJ) still used in structures today, was not rolled until 1848–9, in France. It was this I-section deck beam which was used in shipbuilding, in the arches of one of the huge railway stations of the Victorian age – Lime Street Station, Liverpool – and in the main arches of the Palm House.

GLASS PRODUCTION

The early history of glass-making had much in common with iron-making before the Industrial Revolution. Not only was it hot, dirty, dangerous and hard work, but as it consumed prodigious amounts of charcoal it was, like iron-making, responsible for the loss of many acres of woodland, until James I recognised the dangers and enacted laws requiring glass-making to use coal as fuel.

The main constituent of glass is, of course, sand, but it was soon found that the addition of soda reduced the temperature at which the sand melted. Seaweed was often used as a source for soda, particularly kelp, which was readily available, but some early English glass-makers went so far as to import barilla from Spain. At the time of the Phoenicians, glass was being shaped in the same way as cast iron is today. A mould was formed into sand which was then filled with molten glass. The result, after removal of the central sand core, would be a drinking vessel or vase. The discovery that glass could be blown into shapes ideal for drinking vessels was a great step forward, but only when this technique spread to the colder climes of northern Europe was it used to make window glass – by cutting the blown shape whilst still hot and flattening it out as much as possible. This glass was known as 'broad glass', and the Romans, who knew how to make a crude window glass, probably used this method.

The glass-makers of Lorraine refined the broad glass method. Many of them emigrated to England in the sixteenth century in search of fuel and in England broad glass became the principal method of glass-making until the eighteenth century. The most famous early glass is probably 'crown glass', prized for its brilliant surface. This was developed in Normandy in the sixteenth century. It is said that John

Bowles, the Master of the Vauxhall glasshouse between 1678 and 1691, sent one of his workmen to France as an industrial spy to obtain the secrets of crown glass, but since there is evidence of crown glass production in England from the sixteenth century this is probably nothing more than a romantic story. Nevertheless crown glass owes its name to John Bowles, who embossed a crown at the centre of each pane he produced.

The basic methods of crown glass production were simple. The 'metal' was gathered at the end of a blowpipe and blown into a bubble. A 'punty' or iron rod was attached to the bubble on the side opposite the blowpipe, which was then removed. The metal was then reheated and spun very rapidly until a flat circular 'table' of glass was formed. The most common size of table was 48–55 in (122–140 cm) but because of the central bull's-eye where the punty had been, the size of the piece of glass that could be cut was only about 9 in (23 cm). Normally the bull's-eyes were thrown away, but they have now become so popular that they can be produced by the modern heat method. Although the method sounds simple, by the nineteenth century there were as many as ten specialists responsible for the production of one sheet of crown glass, including the metal gatherer, the blower and the punty spinner.

The major restriction on the demand for glass in the eighteenth century was the iniquitous glass tax. Perhaps even more stringently applied than modern VAT, each glasshouse had its own Customs and Excise Inspector to ensure adherence to the law. Repeal of the tax in 1845 (just after the start of the construction of the Palm House) saw the price per table of crown glass fall from about 6 shillings to 2 shillings.

Apart from plate glass, which was extraordinarily expensive (a large sheet measuring 20 sq. ft (1.8 sq metres) could cost some £2,400 at today's prices), it was not possible to produce large pieces of glass until the broad method was developed further, again by the French, into cylinder glass. Here the initial stages were similar to the production of crown glass except that the glass was blown into a wooden mould – the cylinder. It was then reheated and swung like a pendulum backwards and forwards over a deep pit, still being blown, until the cylinder lengthened to about 5 ft (1.5 metres). After a longitudinal cut the glass was 'ironed' out by a block of green wood at the end of a rod. Robert Chance introduced this method to England in 1832 and improved upon it still further by splitting the glass cleanly with a diamond instead of iron shears and flattening it on a bed of smooth glass. There was still some distortion from the flattening, and the brilliance of the crown glass was lost because of the contact with another surface, but it was possible to cut three panes, each 49 in by 10 in (124 cm by 25 cm), from one cylinder.

In 1847 another type of glass was developed which became commonly used in conservatories and glasshouses. This was James Hartley's rolled plate, produced by ladling molten metal directly onto a casting table. This glass had a dull finish but could be made in sheets as large as the customer required. It was produced for about the same cost as cylinder glass but had the advantage that it could be fluted or patterned.

It is almost certain that the glass for the Palm House was cylinder glass supplied by the firm of Chance in Birmingham and specially tinted green. (See pp. 20–21.) Chance also supplied nearly 1 million sq. ft (about 93,000 sq. metres) for the Great Exhibition Building in 1851, which was followed up by a further ¾ million when the building was moved to Sydenham and renamed the Crystal Palace in 1852.

12 The restoration of the 1950s

Sue Minter and Peter Riddington

THE PALM HOUSE HAD, by the early 1950s, already achieved a hundred years of useful life. A structure made of iron had survived not only the external elements but, an even greater challenge, the high temperatures and humidity that were necessary for the survival of the collections it housed. During this time the house had only one major repair, in 1929, when the feet of the arched ribs were reinforced by encasement in concrete. Regular maintenance had been carried out of course, but the house had probably lasted as long as Turner and Burton would have expected.

The years of the Second World War saw the house deteriorate. Maintenance was minimal, small pieces of flat glass were used to replace broken curved panes and repainting was not carried out at all. In 1951 the house was certainly not the gleaming structure that is so easy to appreciate today. With its battleship grey paint and stained and pitted glass, (clearly visible from contemporary photographs), it must have looked rather like a giant wood-louse. The glass laps were no longer tight, due to a combination of problems including the distortion of glazing bars and the mixture of flat and curved glass. The Palm House was closed to the public in the autumn of 1952 after the engineer's report of August 1951 recommended that the condition of the structure was such that 'a scheme be prepared in the near future for a complete replacement for the house'. A number of designs were indeed mooted. One idea put forward was to replace the house using the arches which had lined the Mall for the Queen's Coronation. Another bizarre proposal was to build a new structure over the top of the existing house. Given the post-war desire for buildings to reflect a new, modern, era, it is surprising that the house was not lost altogether, but saved for us to enjoy.

The poor condition of the Palm House in the early 1950s led to some bizarre schemes for its replacement. This sketch shows the proposal to use the arches which had lined the Mall for the Coronation of Queen Elizabeth II.

That the house was saved at all was due to the efforts of the surveyors of the Ministry of Works. It is evident from correspondence relating to the works that those involved had a real concern for the building, both in terms of its beauty and its historical importance. Messrs Glover, Murrell, Whitaker and Morrell, who were responsible for the completion of the work, should be thanked for their skill and dedication, which allowed the Palm House to be preserved.

Before building works were begun in earnest some experiments were carried out on reglazing the house. Existing glass was of different lengths and some, it was claimed, was the original tinted glass in 3 ft (0.9 metre) lengths. Research showed that this was the original length and an area of glass was replaced in this format, which effected an increase of 27 per cent in light transmission. It was decided to completely replace all of the existing glass with sheets of this size. Various experiments were made with 'plastic putties' but in the end ordinary linseed oil putty was used.

During these deliberations the house was closed to the public for three years before work could commence. The main contractor was Higgs and Hill. They were awarded a contract initially for the north wing and subsequent contracts for the south wing and centre transept. The contractors for the heating installation were Beer and Warren.

The preservation of the plants during the restoration was directed by George Anderson, who had been Acting Temporary Foreman of the Palm House since 1946 and was made Foreman in January 1954. The house was never emptied and the restoration was essentially achieved around the plants. In spring 1955 George and his staff moved the potted palm collection from the north wing into the south to leave it clear for the contractors, who finished there by early November. By the end of December 1955 the contents of the south wing had been moved into the restored north wing and very large plants of *Saraca indica*, *Arenga saccharifera* (the sugar palm) and the famous plant of *Brownea* × *crawfordii* had been lifted from their beds in the centre transept. In the summer and autumn of 1956 all the remaining plants in the centre transept had been lifted to leave only two large palms. These were containerised and the tubs were tilted to allow for access scaffold boarding above them for work on the dome. In 1956–7 the beds were relined and resoiled and replanting commenced when the contractors had finished their work in November 1957, some 31 months after the start.

The actual restoration work carried out was very comprehensive. All of the glass was removed from each area as it was being worked on and all structural elements and the glazing bars were cleaned back to bare metal. The glazing bars were realigned and repaired where necessary by removing glazing bars from beneath the wave moulding at the arches and piecing in. The resulting gaps were replaced by galvanised steel top-hat-sectioned members which provided a bearing to the glass on either side of the arch. At low level the 1929 concrete was removed from the arches and replaced. Some arches had very serious corrosion at this position and major reinforcement was required. These repairs are still visible in the centre transept on the east side of the house. The T-section members on the extrados of the arches were welded in position where they had previously been riveted. The structure was also realigned. The pilasters to the clerestories were repaired, with the fronts removed and replaced by new steel plates bolted to the remaining original material. It was intended that these plates would be removed for maintenance.

All the structure below ground was rebuilt except for the walls to the boiler rooms, the perimeter water

Under the dome of the centre transept several palms were tipped to allow for scaffolding above them. At the far left-hand side of this picture can be seen one of the precarious 'bosun's chairs' or swings used by the gardening staff in the 1950s to get at the crowns of the palms for maintenance.

storage tanks and the tunnel. The supporting structures to the gratings over the heating voids were rebuilt in reinforced concrete, as were the new planting beds constructed in the centre transept. One new feature introduced into the house was the system of perimeter vine beds. These were brick structures built into the stone dado wall. In installing these beds the air circulation patterns for the house were changed and this was possibly the single major cause of the severe corrosion at the feet of the glazing bars found prior to the restoration of the 1980s. By blocking off two out of every three of the low-level ventilators in the dado wall and reducing the area for the warm air to rise behind the perimeter bench, the air currents were reversed. Warm air rose from the front of the bench by convection and then

fell down the glass as a cold draught. This draught was so cold that, before the latest restoration, the low-level glazing had to be lined with insulating material during the winter to protect the plants on the benches. The other effect of the chill was that it created permanent condensation conditions at this level.

It is interesting to note that the house was not painted white at this time, but instead what was known as 'ivorine cream', an 'off white'. The paint system used was very good, being a traditional lead-based system applied over a rust inhibitor. The original paints were completely removed by the use of wire brushes and a patented pneumatic stipple gun, which chipped off the earlier coatings to expose the iron.

The cost of the project was just under £100,000, excluding the cost of scaffolding, and the budget was exceeded by 25 per cent. Although at the time this must have seemed a considerable amount of money to commit to a plant house, looking at the photographs now we can appreciate what a transformation was achieved. In fact the work carried out in the 1950s ensured that the Palm House survived when so many of the other great glasshouses were destroyed.

Given a new lease of life, the plantings established very well and the house was reopened by Her Majesty the Queen on 2 June 1959. The front of the restored house was now guarded by a line of replicas of the Queen's Beasts which had guarded Westminster Abbey Annex during the Coronation and had been donated anonymously to Kew during 1956, at the height of the restoration.

In the New Year's Honours List of 1961, Her Majesty the Queen honoured George Anderson for his long service at Kew and his horticultural work during the restoration by awarding him a British Empire Medal. George retired in 1964, having worked 24 years at Kew, the longest serving Foreman in the history of the Palm House.

13 The 1980s restoration: surveys and reports

Chris Jones

AFTER THE RESTORATION IN THE 1950s the Palm House was painted regularly at three- or four-year intervals both inside and out. This in itself was quite an undertaking, as full scaffolding was required; it also involved great disruption to the plant collection. Despite the best of intentions it was next to impossible to supervise the work adequately, to prevent, for example, paint being applied to surfaces uncleaned and running with water. Access was difficult and if the painters and glaziers wanted to move at high level outside the house they had to stand on the glazing bars to move the ladders with one hand tightly clenched to a gutter.

The first signs that all was not well occurred at the beginning of the 1980s when several pieces of gutter fell through the glass to the floor. Furthermore, up to 600 panes of glass were broken annually through the flexing and corrosion of the wrought iron, costing some £20,000 to repair. Naturally the painters (and subsequently the glaziers) were reluctant to work on an unsafe structure and all maintenance work ceased.

The body then responsible for maintenance of the buildings at Kew, the Property Services Agency (PSA), asked Posford, Pavry & Partners (later called Posford Duvivier) to survey the structure and heating services and report on their condition. Posford had recently finished their work on the Temperate House, where they had been responsible for the surveys, drawings and the design of the structural, mechanical and electrical aspects of that major restoration.

There were several immediate problems with the survey. The first was the lack of information as to how the building was put together. The consulting engineers were handed a set of 'as built' drawings which had been produced after the last restoration, but these were virtually meaningless. Decimus Burton's original 'tender' drawings were examined, but these bore little resemblance to what had actually been built. At this stage, the plants were still *in situ*, creating jungle-like conditions which hindered access to most areas of the house. The humid atmosphere meant that all the glass and metal surfaces were permanently wet. Many of the cracks and crevices had been filled with layer upon layer of putty and other fillers, which appeared sound but when removed revealed badly corroded surfaces.

An examination of the clerestory areas was carried out, working from some scaffolding already fixed in the house. It soon became clear that the cast-iron members were much less substantial than those shown on the tender drawings, possibly because Turner thought he was in danger of losing money and wanted to save weight in iron. Each cast-iron member, whether it was a gutter or other shape, also served to support some of the structure. The clerestory itself was quite a complicated kit of parts. A series of small hollow columns, or pilasters, supported the clerestory roof and also served as rainwater downpipes. They had been strengthened in the earlier restoration by the addition of bolted plates, but rust had built up under the plates and forced them away from the pilasters. When a window was removed the engineers were alarmed to find that the pilaster virtually disintegrated. (See picture on next page.) It was therefore obvious that the windows, rather than the pilasters, were supporting the roof.

Elsewhere the condition of the cast-iron members and covering plates at high level varied considerably. Many of the gutters here were corroded or cracked whereas the dado level gutters (which rested on the stone wall around the house) appeared to be in reasonable condition. However, the cast-iron boxes built into the wall for ventilation had rusted badly and the expansion of the rust had cracked sections of the wall.

The main arch ribs were in reasonable condition, apart from a general loss of thickness throughout, but there were certain areas where strengthening would be required. Between each arch rib was a series of hollow tubes running the length of the building. The glazing bars supporting the glass rest on bars parallel to the tubes and are fixed to them via a series of short rods. A 1 in (2.5 cm) diameter rod running the full length of the building was wedged into each tube so that tubes and arches were all tightened up together by a load estimated by us to be at least 2 tonnes. We subsequently found that Turner had patented his unusual method of tying a building together. It is an early form of 'post-tensioning', but not the earliest; stressed rods had previously been used to strengthen cast-iron beams. Indeed one has been found in a house designed by Decimus Burton himself. Nevertheless the tubes themselves are an advanced example of manufacture in wrought iron and the joints can only be seen under a microscope.

Apart from the clerestories, the wrought-iron glazing bars were the major cause of concern. The end of each bar was tenoned into a wrought-iron flat strip and fixed to form cages between the arch ribs. Many tenons had all but rusted away. Virtually every bar was badly corroded at the ends (the most highly stressed point) and had suffered corrosion along its length. It became clear that it would be necessary to remove the glazing cages before the ironwork could be refurbished, possibly causing further damage to the bars in the process. The rebate supporting the glass was very small (¼ in (0.6 cm)) and the resultant tight fit of the panes contributed to the glass breakage. We also found areas where the glass had been badly cut, leaving protuberances which would have nipped the glass and broken it had any movement occurred, all contributing to maintenance costs.

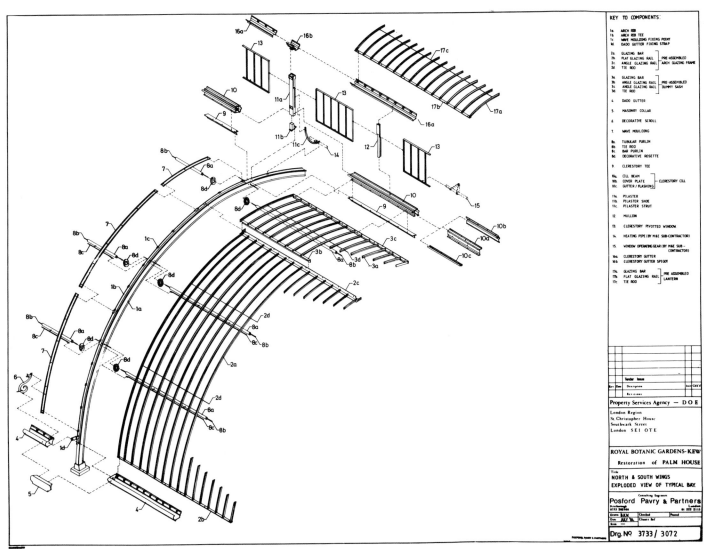

It was essential to check the loads and stresses in the various components of the structure, particularly the arch ribs. Many people have expressed surprise at this because the building had survived for 140 years without failure. However, as corrosion had substantially reduced the cross-sectional area of most of the members an investigation was thought prudent. After finding that wind caused the highest stresses, we needed to check our estimate of wind loads and organised a test in a wind tunnel of a 1:200 scale model. This largely confirmed our assumptions, except that it showed the wind pressures near the main doors to be higher than expected. In the main wings it was clear that wind suction tended to lift the glazing frames away from the building. The centre transept was more complicated. Here we decided that the load from each half arch was transferred by the gallery, acting as a large beam, back to the two main arches. This was probably an original design conception as these two arches were found to consist of the standard arch rib as a base, but with considerable strengthening provided by thick riveted plates. A drilling exercise to discover how the arches had been put together found rusty water. We concluded that it was essential to strip down these two key supports of the building to check which areas had corroded.

Everybody who owns a glasshouse (or who has ever been into one in the summer) realises the importance of ventilation. Originally the building had an inflow of air through the boxes in the dado wall, which was let out via the windows in the clerestories and gallery. In addition, the upper part of each glazing cage was

An exploded view of the components of a typical bay in one of the wings of the Palm House. With very few of the Victorian drawings remaining, these structural drawings formed working plans for the restorers and will record for posterity how the building was formed.

145

designed to slide down the arches on small brass wheels. None of the ventilation systems could now be operated, most of the boxes and all of the windows were wired shut and it is not known whether the sliding sashes were ever operated successfully. The implication is that they were not. Certainly Sir William Hooker stipulated in the brief for the design of the Temperate House in 1859 that 'the building be not curvilinear so that the large openable sashes on a straight roof could be employed to allow maximum exposure to summer rains and the temperature. That these sashes be made of wood as they could be more easily repaired than iron ones could . . .'

The heating system had had a chequered history. As described in chapter 1, the boilers were in the basements of the Palm House in 1848 and fed by coke brought in by small trucks pushed along a railway track through a tunnel from the Shaft Yard by Kew Road. The fumes from the boilers ran back along the tunnel in pipes to the campanile. The system of fume removal was never successful and chimneys were introduced into each wing. The rail track was the subject of an early restoration in 1891, but the boilers were not moved to the Shaft Yard until 1962, when they were renewed. Although in fair condition they were regarded as being towards the end of their useful life. The greater part of the floor in the house was then covered with cast-iron gratings. Heat from the boilers was transmitted by hot water through pipes under the gratings or under the perimeter plant shelf, with some supplementary piping around the clerestories and galleries. The plant shelf limited maintenance access to the pipes, which were found to be in poor condition, and vine tubs built between the plant shelf and the glazing hindered the rise of hot air and caused draughts. This area became a prime candidate for redesign.

The wind tunnel model used to check the loads and stresses on the Palm House and its structural integrity. It was built to a scale of 1:200.

14 Design and specifications for refurbishment

CHRIS JONES and PETER RIDDINGTON

The design brief

FOLLOWING THE VARIOUS SURVEYS and structural analyses, the Property Services Agency (PSA) set up a design team to start the design of the restoration. The firm of Posford Duvivier acted as lead consultant, responsible for structural, civil, and mechanical and electrical design; PSA supervised as project managers and architects; the firm of Ager and Stockwell acted as quantity surveyors; and Kew, as client, monitored the horticultural requirement. The brief and the philosophy for the design emerged from the discussions at design team meetings and also thorough consultation with the Department of Ancient Monuments and Historic Buildings (DAMHB), later to become the Historic Buildings and Monuments Commission (English Heritage).

Kew had certain requirements to be met in the restored house:

- maintenance should be easy and economical in terms both of the plant collection and the building fabric
- the mechanical and electrical services should be renewed and automated as far as possible
- planting beds should be provided for the plant collection throughout the house
- the basement areas should be used to provide staff accommodation and an area to display marine plant life to the public for the first time.

Furthermore the plant collection had to be securely accommodated during the period of the works.

The DAMHB also had requirements to be taken into consideration:

- the structural engineering principles of the Palm House should not be prejudiced
- as much as possible of the original fabric of the building should be kept.

These requirements formed the basic principles of the restoration design, which were twofold. First, the structure of the house itself (effectively everything above ground level) had to be preserved as far as possible, while also being both easily maintainable and requiring of minimum maintenance. Secondly, the ground layout of the house had to be completely altered, with more accommodation provided below ground.

The design philosophy

The philosophy for the restoration had, in part at least, to grow out of the requirements of the client. However, the DAMHB's requirements, which would ensure the integrity of the Grade 1 listed building, were of primary importance. It was agreed that the building should continue to house the palm collection, and as this could be achieved without making major changes to the appearance of the main building fabric, alterations to the ground layout and access to a new basement were not considered too great a price to pay to keep the building as a functioning house. However, there were some refinements as the design evolved.

The Palm House is not a building in the traditional sense of the word, but rather an engineering structure. With a 'normal' building the various philosophies of restoration or repair are well known and documented. They involve, to a greater or lesser extent, piecemeal replacement or repair of masonry, plaster or timber. There have been few restorations of engineering structures of the size and complexity of the Palm House. Even the restoration of the Temperate House, for instance, did not compare, for the Temperate House is in many respects a 'normal' building, with walls, a roof and a supporting structure. In the Palm House there is no differentiation between the walls and the roof, and all of the elements have a structural, as well as envelope function. As all of the elements of the house are therefore interdependent, any decision regarding alterations in one area has a knock-on effect throughout the building. This meant that although the design of the repairs for each individual member could be treated in a discrete way, the replacement and setting out of the glazing bars and the setting of the lines to the secondary structural elements were all interdependent and would not allow a piecemeal restoration of, say, one bay at a time. The house had to be dismantled completely, both to allow all of the structural elements to be examined and all junctions to be protected against rust, and to enable re-erection to common lines.

The ironwork

The design team was naturally concerned about future maintenance of the building and the replacement of iron by aluminium had to be considered. Aluminium is a modern low-maintenance material, easy to cast and extrude, and its low weight helps erection considerably. However, as its movement when bent is three times as much as iron, larger structural members would be needed. Moreover it became clear that the various external bodies preferred (and would possibly insist on) replacement of like with like. The Palm House is a famous *iron* building after all.

The longitudinal section through the restored house shows the subterranean position of the Marine Display with its twin helical staircases. The stippled areas denote the planting beds, parts of which benefit from rising heat from the occupied areas below.

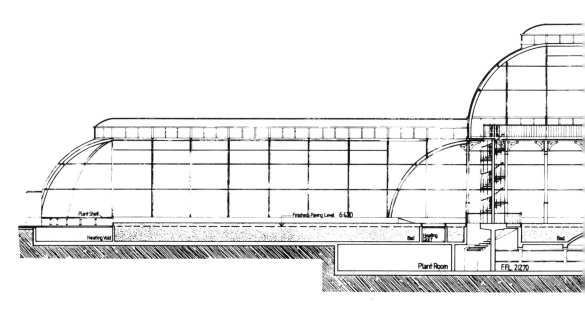

148

Cast iron is, of course, still readily available. Indeed a visit to a foundry might lead one to suppose that the technology had not changed since 1848. Black foundry sand (or the modern epoxy-based equivalent) lies everywhere and gives the average foundry a decrepit and Dickensian air. Our early visits were at the beginning of the 1980s and many foundries were going out of business. However, the range of irons available was interesting. As made clear in chapter 11, the disadvantage of cast iron is its brittle nature. In the 1940s an alternative had been developed, ductile iron. By adding magnesium the 'crisps' of carbon formed little balls within the iron, thus removing the fracture planes which led to the brittleness. In fact, ductile iron was the nearest available material (in behaviour) to wrought iron, except that it was still a material for casting and could not be rolled. It is possible to extrude it, but only for members larger than glazing bars.

We felt that ductile iron was the right material to replace the structurally important cast-iron members, since if corrosion did occur in the future, the loss of material would not cause cracking or failure for a long time afterwards. There was also some evidence to confirm that ductile iron had, of itself, a greater resistance to corrosion than cast iron. We also specified ductile iron to replace badly corroded wrought-iron sections such as tees and angles. We also investigated austenitic iron, which is a form of 'stainless' iron incorporating chromium and nickel. This material would have given a much enhanced corrosion resistance but the fall in the value of the pound at the time dramatically changed the cost ratio of austenitic to ductile because of the imported raw materials, and we decided that it would be uneconomic.

The building contains some 7500 castings, of which about one-third are structural, the remainder (roses and the like) being purely decorative. From the survey results we assessed the amount of replacement required. For the structural elements this varied from 20 per cent for the dado gutters above the stone wall to complete replacement of the clerestory components. We prepared a drawing for each of the structural components to such detail that it could be worked to by a foundry, although as the information was based on limited surveys we asked the future contractor, in the tender document, to check the members as they were dismantled and amend the drawing if necessary. We recognised that Turner had designed a masterpiece in iron. Nevertheless it was tempting (and we are only human) to want to change

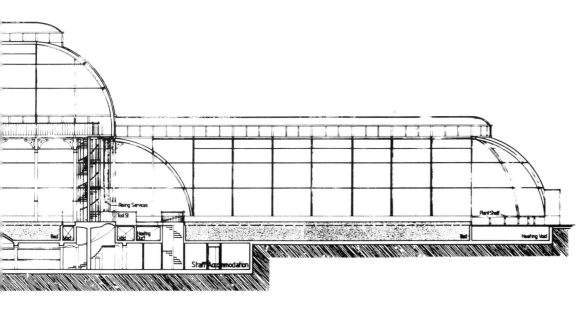

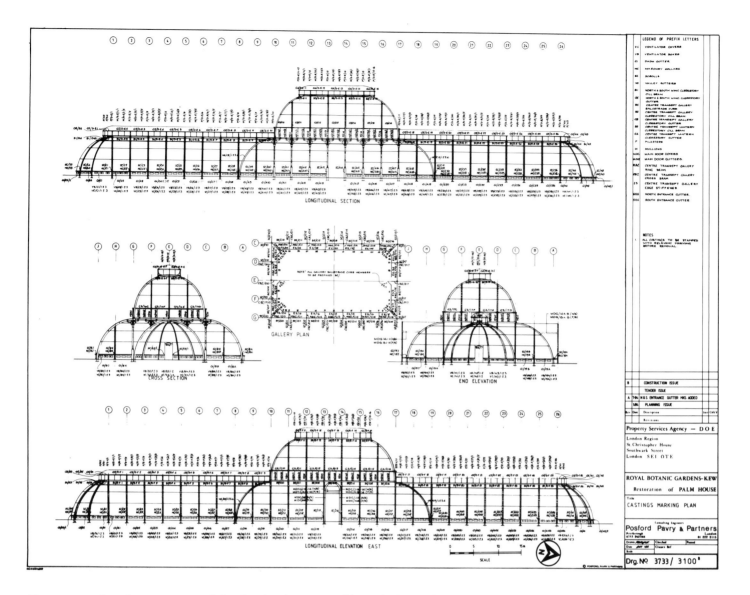

The castings marking plan provided codes for the 7500 structural and decorative castings of the building. Each piece was tagged on disassembly so that its location in the huge jigsaw could be found again after repair.

some of the details when we could see faults, such as components which had trapped water or cracked because they were simply too thin. Apart from the historical aspect, which we felt was very important, we were largely prevented from change because each component fitted neatly to its neighbour and any change, however minor, had a knock-on effect down the line. We would have liked, for example, to completely change the gutter splice detail because the spigot sits above the gutter. This means that the water level in the gutter must rise above the thickness of the spigot material before it will flow, leaving the gutter constantly part full. Consequently water seeps between the spigot and the gutter, causing corrosion. After much thought it became clear that such a change would destroy the character of the building and we therefore contented ourselves with some thickening in places and substantial sealing.

From our surveys we realised that the distance between each arch could vary by up to 12 mm and that the tops of the arches were not level. We presumed from this that most of the components would have been adjusted in length by some means or other. We were, therefore, keen to put each casting back exactly where it came from, and so each one was tagged with its individual number before removal. New castings were to have their number cast in or stamped on. As the quality of fit and control of supply were of paramount importance, we limited the contractor to a maximum of two foundries to provide all the new

150

castings. We found that there were few foundries who were large enough to cope with the volume and size of members, particularly in ductile iron, and who were interested in this type of work. Two that we visited who were keen to try mainly produced engine components. Eventually we chose five but by the time the tender documents were released, three of these had ceased trading.

Where the repair of existing castings was possible, we specified the Metalock method of repair, since cast iron is very difficult to weld. This process was developed about 40 years ago in the Texas oil fields and is really a form of stitching across the cracks using a nickel alloy as the thread. The repair is invisible after painting and can be as strong as the parent metal. We were a little sceptical about this until we load-tested a repaired floor grille which had been badly cracked and found the collapse load to be identical to that for an uncracked grille.

Most of the Palm House – the main arches and the miles of glazing bars – was constructed in wrought iron. Repair or replacement for these sections was difficult because of the shortage of this material. Wrought iron was so labour-intensive to produce that demand slackened soon after the invention of reliable steel-making, but surprisingly the craft of puddling (see p. 136) stayed alive until the closure of the Atlas Forge at Bolton, Lancashire in 1973. We were told by various people that the Ironbridge Museum was about to produce wrought iron and visited that remarkable place. However, its Director, Stuart Smith, very helpful but honest, was sure that the museum would not be able to puddle iron in sufficient quantities for our purposes until the late 1980s.

One alternative was to use second-hand wrought iron, of which large amounts often come onto the market. We visited a rolling-mill in Sheffield, which has now moved to the Black Country. This is the only rolling-mill in the country which regularly rolls in wrought iron. Their expertise, however, was limited to squares and rounds for balustrading and it was felt that the rolling of a more complicated section (such as the glazing bar, for instance) would be difficult. Also there was not enough wrought iron available.

We turned our attention to stainless steel. This is a low-maintenance material which can be rolled, extruded or cast. Its main disadvantages are its high cost per tonne plus its high fabrication costs, as it is difficult to work. We also recognised the possibility of bimetallic corrosion between stainless steel and iron. There are a variety of stainless steels on the market and it was important to choose a type which did not pit.

Following a timely visit to the recently restored Belfast Palm House we found that the glazing bars there had been extruded from mild steel at the Low Moor Ironworks at Bradford. We thought that mild steel could give Kew maintenance problems in the future but the Low Moor Works, originally famous for high-quality wrought iron, is the only plant which extrudes stainless steel in the United Kingdom. We were able to reuse the Belfast dies to produce small samples of stainless steel bars to discuss with interested bodies.

We were also keen to suggest rolling as an alternative to extrusion to any contractor. Although the initial costs were higher (a set of rolls would cost £20,000 to cut) the overall rate per tonne was cheaper than extrusion. Rolling also provides a 'cleaner' shape with sharper corners. In the event the successful contractor elected to extrude as he could then call off whatever quantities he wanted to suit his timing, as against rolling, which is a 'once and for all' operation.

Decisions on glazing

At first glance polycarbonate seemed the ideal material to replace the glazing. It is shatterproof and easy to bend. It could be possible, for example, to use a single sheet for one half arch – when laid on the bars this would take up the right shape without cold or hot forming. However, after discussions with other users and a visit to a production plant in Germany, we soon found that there were many drawbacks:

- thermal expansion is ten times as much as glass, so special glazing bars would be necessary
- during our investigation some thin-walled polycarbonate-covered glasshouses were badly damaged by hail
- the manufacturer could not guarantee colour fastness. There was a tendency for polycarbonate to go opaque after ten years
- all polycarbonate is imported
- last, but by no means least, the architect expressed concern that a single sheet spanning down an arch would not 'twinkle' in the sunlight in the same way that shorter sheets do.

After the rejection of polycarbonate, toughened glass was considered, both in view of the safety of the public and to reduce maintenance costs. As with the foundries, glass-makers in the United Kingdom were suffering from the effects of the recession in the early 1980s, as volume car manufacturing had slumped and with it production of toughened glass for windscreens. Pilkington Glass in particular were

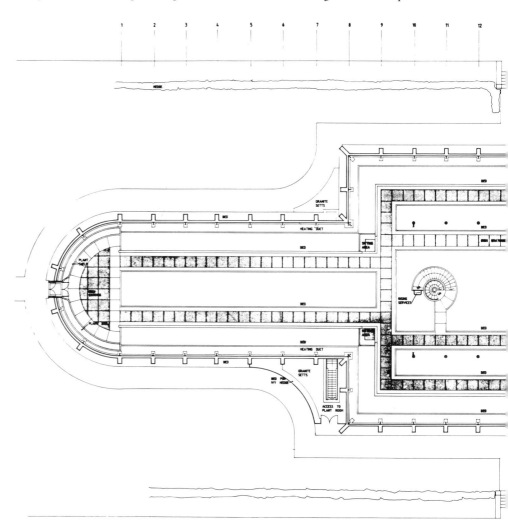

keen to help and gave us what appeared to be a very reasonable price for the supply of toughened (or tempered) glass. Indeed, it was less than other manufacturers were quoting for ordinary bent annealed glass. This is perhaps not as surprising as it seems, since the toughening of bent glass is a relatively minor extra process. For both, the glass is heated over a saddle mould until it drops into and forms the shape of the mould. The glass is then quickly cooled to toughen it. The main problem is that it cannot be cut after manufacture, and it would therefore be necessary to provide individual templates cut on site for the special shapes in the hips, valleys and apse ends. Eventually, however, the time to prepare the individual jigs for each shape was much longer than originally envisaged and these areas were glazed with annealed glass cut on site.

Toughened glass is extremely flexible and we enjoyed demonstrating this by standing on a pane of the curved glass spanning between two curved blocks. This finally led to a very embarrassing moment when the engineer was showing it to Kew, as the corner of the glass caught on a table and shattered. In a car windscreen the small pieces are held together (as they will be in the Palm House) but this pane broke into several thousand pieces thrown all over the room.

Various alternative methods of holding the glass in were also considered, but a dry or clip system, as used now on most glasshouses, could not be made to match the original. The main disadvantage of putty is that it should be painted at five-yearly intervals. There are many proprietary sealants currently on the market but few are white. We eventually decided to use silicone but specified a fungicide to prevent algal

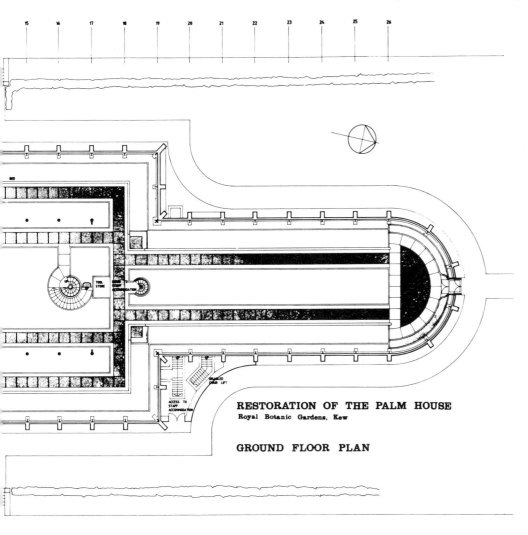

The ground floor plan of the restored house shows the new system of planting beds, while the apse ends retain the original arrangement of gratings and plant shelves. The shaded areas denote the new, wider, paths, which are made of reused gratings and York stone.

RESTORATION OF THE PALM HOUSE
Royal Botanic Gardens, Kew

GROUND FLOOR PLAN

growth. This is the same kind of material as that which is used to seal bathrooms and as it happens the type eventually used was designated 'Sanitary'. We were not sure at first whether to seal the glass laps but our heating engineer assured us that there would be a tremendous heat saving. Accordingly we decided to seal the upper edge only of each lap with a clear silicone, as often used in fish tanks. The intention was to avoid trapping algae.

Revised floor layout

The design of the revised floor layout arose out of three requirements. First, it had been found over the years that the width of paths in the house was very restrictive for visitors. This meant that the house could become uncomfortably crowded and that in extreme circumstances the plant collection could be damaged. Therefore the client brief was for wider paths, and also for areas where visitors could sit to rest in the stifling heat.

Secondly, the requirement was for the plants to be grown in beds in the wings as well as (as before) in the centre transept. Thirdly, the redesign of the heating system called for a perimeter service adjacent to the dado wall. This was required to allow heating to be installed on the perimeter of the house to counter the down-draught effect of cold air falling from high level. Also the main heating source for the house would now be relocated from under the main planting area of the house to under the paths. The revised floor layout had to take these aspects into account.

The Palm House has a strong geometry, based on multiples of a square grid of 12 ft 6 in (3.8 metres) or 150 in (381 cm) bay widths, broken down into 50 in (127 cm) modules (the cast-iron grating dimension), and indeed broken down further to 10 in (25 cm) glazing bar spacings. Thus it was appropriate that any revised floor layout should reflect both this geometry and the symmetry of the house. It was decided that the cast-iron gratings on which the palms and cycads used to stand should be reused in the new walkways, to allow the heat to pass upwards from the heating void below and to reuse an important element of the original floor construction. Other materials for the paths and the bed edgings were chosen to reflect the original materials: York stone for the horizontal finishes – path edgings and pavings, and Portland stone (to match the original dado) for the vertical elements – bed edgings and walls.

Externally the paving layout was also revised. The need to have close access to the house for a maintenance platform (hydraulic lift) meant that the elliptical path installed in the 1950s would not be suitable and a path relating to the perimeter of the house was designed. The original designs included a ramp to provide access to the basement for people with disabilities. This was to have led from the Rose Garden to the north end of the Marine Display. Unfortunately this had to be abandoned as a cost-saving exercise, and it was replaced by a chairlift situated in the service area for the staff accommodation.

Mechanical and electrical services

In a building like the Palm House a successful restoration design can best be assessed by how well the modern services have been integrated into the original fabric. The Palm House is a very highly serviced building. Not only does it have an enormous amount of heating surface to maintain temperatures during

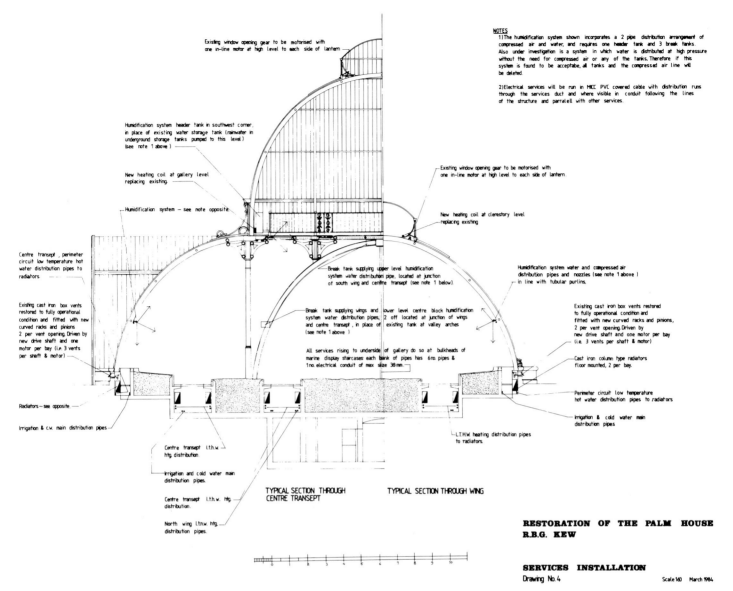

Existing window opening gear to be motorised with one in-line motor at high level to each side of lantern.

Humidification system header tank in southwest corner, in place of existing water storage tank (rainwater in underground storage tanks pumped to this level) (see note 1 above)

New heating coil at gallery level replacing existing.

Humidification system – see note opposite.

Existing window opening gear to be motorised with one in-line motor at high level to each side of lantern.

New heating coil at clerestory level replacing existing

Centre transept, perimeter circuit low temperature hot water distribution pipes to radiators.

Break tank supplying upper level humidification system water distribution pipe, located at junction of south wing and centre transept (see note 1 below).

Humidification system water and compressed air distribution pipes and nozzles (see note 1 above) in line with tubular purlins.

Existing cast iron box vents restored to fully operational condition and fitted with new curved racks and pinions, 2 per vent opening. Driven by new drive shaft and one motor per bay (i.e. 3 vents per shaft & motor)

Break tank supplying wings and lower level centre block humidification system water distribution pipes, 2 off located at junction of wings and centre transept, in place of existing tank at valley arches (see note 1 above)

All services rising to underside of gallery do so at bulkheads of marine display staircases each bank of pipes has 6 no. pipes & 1 no. electrical conduit of max size 38 mm.

Existing cast iron box vents restored to fully operational condition and fitted with new curved racks and pinions, 2 per vent opening. Driven by new drive shaft and one motor per bay (i.e. 3 vents per shaft & motor)

Cast iron column type radiators floor mounted, 2 per bay.

Radiators – see opposite.

Perimeter circuit low temperature hot water distribution pipes to radiators

Irrigation & c.w. main distribution pipes

Irrigation & cold water main distribution pipes

Centre transept l.t.h.w. htg. distribution.

Irrigation and cold water main distribution pipes.

Centre transept l.t.h.w. htg. distribution.

North wing l.t.h.w. htg. distribution pipes.

L.T.H.W. heating distribution pipes to radiators.

TYPICAL SECTION THROUGH CENTRE TRANSEPT

TYPICAL SECTION THROUGH WING

RESTORATION OF THE PALM HOUSE R.B.G. KEW

SERVICES INSTALLATION
Drawing No. 4
Scale 1:60   March 1984

the winter, but it has ventilators, irrigation pipes, humidistats, thermostats, lighting and power supplies, water tanks and a proliferation of other wires, pipes and control boxes necessary to maintain the climate in the house. Added to all the usual paraphernalia of a glasshouse, Kew also required a new humidification system to be installed to provide a constant humidity level 24 hours a day, 365 days a year and of a standard to ensure public health. The co-ordination of the services with both the new and the original architectural features of the house was a painstaking exercise.

The new humidification system required two pipes to run horizontally throughout the house, with further pipework below the gallery, as well as various tanks to be incorporated at different positions in the house. All of these items were specially designed, with purpose-made brackets and water tanks. To irrigate the house, two 50,000 gallon (227,300 litre) tanks were constructed under the terraces in front of the building to collect rainwater from the roof for a supply of soft water. In times of drought this would be topped up by a deioniser water-treatment plant located in the south plant room. The ventilation of the house, which over recent years had been accomplished inadvertently by the broken and missing panes of glass, was to be by the automation of the original windows and the low-level ventilators set in the dado wall. However, the motors and cables had to be discreetly positioned in the house and the original

The services installation drawing shows the arrangement of the heating, ventilation and humidification systems in the centre transept (left) and in the wings (right). Note the suspended floor, the loading limits of which affected the choice of machinery for replanting.

155

opening gear for the windows refurbished for reuse. The services to the low-level vents are hidden within the perimeter service area.

The heating system

The new heating system was designed to be fully integrated with the revised floor layout, and Kew felt that the minimum temperature requirements could be reduced. The boilers in the Shaft Yard (about 400 metres from the house), now near the end of their useful life, were to be replaced, and hot water was to be piped along the underground tunnel to radiators set along the perimeter of the house and in the service trenches below floor level. Supplementary heating was to be provided by pipes along the wings at clerestory level and around the gallery, following the successful system originally introduced by Dr Hooker. The various controls for these services had to be integrated with the building. What look like lamp standards in the planting beds are in fact devices for holding at the required height aspirated humidification and heating sensors. Doors in the seating areas hide controls to the ventilators.

In summary, as well as the boiler house in the Shaft Yard the Palm House has a generator house, a compressor house to serve the humidification system, a large plant room in the south basement containing water-treatment plant, pumps, air-handling equipment and switchgear and, finally, a small plant room in the north basement servicing the staff accommodation.

The consultations with planning and conservation bodies

Although the Palm House is a government building and therefore not subject to the same planning regulations as other buildings, the PSA still had to go through a planning procedure similar to that for other buildings, submitting its proposals to the London Borough of Richmond, who in turn consulted with the then Greater London Council. As the building is of outstanding importance the Royal Fine Arts Commission and English Heritage also had to be consulted. Notwithstanding this requirement, we were aware of the considerable amount of affection the house engendered and were sensitive to the feelings of the various interested bodies, from the Kew Society to the Victorian Society. A reception was held for all of the learned and other societies at Kew, where a brochure describing the proposals was presented. Further presentations and other meetings were held during the design process and eventually the proposals were accepted by the planning authority.

The design team had expected that the proposals to change the glazing bars would create controversy. However, we had not thought that the alterations to the ground-floor layout would prove to be the most contentious aspect of the proposals. Feelings were particularly aroused by the proposals to remove the perimeter plant shelf and to put the plants into beds. Following the consultations it was agreed to modify the plan slightly by maintaining the original layout in the apse ends which are, in effect, 'conservation areas', relocating the access to the Marine Display basement so that none of it is visible from the ground floor and incorporating the redundant cast-iron shelf legs into the design of the perimeter bed.

The overwhelming consensus on the paint colour of the house was that white should be used, and that the glazing bars (though stainless steel) should also be white, as they had been immediately prior to the restoration. This decision was contrary to the historical knowledge provided by the DAMHB, who carried out limited investigation which showed the house to have been originally painted a deep blue-green colour, a discovery later confirmed by scratchings on the castings as the house was disassembled. This was in many ways to be expected, as the Victorians preferred their iron to look like bronze. The decision to maintain the white paint was based on the prevailing feeling that the house had been white for so long that it would be a culture shock to change it now. However, the high reflectivity of the paintwork was one factor behind Kew's decision to provide shading for the plant collection during the period of replanting.

Design for future maintenance

Naturally considerable thought was given to the future maintenance of the building. Although we hoped that for some time after the restoration the amount of maintenance would be minimal, there would still be a need to touch up paint and replace panes of glass. Continuous walkways at high level were initially suggested but rejected as being too obtrusive. Mobile gantries moving up and down the inside of the house were similarly rejected because of appearance and the possibility of obstruction by the hopefully prolific growth of plants.

The full range of maintenance platforms was assessed and some helpful guidance was obtained from other houses, such as Belfast, where external mobile gantry ladders had been installed. There are two basic sizes of hydraulic platforms: the smaller are self-propelled and the larger are lorry-mounted. There was, at the time, only one self-propelled platform which could reach up to the gallery level outside, and yet could be folded down and taken through the small doors while also being capable of reaching everywhere within the building. Only a lorry-mounted machine would cover the whole building outside but this would cost at least eight times as much as the smaller machine. Even the daily hire would be very expensive and would require the cost of road access round the house. We therefore designed mobile gantry ladders to give access to the upper centre transept. These were necessarily more obtrusive than the ones they replaced due to the requirements of recent health and safety legislation. There is one ladder for each side, running along a track sitting on the gallery gutters and operated by turning a wheel. As at least one-third of the side could not be reached if the ladder was supported at the clerestory, we provided a rail at about two-thirds the way up so that the ladder cantilevers over the remainder. A small aluminium curved ladder was designed to span over the roof of the clerestory and run along the gutters, which were specially cast to support the wheels.

Tender stage

As in all construction projects there were various types of documentation to consider. For this project it was felt that the survey and subsequent detailed drawings justified a lump sum tender. There would have been some advantages in having a two-stage contract split into dismantling and re-erection, but the time span given for the temporary housing of the plants did not allow for this. Furthermore, it was felt advisable to have the same contractor re-erect whatever he had dismantled. As the budget exceeded £0.5 million the project was advertised in the EEC. There were 42 replies, none from outside the United Kingdom. Of these 19 were interviewed, a figure which was whittled down to 9 tenderers. The main contract was finally awarded to Balfour Beatty in 1985.

15 The Marine Display

PETER MORRIS and PETER RIDDINGTON

WHAT ON EARTH has a marine aquarium got to do with Kew Gardens? This was the question we were to hear time and time again when we started to develop the Marine Display in 1985. To answer it we have to go back to the original purpose and philosophy behind the gardens.

The Royal Botanic Gardens, Kew has always maintained that it holds a scientific living collection of the plant kingdom and there has always been an implicit determination to increase the collection continually to include those plants which are not grown in most botanic gardens.

So how well does the present collection of plants at Kew represent the groups of plants found in the plant kingdom? If we forget the fungi, the plant kingdom can be divided into five major groups: flowering plants, conifers, ferns, mosses and liverworts, and the algae. Up to 1985 Kew already had good representations of flowering plants, conifers, ferns, and even a few mosses and liverworts in the Filmy Fern House, but nowhere could be seen any living representatives of the very important plant group known as the algae. The Marine Display aims to redress the balance.

ARCHITECTURAL DESIGN

The Marine Display, a new concept involving new technology to display the plant life of the oceans, has been a project requiring imagination and vision. This is the architect's visualisation, drawn up early in the design process.

The Palm House originally had two small basements which housed the boilers. These were sited at the north and south ends of the centre transept at the intersections with the wings. Because the new planting beds were being built over them and the weight of these would have been too great for the crumbling

Victorian brickwork, the decision was made to rebuild these areas completely. This created a new opportunity. As the basements were to be rebuilt, major engineering works had to be carried out below ground in any case. So the decision was taken to excavate the whole of the area below the centre transept between the basements and construct an area which would house the 'Marine Display'.

At this stage of the design no one really knew what a 'Marine Display' would be, let alone what it should look like. We could design a new basement like a big box below ground and put things into it later. The Palm House was the first priority and the integration of the new facility into the Victorian glasshouse was of primary importance.

The design of the structure itself was governed by three parameters. First, the structure had to avoid the columns in the centre transept of the house and their brick and granite foundations. Secondly, all of the height restrictions imposed by the depths of planting beds and the heating trenches below the paths had to be accommodated. Thirdly, the new excavation obviously had to be within the space between the original basements. The engineer's solution was to design a reinforced concrete structure with diaphragm walls, braced by roof and floor slabs. The excavation method was to install two rows of sheet piles, which would just miss the foundation blocks of the two rows of columns, and then dig out the earth between, providing temporary bracings to the piles while the excavations were being undertaken. The efficacy of the design and construction procedure was evident after the new basement was completed, as a check survey of the iron structure showed minimal movement. This must have been the first time that such extensive sheet piling has been done within a glazed glasshouse.

The first architectural design problem was how access to the new basement structure could be arranged without detracting from the house itself. Various schemes were investigated. Initially a single staircase was proposed in the centre of the house. This was designed to wrap around an aquarium tank which would have formed a pond at ground level. This proposal was abandoned because the planning authorities requested something more discreet. It was finally decided to construct two new helical staircases which would start at the feet of the original cast-iron spiral staircases. This would both provide an efficient circulation pattern and effectively hide these new elements in the planting beds, while providing an attractive staircase feature below ground. Having ascertained the position of the access and knowing the size of the 'box' (as our newly designed basement came to be called), the layout and treatment of the engineering structure was the second architectural problem.

Since the whole project was so innovative, it was hard to imagine what a Marine Display would look like. Visits were made to various public aquaria to see how they were designed and serviced, but it became increasingly apparent that nowhere was there any installation which came anywhere near what we were trying to achieve. Not only do public aquaria not grow marine algae, but many use plastic seaweed as decoration. It was at this stage that Kew decided that it would have to appoint its own marine biologist, Mr Peter Morris, to brief the design team. However, in the interim, decisions on the basic layout of the basement had to be made based on the limited information gathered. All public aquaria need considerable space behind what the visitor sees, to be used for servicing the tanks, storage of water, mixing of water, the provision of back-up materials, propagation and administration. All of these activities had to be included in our installation. It was decided to divide the proportion of public and service space equally. Kew insisted that there should be a large central feature and the plan form that developed was based on two aisles, one leading from each staircase, meeting in the central colonnaded area and thus mirroring the overall ground plan of the Palm House.

The staircases had to have minimal headroom due to the aggregation of adjacent serviceways and the basement itself was very low because of the plant beds above. In the treatment of the structure it was decided to turn the low ceiling heights to advantage. By accentuating the low ceilings with vaults and the main structural elements with rough white concrete, the feeling of being below ground was heightened rather than concealed. The low dome over the central circular area lightens this effect while retaining a definitely subterranean atmosphere.

The marine biologist's brief was crucial in deciding the detailed layout of the display. Having decided his priorities in the kinds of environment to be displayed, it was possible to arrive at tank sizes and locations within the basic parameters already decided. He was also able to give precise information on the different climatic conditions required in each tank and the different items of equipment necessary to produce them. All materials specified had to be suitable for use in a marine environment, the most corrosive environment for building materials. This included all of the light fittings, the pipework and other items of equipment likely to be regularly splashed by the salt water. Of primary importance was the wall into which the tanks would fit. It was decided that for durability and to allow the possibility for future alteration, a wall fabricated from vitreous enamel panels on a stainless steel frame would be used.

The new area has been designed for the display of the exquisite miniature landscapes contained in the aquarium tanks. The architectural treatment is intended to complement and provide a backdrop to these in much the same way as an art gallery provides a setting for its pictures. The structure is highlighted by the background lighting, to give a sense of place, but the cladding materials are deliberately not intrusive and the primary lighting is from the tanks themselves and from the small panels of identifying text.

THE MARINE ENVIRONMENT

Seawater covers 70 per cent of the earth's surface. Throughout this vast area plants live and grow in great abundance, providing 50 per cent of the earth's oxygen and originating all marine food chains. Many groups of plants have representatives which live partially in seawater but, in the main, our seas and oceans are the home of the very first plants, the algae or seaweeds. Algae do not, however, exist throughout the length and depth of the oceans. Like all plants they need light to survive, so they are only able to grow in the areas of the oceans lit by sunlight. This rarely exceeds depths of 100 metres even in the clearest waters. The oceans are, of course, mostly much deeper than this, so most marine plants either float or swim. These are single-celled plants known as the phytoplankton or microalgae.

Microalgae are invisible to the naked eye but their presence is sometimes marked by phenomena such as green water or red tides, where populations can be as high as a billion plants in a few cubic centimetres of water. Sadly they are impossible to exhibit in an aquarium situation. Plants which we can see easily are limited to the areas where the sea-bed is not deeper than 100 metres. These are the continental shelves and the margins between the land and the sea which also incorporate the tidal zone. Although this narrow strip of water between land and sea represents such a small area, it gives rise to some of the most productive, unusual and inaccessible habitats in the world. The Marine Display shows in miniature four intertidal habitats, two from around our shores and two from tropical areas.

BRITISH NATIVE HABITATS

There are four common types of shore around the British Isles: sandy beaches, rocky shores, shingle beaches and muddy shores. Sand and shingle beaches are too impermanent to allow any real plant establishment but rocky and muddy shores are quite different.

The rocky shore

Rocky cliffs emerging from the sea can be seen around much of Britain's coastline. This environment is extremely harsh, as plants and animals living here have to withstand waves crashing against them at high tide and severe desiccation when the tide is out. They have to survive baking-hot conditions in the summer and frost and snow in winter. The amount of desiccation a plant can withstand determines where it appears on the intertidal rocky shore. For instance, it takes approximately five hours for a tide to go out and seven hours for it to come in. Plants at the very top of the tide-mark could be out of the water for 23 hours of every day. As we go down the rockface the time spent out of the water gets progressively less, and plants and animals appear at the points which correspond to how much time they can survive out of the water. This banding effect is a characteristic of rocky shores throughout the temperate environment. The only group of plants to survive in this harsh habitat are the brown seaweeds known as fucoids or wracks. They have thick rubbery fronds filled with mucilage which keeps water loss to a minimum. Some of the upper banks of plants have air bladders, causing the plant body to float away from the rockface at high tide. All of them have thick strong holdfasts to grip the rock surface.

Two other habitats can be found within the rocky shore environment. One of these is the rock pool. These pools do not empty at low tide so the habitat is less severe than the open cliff face, allowing a variety of red and green algae to flourish. The other habitat lies at the foot of rocky cliffs and is exposed at extreme low tides. Here we find forests of the largest algae, the kelps. Around our shores these grow to quite modest sizes but in California the giant kelp grows to over 100 metres, rivalling the giant redwood as the longest plant in the world.

The muddy shore

The second native habitat features the temperate estuarine system. This occurs where rivers empty soil and organic waste into the sea, creating a muddy environment. The plants which dominate this habitat are not algae but land-evolved plants which have adapted to live in a salt-water habitat. Collectively these plants make up a salt-marsh. Here the land is advancing on the sea and mud is turned into soil as each successive group of plants establishes and raises the mud level, allowing more plants to gain a hold. The most seaward plant colonising the bare mud is *Salicornia*. Its seedlings germinate on the parent plant and then drop into the mud, ready to establish and grow much as mangroves do. This is vital, as ungerminated seeds would simply be swept away with the receding tide. As *Salicornia* grows, putting down its long roots, the mud becomes firmer and allows more plants to establish. Many flowering plants have representatives in the salt-marsh: grasses, composites, lilies and plantains, to name but a few. In summer the marsh is a blaze of colour and variety. Behind the main body of the marsh the landward advance continues, consolidating the ground until totally terrestrial plants can colonise the new soil habitat.

The so-called red algae live in the deepest water and survive with comparatively little light. Their true colours range from pink to near black or the maroon of this species of Grateloupia.

Of the green algae, species of Caulerpa *are perhaps the easiest to grow in an artificial environment. They are adapted to live in sand or mud, with structures resembling roots, and fern-like fronds.*

The areas of anoxic mud preceding a salt-marsh host vast quantities of shellfish such as cockles and ragworms. They are also the home of our only native flowering plant which lives totally immersed in the sea, the eel grass, *Zostera marina*. This is a true higher plant, with roots, leaves and flowers, and is one of the seagrasses. Only 50 species of seagrass are found worldwide, and therefore we give them special consideration in our displays. Estuaries are highly productive, being very important feeding grounds for young fish and wading birds.

TROPICAL MARINE HABITATS

In the tropics there is not much of an intertidal zone as average tides are only about 60 cm. There are, however, two important habitats where plants feature highly: the coral reef and the mangrove swamp.

The coral reef

Where the seas are above 20°C with plenty of calcium in solution, coral reefs sometimes develop. Coral reefs are perhaps the most unique and beautiful habitats in the world. They are unique because they create themselves, continually evolving and developing more and more niches for plants, invertebrates and fish to use. The variety of flora and fauna on coral reefs is staggering. For instance, the Great Barrier Reef in Australia is only tiny when compared to the rest of the oceans, yet it contains 20 per cent of all the world's species of fish. So how does it all begin? Tropical seas are nutrient poor, since most nutrients are locked below a permanent temperature barrier. In such an environment, symbiosis (the joining of two different organisms in a mutually beneficial partnership) becomes highly favoured. Coral is the symbiotic relationship between an animal cell, the coral, and a single-celled alga. Once the two are united all they need is sunlight. The plant photosynthesises, passing on excess products as food to the animal, which uses the food and passes waste products back to the plant as nutrients. This simple relationship, along with the ability to extract calcium from the water to create a rocky body, gives rise to the huge length of the Australian reef. As the reef develops, plants and animals attach themselves to it, boring organisms drill holes in it and so it goes on, ever growing, changing and evolving.

Coral is the result of a symbiotic relationship between an animal cell, the coral, and a single-celled alga. By extracting calcium from seawater this partnership creates huge fringing reefs, home to many species of other algae as well as fish and invertebrates. This is a green brain coral.

Within the reef environment there are many habitats where plants have a vital role and are well represented. Algae are divided into three major groups based on their colour: brown, red and green. Brown algae, generally the biggest and toughest of the three, are poorly represented in the tropics except in two specific places: on the reef flats and floating out in the ocean. On reef flats living in the breaking surf we find *Sargassum* and *Turbinaria*. *Sargassum* lives attached to rock, but one species forms vast floating colonies sometimes as much as 160 km offshore. These colonies form very important nursery grounds for fish, but also have their own unique fish and invertebrate fauna which never leave the *Sargassum*.

Red algae are the most beautiful and deepest growing of all marine plants, often existing in very little light. We call them red but their true colours range from delicate pinks and purples to almost black. They are found generally in sheltered places around the reef, but one group, the calcified red algae, covers vast areas of old reef flats, turning them red and keeping the reef from crumbling. These plants are as hard as rock, able to withstand extreme wave movement and desiccation. They generally appear in such numbers that they are thought to be one of the primary producers of the coral reef system itself.

On the landward side of reefs one often finds lagoons. These muddy areas protected from the sea are dominated by green algae and seagrasses. The green algae are shallow-water plants with the ability to colonise mud. They do not look much like our seaweeds. Some, like *Halimeda*, could be mistaken for cacti, and *Cladophoropsis*, which grows into a ball of interwoven threads, looks like a pan scourer. Perhaps the most beautiful are the caulerpas, which have evolved to live in mud or sand. Their holdfasts are very similar to roots and their fronds to the fronds of ferns.

A typical coral reef is preceded at its landward end by a coral sand beach. This coral sand is the end product of corals and algae which have been eaten by reef animals. The beach provides a special environment which is colonised by many tropical flowering plants. Conditions in this habitat are far from ideal. Sandy beaches are characteristically nutrient poor, subject to extreme temperatures and seawater spray, and devoid of fresh water. Despite these harsh conditions, most tropical beaches are bordered by a lush mixed community of tropical plants. Perhaps the most common is *Ipomoea pes-caprae*, a pantropical creeper with distinctive leaves and pink to violet flowers.

The mangrove swamp

Like the salt-marsh, this habitat is dominated by land plants adapted to live in seawater. However, whereas salt-marsh plants are relatively small, mangroves are mostly bushes and trees. Two mangroves are common, the black mangrove, *Avicennia*, and the red mangrove, *Rhizophora*. They both show interesting adaptations to their habitat, including prop roots to anchor themselves in this muddy world, and pneumatophores, botanical snorkels passing air down to roots searching for nutrients in an airless environment. Mangrove seedlings are borne live, like those of *Salicornia*. The large root/shoot drops like a bayonet into the mud with sufficient force to anchor itself. If the seedling drops at high tide it floats away, drifting and photosynthesising for up to a year. In this way mangroves are able to colonise new areas.

The mangrove habitat is highly productive, yielding an important source of food both for the resident animal species and their sea-dwelling cousins who visit the swamp at high tides. The animal community is made up of two types: those such as fiddler crabs and mudskipper fish which live out their whole lives in the mangrove swamp, and others which use the swamp as a nursery facility, moving out onto the reefs at maturity. Mangrove swamps literally teem with life. Oysters attach themselves to the mangrove roots and crabs, worms and lobsters burrow in the mud. Perhaps the most bizarre animal is the mudskipper, with its pronounced eyes and fins adapted to hop or crawl over the mud, a creature intermediate between land and sea, as indeed are the plants.

CREATING A HABITAT

For our purposes plants can be divided into two groups: those which will grow in habitats the gardens can provide and those which will not. Throughout the gardens can be found available a vast variety of environmental conditions – temperatures ranging from arctic to tropical, endless combinations of soil types, and humidity levels ranging from 100 per cent to the dry air of arid deserts. Despite this enormous variety of conditions, plants still exist which need even more specialised environments. In these cases research must be undertaken to provide the plants with a new habitat, one which supplies, as near as possible, the conditions necessary for their successful growth and reproduction.

When it comes to providing specialist environmental conditions there can be no group of plants which provide a greater challenge than the marine algae. To begin with they all live in seawater, which is in itself a complicated mixture of chemical and biological substances. For the most part they need to be supplied with nutritious plant foods in a totally different form from land plants and they need varying degrees of illumination and quality of light depending on where they grow in their natural environment.

The starting point for the creation of a habitat is to look at how the plants grow in the wild and to pinpoint the major environmental factors involved therein. To illustrate this point I would like to look at the one major marine habitat from which 70 per cent of our display plants come, the tropical coral reef.

As you stand gazing across a tropical coral reef the first thing that strikes you is the intense sunlight which hits the water surface; something in the region of 100,000 lux. However, as soon as sunlight hits seawater its illuminating qualities drop off drastically, gradually decreasing until at around 100 metres, in clear water, all illumination ceases. Water clarity differs not only between reefs but also between different parts of one reef and even between the same parts of one reef at different times of the year. This variation of clarity works very much in our favour, allowing us to collect plants from areas of low illumination which we can successfully recreate in an artificial environment.

There is another major problem associated with sunlight and seawater. Different parts of the colour spectrum are absorbed at different depths. For instance, ultraviolet light is absorbed within the first few centimetres of surface water. Next to go are red, orange and yellow light until only blue-green light remains. Marine algae live at all depths, from the surface right down to 100 metres, where only the last gleanings of the sun's rays persist. To make full use of their environment the algae have developed a range of pigments enabling them to absorb whatever light is available. Most commercial lighting units only emit yellow light, so our challenge was to find a lamp of high intensity which would emit the full colour spectrum from infra-red to ultraviolet.

Water quality is another major consideration. The coral reef environment is incredibly pure, unlike our rather dirty coastline where excessively high nitrite levels have caused the marine life to evolve to live in a more polluted environment. On reefs even moderate nitrite levels kill corals and fish. Whilst the nitrite will not in itself harm the plants it can cause single-cell algal blooms which literally smother everything. Therefore filtration systems had to be designed that would not only ensure a pure, unpolluted environment but also the excellent clarity essential both for light penetration for the plants and for the enjoyment of our visitors.

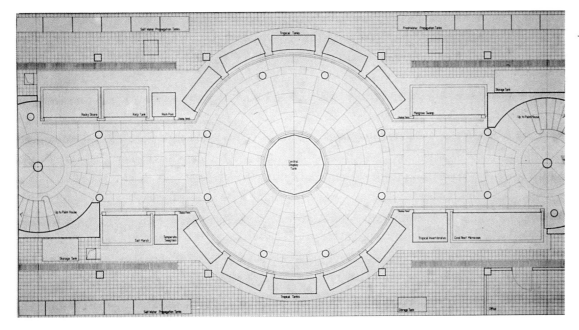

The architect's ground plan for the Marine Display.

Snorkelling along a coral reef enables you to see the varied local habitats which exist within the coral reef environment. *Caulerpa* and seagrass live in shallow-water lagoons rooted in mud. Their habitat is protected from the crashing waves by a seaward reef. This environment is totally different from the top of reef flats, where waves constantly crash over *Sargassum* or *Turbinaria*. *Halimeda* is a plant which often grows rooted in sand. All these examples are plants which share the same major requirements of light and water quality but have quite different local habitats.

To be successful in keeping marine algae one must try to create artificially as near as possible the same conditions as in the wild. This becomes especially difficult when we consider, say, the temperate rocky shore. Its intertidal brown seaweeds require to be out of the water twice a day and need strong water movement to develop healthy holdfasts and keep the plant body clean from parasitic plants and animals. In addition they will rot off in water above 13°C.

This challenge is very rewarding, especially when the plants carry out their reproductive cycles at the same time as their cousins out in the wild. What better recommendation could you have than from the plants themselves, assuring you that, as far as they are concerned, you have got the habitat right.

The habitats we show are not large. On the contrary, many would argue they are far too small. But at least they give a glimpse of four of the most unique and inaccessible habitats in the world. The collection of algae provides a long-needed window into the tropical seas, a window which hitherto has not been available either to the public or to students of marine biology or botany. The completed marine display should prove to be a valuable scientific collection, providing a unique resource to scientist and horticulturist alike.

The stilt and breathing roots of the red mangrove, Rhizophora mangle, *in the Florida Keys. Mangrove vegetation with its mass of stilt roots stabilises the coastline it fringes and protects it from erosion. The mangrove habitat is one of several marine environments recreated in miniature in the Marine Display.*

16 The restoration of the Palm House 1985–1988

CHRIS JONES

October 1985. Removal of the floor grilles reveals the concrete floor supports reconstructed in the restoration of the 1950s. The underfloor heating pipes have been removed.

167

THE RESTORATION OF THE PALM HOUSE by the contractors Balfour Beatty (later to become Balfour Beatty Building) commenced in the autumn of 1985, a year after the building had been emptied of plants.

It was in many ways a difficult site for a contractor: right in the middle of gardens which attract over 1.25 million people a year. The contractor used the Shaft Yard and a small area of the gardens at the base of the campanile and accessed the Palm House terrace by a ramp in the south-east corner, a section of the hedge having been removed. Contractors' traffic had to negotiate narrow entrances to the gardens and cross busy public walkways. Later in the contract, at the reconstruction stage, it proved necessary for Balfour Beatty to overflow the site boundaries into the Rose Garden to store the glazing frames awaiting lifting onto the house.

Throughout the autumn and winter of 1985–6 the disassembly of the house continued, with priority given to the stripping out of the interior. Access was via a section cut into the north apse end. From November onwards the site echoed to the sound of sheet piles being driven into the ground for the construction of the Marine Display.

Throughout the spring and summer of 1986 the glass was broken out in sections (a popular job) and the old wrought-iron glazing bars were removed. As soon as the main frame was ready the gardens reverberated to the noise of grit blasting, which rapidly removed all the old paint. It also showed up worse corrosion than had been anticipated on survey and substantial local reinforcement had to be done, delaying the work.

Throughout 1987 the site appeared forlorn; so much dismantling had been done and the grit-blasted arches were covered with a superficial layer of rust. Below ground, however, an enormous amount of work was going on, with the new Marine Display, the new basements, the new planting beds and the water storage tanks all being constructed. Much of this was not visible to the general public. However, the enormous tower crane on site caused much interest, as did several of the tricky operations involved, including the lifting out of the central columns of the spiral staircases.

In the winter of 1987–8 substantial progress was made in reconstructing the house, with the glazing frames fabricated and painted in tented workshops on site and gradually replaced on the house using the tower crane. Suddenly the house seemed to come together. Glazing progressed rapidly from late spring onwards and, inside the house, masons laid the new York and Portland stone. From late summer onwards the mechanical and electrical commissioning began and the beds were filled with their drainage and subsoil layers to await the plants. The campanile flue was relined using a lorry-mounted crane and the external paths were laid. In November the building was finished and beautifully floodlit for a completion ceremony.

In the course of the restoration men of many different trades (and one woman) had worked on the site, varying in number from 35 to over 150 in the closing stages. The story of their progress is given here in pictures.

November 1985. Sheet piles are driven into the ground to protect the foundations of the centre transept columns before the Marine Display basement can be excavated. The piling was done before the glass was removed.

February 1986. Glass is knocked out section by section and cutting equipment is used to remove the rusted wrought-iron glazing bars.

169

Spiral staircase components. Every piece of iron was laid out and tagged with an individual number before a decision was made on whether to repair or replace it.

Below right: some of the gutters were repaired by the 'Metalock' method of metal stitching.

171

Parts of the Palm House
were distributed around the
country for off-site repair.
The curved gutters cost more
to replace than the straight.
Here the weld repair method
is being used, an expensive
technique which involves the
building of a furnace around
the component to bring it up
to the required temperature.

The grit-blasted metal had to be primed immediately after blasting. Here the apse end crown is being primed.

After strengthening of the main ribs the service trench base slab is cast in the south wing. A surveyor checks for correct levels.

February 1987. Progress on the reinforced concrete roofs of the Marine Display and south basement plant room.

July 1987. Joiners complete the wooden formwork to the Marine Display dome before the concrete is cast around it.

Re-erection of the ironwork to the upper centre transept commences.

The main ribs are post-tensioned together by a wedge driven into the end of a continuous rod running inside each purlin. This straps all the main arches together and, together with the glass, provides some of the stability of the building.

Construction of the Marine Display continued whilst remedial works were being carried out above the gallery level.

One of the new Marine Display staircases. The columns are white concrete.

Opposite: the white concrete used throughout the Marine Display prepared for blasting to final finish.

Each pin was removed from each spandrel bracket to check for corrosion before primer was applied.

General view, September 1987. Every part of the site could be accessed by the reach of the tower crane, which operated on a rail at the back of the site.

The new boilers in the Shaft Yard (Kew Road) boiler house.

The Victorian tunnel from the Shaft Yard to the Palm House. Originally used to transport fuel, it now carries hot water from the boilers to the house and flue gases to the campanile.

Left: stonemasons reconstruct the dado walls and build in newly recast ventilation boxes.

Right: ventilation ductwork is installed in the new staff accommodation area in the north basement.

A jig is used to fabricate the glazing bars into cages for the north and south wings. This took place in a specially erected building within the Palm House site.

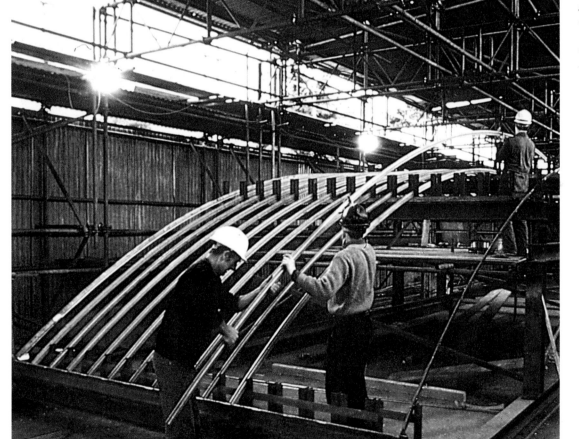

A glazing cage is lowered into the paint shop from the tower crane.

The cages were painted and stored alongside the site in the Rose Garden.

The final positioning of a glazing cage over the new south wing porch.

February 1988. The glazing cages of one wing and its clerestory nearly complete.

Opposite: the fabrication of glazing cages for the hips and valleys is done in situ.

Left: the re-erection of the spiral staircase commences.

Right: the final coat of paint is applied to the ironwork in one of the clerestories.

The south apse end prior to the fabrication of its glazing frames.

A welder fabricates the apse end glazing frames in situ. *The curve on these is taken up by elegant tridents and they are spaced by delicate horizontal lacing bars.*

Left: glazing the clerestory windows in toughened glass, most of which was made in Australia.

Right: the mason prepares stone for lining the walkways in the house. York stone was used on the flat and Portland stone for the risers.

The apse ends, hips and other 'specials' were glazed in annealed glass cut on site.

A crane is used to lift the gantry maintenance ladders onto the centre transept.

One of the new seating areas. The Victorian floor grilles were reused in the new, wider, pathways and the original bench legs now line the new perimeter planting beds.

The Supervisor's office, staff accommodation area. Outside is the chairlift which provides access to the Marine Display for people with disabilities.

Opposite: the north wing, showing the new staircase down to the staff accommodation area.

17 Plants on the move

1984 WAS THE YEAR that the Palm House was completely emptied of its plants for the first time in its history. This was a long operation but culminated in the bulk of the collection being moved in nine days under the direction of the Supervisor, Sue MacDonald. For over a year beforehand plants which could be propagated had propagules taken so that the parent plant could be discarded. The collection was thinned of duplicate plants, many of which went to other botanic collections, including a large containerload which was expertly packed by the staff of the Frankfurt Palmengarten. Small plants were sent to the temperate nursery and large plants in tubs were resoiled, using a tripod and block and tackle, so as to last them for their anticipated period in storage. Some very precious plants, including the giant bamboos, the two leguminous trees, *Brownea* × *crawfordii* and *Brownea coccinea* × *latifolia*, and the ebony (*Diospyros ebenum*) were lifted from beds in the centre transept and containerised. Many plants were planted in grey plastic barrels for temporary storage, and all plants were lifted onto wooden pallets.

Meanwhile a large commercial widespan glasshouse was erected with temporary planning permission as a Temporary Palm House close to the Lower Nursery. This house provided the 1000 sq. metres of growing-space needed. It was heated with a warm air heater, supplied with deionised water and had a floor of stone chippings. In September 1984 the containerised plants were wheeled out of the Palm House on pallet trucks, loaded by forklift onto a trailer, driven to the Temporary Palm House and unloaded with another forklift operating through the opened gable end of the house. The house began to fill up within several days but the process was halted while a large pit 1.8 metres deep was dug and shuttered. This was to house some of our tallest palms, including a 7-metre *Ptychosperma* from Samoa and a rare *Ravenea moorei* from the Comoros. Some of these had to be tipped onto their sides to get them out of the Palm House and had to be lowered into the pit using a jib.

In the Palm House itself the sad job of felling the palms which were too large to get out of the house was begun. The largest were *Phoenix sylvestris* var. *exilis* and a *Caryota urens* which had an inflorescence 2 metres long at the time. Other losses were *Syagrus schizophylla*; *Caryota mitis*; *Chamaedorea concolor*, *C. ernesti-augusti*, *C. klotzschiana* and *C. oblongata*; a *Chrysalidocarpus*, *C. madagascariensis* var. *lucubensis*; *Coccothrinax argentea*; two coconuts; *Polyandrococos pectinata* just renamed with a long-forgotten name; a *Ptychosperma*; *Sabal beccariana* and *S. causiarum*; another *Syagrus*; *Veitchia merrillii* and a *Washingtonia robusta*. Specimens from all of these felled palms were collected for the herbarium. The Tropical Development Research Institute took the opportunity to analyse the sago content of the felled trunks of the two *Caryota* species. But the visual impact was dramatic. Within a few days the famous silhouette of palms through the central dome had gone. One of the staff went home in tears.

As the nearly emptied house began to echo to people's footsteps one difficult job remained. This was to move out the largest of the cycads, several of which leaned out of their tubs and were propped to support their weight. A student on the diploma course, Andrew Jackson, devised scaffolding cages to make their weight act as a single unit. It was in this way that *Encephalartos altensteinii*, the 'oldest pot plant in the world', first emerged from the Palm House, having been cultivated within its frame for over 130 years. Its move to the Temporary Palm House was slow, due mainly to the interest of the BBC.

In the Temporary Palm House the canvas curtain on the gable end was removed and it was reglazed, signalling that the move was complete. In the Palm House the climbers were cut down, the bulbous

*Chain saws enter the Palm
House in September 1984
and a mature specimen of*
Phoenix sylvestris *var.*
exilis *is felled.*

plants outside were lifted and planted in the nursery and the house was more or less abandoned from the horticultural point of view. In the Temporary Palm House, paths were laid, barriers were built around the pit and the house was opened to the public. It soon became a popular venue. As a growing-house, however, it has proved less than optimal. The warm-air heating system, designed for dry warehouse storage, would only function for plants when excessive damping down was done. In the first summer it proved essential to shade the roof to prevent soaring temperatures and the subsequent loss of humidity when ventilation had to be given. This was an expensive and unforeseen operation and was the main factor (along with the experience of planting the Conservatory) which led to the design of a system of thermal screen shading for the initial establishment of the plants in the Palm House after restoration. The pit successfully accommodated the taller palms but one or two suffered from the lower temperature below ground-level which reduced the warmth around the roots by about 2°C. Thermosensitive species such as the double coconuts went into a prolonged decline without the heat which used to rise around them from the Palm House underfloor heating.

Despite the initial problems of managing this new environment, however, the growth of many of the plants was considerable. With the delay in the restoration contract the house and the nursery facility had to contain the collection for twice as long as had been planned. In March 1988 the Aroid House was temporarily taken over to store some of the burgeoning material. Plants moved there from the Temporary Palm House took on a new lease of life, showing that there is nothing to surpass a piped hot-water system and a very humid atmosphere to benefit tropical plants. The collection of *Costus* and Zingiberaceae which was being grown on for ground cover in the Palm House did particularly well there.

A unique view of the unheated house cleared of plants in early 1985. Covered in snow, it awaits the attention of the restorers.

The period during which the Palm House collection was housed in the Temporary Palm House was the last time that the bulk of the plants were to be seen in their moveable containers. A chance to show some of them at the 1987 Chelsea Show proved irresistible and an exhibit was designed called 'Plants under Glass'. This was the largest exhibit ever staged at Chelsea by Kew and was managed jointly with the Morris Arboretum of the University of Philadelphia to celebrate their centenary and the proposed restoration of their Victorian fernery house. The Morris staged their exhibit at the Philadelphia Flower Show in March against a painted backdrop of the Palm House and with plants grown at the United States Botanic Garden, Washington, DC. Kew's counterpart exhibit at Chelsea consisted of a large

The exhibit 'Plants under Glass' at the 1987 Chelsea Show made use of some of the structural elements of the Palm House and part of the plant collection while the restoration was under way. Staff appeared in Victorian dress.

plywood-sectioned structure designed to imitate the enormous doors of the Palm House. The visitor walked through the doors into a paved conservatory 15.6 by 13.5 metres and surrounded by palms, cycads and other endangered and decorative tropical plants. Specially lit graphic displays illustrated the history of plants under glass, the restoration of historic structures and the conserving role of botanic gardens in maintaining the plant collections within them. Models of the Morris's fernery and Kew's Princess of Wales Conservatory were included and a special feature was made of a Wardian case filled with rubber plants, to commemorate Kew's role in the introduction of the rubber industry to Malaya and the transport of quinine, coffee and tea plants around the world. This stood on four of the 1-ton floor gratings brought from the Palm House, which created an authentic period effect, along with the Victorian dress worn by all the staff, an original urn from Paxton's Crystal

Palace and many other detailed features. The work in staging this exhibit involved 28 staff, and seven 17-tonne pantechnicons were used to transport it. We were rewarded with a Gold Medal.

With this great effort out of the way, the plans for the real Palm House began to assume renewed importance. The challenge of designing planting plans to furnish the Palm House into the twenty-first century was quite unique. Never before had the house been completely emptied of plants, leaving a totally clear canvas for design. The large empty beds seemed begging to be filled but it was obvious that in order to get the structural planting right much research had to be done. With the majority of the plants no longer in containers it would not be easy in the future to move something which proved to be in the wrong place. Most people seemed to feel that an informal approach to the planting of the Palm House was inappropriate in an elegant Victorian building of this kind. The rockwork and flowing water that had been used in landscaping the Temperate House as a 'winter garden' was never proposed. Nor were the winding paths and steps that had been used in the Princess of Wales Conservatory. Essentially Kew was planting out its collection in formal beds in order to obtain better growth. This meant that the planning was limited to placement of the plants. We also anticipated having to use a spanning gantry to lift the plants, many of which weighed 1 or 2 tonnes or more, up and over the bed edges and across and down into the beds. This would mean producing complete planting plans, so that the planting could be done systematically without fouling the span of the gantry by the tall stems of the palms.

Between December 1984 and January 1987 a considerable amount of my time was taken up accumulating information on the ultimate height and spread and precise habitat requirements of the plant collection and how each accession was likely to respond once planted out. This required some vision, particularly as the Palm House then stood totally devoid of glass, a rusting skeleton. In July 1986 preliminary proposals for the landscaping of the house were submitted to Hans Fliegner, the Assistant Curator in charge of the section and to the Curator. The proposal was to plant the house as one habitat, tropical rainforest, and to show the tropics of the three continents of the world in the three sections of the house. The centre transept was to house the richest and most diverse American flora, including the enormous wealth of Amazonia; the south wing would house the African flora and the north wing the floras of Asia, Australasia and the Pacific. This phytogeographic design essentially mirrored that of the Temperate House. It contrasted with the approach of the Princess of Wales Conservatory, where geography takes a back seat compared to habitat and where a number of different computer-controlled habitats are accommodated in different sections under one roof. In order to accommodate to maturity some of the larger palms, our palm taxonomist, Dr Dransfield, suggested using the two large beds in the centre transept which were directly under the dome for the tallest tree palms of the tropics worldwide. This underlined, and commemorated, the original reason for the building of the Palm House to such a height and was the only deviation from the phytogeographic plan.

It soon became obvious that a major decision had to be made on the future of the very valuable cycad collection. Traditionally these had been kept in square teak tubs placed on the south wing gratings and periodically resoiled by removing each side of the tubs in turn. They were a comparatively trouble-free collection and took little labour input. With the provision of planting beds throughout the house the area of gratings available for standing down was vastly reduced, from just over 643 sq. metres to just over 38 sq. metres. Many of the cycads were unlikely to do well included in a mixed tropical planting and would prove ferocious obstacles to maintenance. The Curator felt that far too much heat was wasted maintaining the hardier of the cycads in the Palm House and that the space could be better used housing

The replanting of the Palm House was accomplished using a gantry capable of lifting 3 tonnes. This spanned the beds in the wings and the corners of larger beds. The bed edges had to be carefully protected.

tropical woody plants which really needed the heat. Since Kew was constrained to save 30 per cent of its energy costs, this was an important consideration. Others felt that it would be a shame to split the collection which had been housed in the south wing for so long, a misgiving which did not accord with the speed at which the nursery collection was growing and with likely demands on space in the future. After a visit to Fairchild Tropical Garden, Florida in November 1986, it became clear to me that many gardens managed their cycads by dividing the species into rainforest types and those from semi-desert areas of xerophytic scrub, most of which are nearly frost-hardy. That winter the cycad collections in the Temporary Palm House and the nursery were divided into two, with the rainforest species given more water and shade. It was decided to plant out only the latter in the Palm House. The xerophytic cycads could be housed elsewhere at Kew in space for arid-zone plants, where lower temperatures, a drier atmosphere and brighter light than was planned for the Palm House would offer better cultivation conditions. This decision was in line with the gradual movement of many of the more temperate palms from the Palm House to the Temperate House. It was also part of the movement towards showing landscaped ecosystems to the public, rather than collections based only on systematic botany.

With these decisions made, it became possible to look at the pool of material available for planting. In summer 1986 the temperate nursery had developed computer stock-control systems for the hardy arboretum plants and for the tender glasshouse material. These were linked to our main computer database and the tender plants were listed on a system code-named 'Palm'. In January and February 1987 I coded all the Palm House plants according to their continental origin and added details of their height and spread, so that by the summer it was possible to list all the plants for the three sections of the Palm House in a matter of minutes, a job which had taken hours of painstaking sorting of record cards when the Temperate House was planned prior to replanting between November 1979 and July 1981.

Starting in November 1987, I used the architect's sectional drawings through the Palm House to measure the planting heights available in the various parts of the building between the final soil surface and the curvature of the glass. A student on the diploma course, Allan Forrest, enlarged the architect's ground plans in six sections, blowing them up from a 1:100 scale to 1:25. Dyeline prints were made of his enlargements. Working from the 'Palm' programme printout I could now begin plotting the planting. The vines were marked and assigned to the supports around each arch rib and each pillar in the centre transept. All plants growing under 4 metres, or easily pruned to that height, were assigned to the perimeter beds. Since the Palm House is not aligned exactly north–south, the planting in the north wing was carefully considered as to shade. Those plants needing the most light were assigned to the eastern beds and shade-tolerant species to the west, using the experience of Victorian gardeners who found that, particularly in the north wing, tall plants in the centre of the house shaded the north-western perimeter areas. Particularly architectural specimens were marked as focal point plants, destined to catch the eye at the end of each walkway in the house, an element of formality which I thought appropriate for a Victorian house. Plants particularly well adapted to growing in pots were marked for display on the north and south grating areas and benches, areas designated to reproduce a classic Victorian display showing how the house would have looked in the middle of the nineteenth century. Spreading canopy trees were identified and those of maximum interest were plotted at the maximum distance available in the centre beds. Throughout the planting the specimens were distributed to give a balance of existing size for immediate effect, as well as with regard to their potential size. Wherever possible, preference was given to material of natural source origin, which is more scientifically valuable in any plant collection that forms a bank of living material for genetic research.

196

The distribution of economic plants was carefully planned so that educational labels, tour guide points and possible 'trails' of interest could follow logically around the house. Fast-growing plants were plotted with their eventual spread so that several of each species could be planted and then reduced as the area allotted to them became filled. The aim was to build up the multi-layered nature of a tropical rainforest, with canopy palms and trees, climbers and then shorter understorey trees and shrubs. Finally the understorey forest-floor layer of herbaceous plants and palmlets was plotted on overlays to the main plans. Much thought was given to the genus *Ficus*, with 87 accessions compared to the 160 or so of palms of all genera. A few of the most representative were planted in the centre beds but most were planted in the side beds with a view to pruning them to 4 metres to contain their potential dominance of the house, while still showing their diversity of form in foliage and in fruit. The species from semi-arid zones were not included in the planting. Much thought was given to the placement of the young, natural-source palms in our nursery, many of which would reach plantable size in 1989 and would make the Palm House collection the finest in Europe. To assist in the growth of some of the young palms from Madagascar and in particular of the double coconut, an area of electric soil-warming blanket was planned for the south wing's centre bed.

After the completion of the ground plans, some perspective drawings were done. This was achieved by taking 35-mm slides at average eye level of key vistas in the Palm House. The slides were projected onto paper and the rib, pillar and bed outline details of the 'ironmongery' of the house were traced in. The outlines of key plants were then sketched in on these 'as seen' visual perspectives and the ground plans were changed whenever an effect was not quite as desired. Unfortunately it did not prove possible to use computer-aided design.

When the planning had been substantially completed it became obvious that we were getting much less back into the house than we had got out, perhaps as much as 25 per cent less. This has happened in most houses at Kew, including the Australian House, and is even more the case in tropical houses, where the plants romp away unrestricted by pots. Their increased spread has to be accommodated. The restored house has quadruple the area of beds of soil and only one-sixth the area of benching. The total area for plant display has been reduced from about 1134 sq. metres to 1004 sq. metres, the difference being exactly accounted for by extra service areas and wider paths to enable better access for care and for viewing of the plants.

Left: the resoiling of the beds was done around the rootballs of the plants. Compost was supplied in pallet bins lifted by a hand-operated forklift truck. In the hot summer, temporary shading under the dome was supplied by a series of baffles made of shade cloth.

Right: a powered grinder was used to remove plant containers.

197

Horticultural diploma students lift and tip compost into the beds. Further shading had been installed in the curved areas of the house prior to planting.

198

The contract to restore the building was finished in November 1988, too late in the year to start moving tropical plants from one heated structure to another. It was opened to allow the public to see the beauty of the structure and for a carol concert on 18 December 1988. Kew staff took the opportunity to dig, resoil and prepare the terraces for grass seeding in the spring of 1989 and to replant the collection of *Kniphofia*, *Agapanthus* and other tender South African bulbs which have long been grown around the base of the house to benefit from proximity to its heat.

The replanting of the house did not commence until 4 April 1989, when *Encephalartos altensteinii* was carefully manœuvred into its position in the south apse end. The West German gantry, of a design which erected itself by the use of winches attached to the legs, proved invaluable in this operation. The compost was added around the rootballs of the plants after removal of their containers, many of which had to be cut off using a grinder. The resoiling was mechanised as far as possible, using pallet bins which could be partially tipped, and then manhandled, into the beds using a small, hand-operated forklift truck. Movable panelling was used to protect the bed edges during these operations and the floor was protected by marine ply and locally reinforced by the use of checkerplate. Cabling was used to guy the root systems of several palms underground to assist their stability. During these operations, the shading proved its worth as the summer was one of the hottest in recent memory and there were initial problems in the use of the new humidification system. (The frontispiece and the picture on p. xi show the new planting.)

Replanting was substantially completed by the middle of August 1989 and the Palm House was opened on 1 December 1989. A separate contract for the Marine Display had commenced in May 1989 and it is due to open in the autumn of 1990.

The silhouette of palm crowns through the dome of the Palm House in the early 1980s. Destroyed by the need to empty the building totally for restoration, this view will take a quarter of a century to restore.

ostscript

THE ARCHITECTS AND ENGINEERS of the 1980s have given back to the nation Turner and Burton's masterpiece in iron, now in full working order. In terms of planting, however, it is a very different Palm House. The collections have evolved from the taxonomic emphasis of the early Victorian era and now reflect the educational and conserving role of a glasshouse planted to show the palm-rich tropical rainforests of the world.

The priorities for development in the collections will be: in the south wing to augment the least well represented flora of West Africa and the highly endangered flora of Madagascar; and in the centre transept to enrich the representation of the Amazonian flora – before it is too late. A strict renewal policy will be necessary as the collections grow, in order to conserve and improve the genetic base and to demonstrate the importance of rainforest in terms of sustainable economic products.

The Curator has likened the Palm House to an ark, both because of its architectural structure (functionally an upturned boat) and on account of the high proportion of rarities it contains. This analogy is painfully accurate, with several plants now extinct outside the confines of this glasshouse and several dioecious plants which have literally 'come in two by two'. In looking to the future we hope that this little piece of tropical rainforest in suburban London will demonstrate why it is important to conserve the world's rainforest – for the peoples who live in them, for the long-term benefit through 'sustainable use' of the countries where rainforests exist and for the global climatic environment of us all.

Notes

1 Charles M'Intosh, *The Greenhouse, Hothouse and Stove*, (London, 1838), p. 362

2 Berthold Seemann, *Popular History of Palms and their Allies*, (London, 1856), p. 38

3 J D Hooker, *Report on the Progress and Condition of the Royal Gardens at Kew during the Year 1882*, (London, 1882), p. 10. Loddiges' palm collection was sold when the nursery closed in 1854 and was bought by Paxton for the ill-fated Crystal Palace at Sydenham. Wendland, who had worked at Kew, exchanged plants often with his alma mater and became unfortunately involved in the episode of the thief palm. (See p. 11.)

4 John Smith, 'History of the Royal Gardens at Kew', 1880, pp. 54–8. Kewensia Collection, Royal Botanic Gardens, Kew

5 Thomas Drew, cited in Smith, 'History', p. 268

6 Sir Arthur W Hill, 'The Royal Botanic Gardens, Kew', *Journal of the Kew Guild* VI, xlviii (1941), 12

7 See also Peter Ferriday, *Architectural Review*, 21, 721 (1957), 127–8

8 Edward J Diestelkamp, 'The design and building of the Palm House, Royal Botanic Gardens, Kew', *Journal of Garden History*, 2, 3 (1982), 233–72

9 W J Hooker, 'Report on the Present State of the Gardens, 1844', in *Kew Gardens Annual Reports, 1844–70*, p. 7. Kewensia Collection, Royal Botanic Gardens, Kew

10 Ibid. pp. 1–2

11 Smith, 'History', pp. 64–5

12 Ibid. p. 65. Smith must surely have been exaggerating in his estimate of the weight of the palms.

13 Charles M'Intosh, *Book of the Garden* (Edinburgh, 1853), p. 119

14 Figures from W J Hooker, 'Report for the Year 1847–48'; 'Report for the Year 1850'; 'Annual Report on the state and progress of these Gardens, 1851' in *Kew Gardens Annual Reports 1844–70*, p. 13, p. 15, p. 19. Kewensia Collection, Royal Botanic Gardens, Kew

15 W J Hooker, 'Annual Report on the state and progress of these Gardens, 1851' in *Kew Gardens Annual Reports 1844–70*, p. 20. Kewensia Collection, Royal Botanic Gardens, Kew

16 Ibid.

17 W J Hooker, 'Report on the state and progress of the Royal Gardens and Grounds, 1852' in *Kew Gardens Annual Reports 1844–70*, p. 23. Kewensia Collection, Royal Botanic Gardens, Kew. According to Smith, 'History', p. 71, the two plants which had reached the roof were a vigorous rattan palm, *Plectocomia elongata* and the kapok tree, *Bombax ceiba*.

18 Smith, 'History', p. 64

19 *Papers relating to Kew Gardens*, p. 94, no. 55 (1867). Kewensia Collection, Royal Botanic Gardens, Kew

20 'Greenhouse plants' were temperate species needing lower temperatures.

21 W J Hooker, *Report on the Progress and Condition of the Royal Gardens at Kew during the year 1866*, (London, 1866), p. 2

22 J D Hooker, *Report on the Progress and Condition of the Royal Gardens at Kew during the Year 1868*, (London, 1868), p. 3

23 Smith, 'History', pp. 60–61

24 W J Hooker, *Report on Kew Gardens for 1860*, (London, 1860), p. 2. According to Smith, 'History', pp. 71–2, the centre transept had six beds installed, three on each side of the central path and each 8 ft (2.4 metres) wide. Sir William Hooker had, in fact, lobbied for beds in the centre transept in 1847.

25 J D Hooker, *Report on the Progress and Condition of the Royal Gardens at Kew during the Year 1868*, (London, 1868), p. 3

26 Smith, 'History', p. 70

27 Ibid. pp. 74–5. This conflict between architects and horticulturists is often heard today!

28 Ibid. pp. 75–6

29 Ibid. p. 81

30 Ibid. p. 261

31 Ibid. p. 262

32 J D Hooker, *Report on the Progress and Condition of the Royal Gardens at Kew during the year 1880*, (London, 1880), p. 6

33 Cited in Georg Kohlmaier and Barna von Aartory, *Houses of Glass* (Cambridge, Massachussetts, 1986). Many early Victorian growers considered (wrongly) that *all* palms were either male or female.

34 James Duncan, letter to W J Hooker, 7 September 1859. Archives, Royal Botanic Gardens, Kew

35 *Kew Collectors Papers relating to 1791–1865*, XI (160). Archives, Royal Botanic Gardens, Kew

36 H Wendland, letter to W J Hooker, *North Europe letters NAE–YOU, 1845–1900*, vol. 137, pp. 1978–9. Archives, Royal Botanic Gardens, Kew

37 Berthold Seemann, *Die Palmen*, (Leipzig, 1863)

38 W J Hooker, 'Report on the state and progress of the Royal Gardens and Grounds, 1852' in *Kew Gardens Annual Reports 1844–70*, p. 24. Kewensia Collection, Royal Botanic Gardens, Kew

39 J D Hooker, *Report on the Progress and Condition of the Royal Gardens at Kew during the Year 1881*, (London, 1881) pp. 6–7

40 'Miscellaneous notes', *Royal Gardens, Kew. Bulletin of Miscellaneous Information*, (1895), 320–21

41 J D Hooker, *Report on the Progress and Condition of the Royal Gardens at Kew during the Year 1874*, (London, 1874) p. 2

42 Conrad Loddiges and Sons, *Catalogue of Plants in the collection of C Loddiges and Sons*, 15th edition, (London, 1830)

43 W J Hooker, *Report on the Progress and Condition of the Royal Gardens of Kew, from 1853–1857*, (London, 1857) p. 6

44 Thomas Meehan, 'Kew, as I Knew it, nearly 50 years ago', *Journal of the Kew Guild*, I, ii (1894), 38–43 (p. 42)

45 Betty Cooper, 'Impressions of Kew from the Women Gardeners', *Journal of the Kew Guild*, VI, xlviii (1941), 56–61 (pp. 58–9)

46 'Notes and Gleanings', ibid. V, xliii (1936) 531–4 (p. 533)

47 'Supplement', *Gardeners' Chronicle* 6, 136 (1876)

48 William Dallimore, 'A Gardener's Reminiscences', (2 vols.), vol. 1, pp. 318–321. Kewensia Collection, Royal Botanic Gardens, Kew

49 'A Present Kewite on Kew', *Journal of the Kew Guild*, I, v (1897), 30–32 (p. 31)

50 Dallimore, 'Reminiscences', vol. 1, p. 318

51 Ibid. vol. 1, p. 286

52 'Notes and Gleanings', *Journal of the Kew Guild*, IX, lxxviii (1973), 233–44 (p. 237)

53 Ibid. III, xxiv (1917), 359

54 Dallimore, 'Reminiscences', vol. 1, p. 287

55 'Notes', *Journal of the Kew Guild*, III, xx (1913), 84–91 (p. 91)

56 'Notes and Gleanings', ibid. III, xxv (1918), 408–10 (p. 409)

57 See for example in J C Loudon, *Encyclopaedia of Gardening* (London, 1825 and 1878) and in *The Gardeners' Chronicle and Agricultural Gazette*, no. 9 (1848), 138

58 Smith, 'History', pp. 61–2

59 *The Gardeners' Chronicle and Agricultural Gazette*, no. 9 (1848), 138

60 *The Gardeners' Chronicle*, 13, 323 (1880), 307–8

61 Dallimore, 'Reminiscences', vol. 1, p. 276

62 'Green-glass in plant houses', *Royal Gardens, Kew. Bulletin of Miscellaneous Information*, (1895), 43–5 (p. 44). The placing of the chimney stacks in the wings in the 1860s cannot have helped either.

63 'The February Blitz', *Journal of the Kew Guild*, VI, li (1944), 397

64 J D Hooker, *Report on the Progress and Condition of the Royal Gardens at Kew during the Year 1879*, (London 1879) pp. 5–6

65 W J Bean, *The Royal Botanic Gardens, Kew: Historical and Descriptive*, (London, 1908), p. 131

66 Dallimore, 'Reminiscences', vol. 2, pp. 563–4 and pp. 591–2

67 'Notes, Correspondence, etc.', *Journal of the Kew Guild*, I, ix (1896), 6

68 Seemann, *Die Palmen*, p. 42

69 *Curtis's Botanical Magazine*, 125 (1899), t. 7623

70 N Wallich, quoted in ibid. 75 (1849), t. 4453

71 Ibid. 96 (1870) t. 5838

72 Ibid. 104 (1878) t. 6373

73 Ibid. 5 (1791) t. 158

74 Ibid. 5 (1791) t. 169

75 Ibid. 118 (1892) t. 7260

76 Ibid. 76 (1850) t. 4549

77 Ibid. 68 (1842) t. 3952

lossary

Algae	Uni- or multi-cellular lower plants, e.g. seaweeds.
Alternate	Leaves arising singly, one at each node, not opposite or whorled.
Angiosperm	A flowering plant; members of the class Angiospermae, characterised by their true flowers and the development of seeds within a usually enclosed carpel or ovary.
Axil	The upper angle formed by the junction of a leaf-petiole or branch and the stem that bears it.
Bifid	Divided into two, usually equal, parts.
Bipinnate	Twice pinnate.
Bract	A modified leaf which subtends an inflorescence or flower.
Calyx	The collective name for the sepals.
Campanulate	Bell-shaped.
Canopy	The uppermost layer of foliage in forest vegetation, formed by the crowns of trees.
Carpel	The female reproductive organ of flowering plants, consisting of ovary, style and stigma.
Cauliflory	The production of flowers directly on the trunk or woody stems. (See p. 27.)
Cirrus	A climbing organ in palms, structurally a spiny whip-like extension of the rachis.
Clone	One of a group of plants derived from a single individual by vegetative propagation, and all therefore genetically identical, e.g. oil palm derived from tissue culture, used for uniform plantation cropping.
Cordate	Heart-shaped.
Corolla	The collective name for the petals of a flower.
Corymb	A flat-topped or rounded inflorescence with the outer flowers opening first, as in some jasmines.
Costapalmate	Shaped like the palm of the hand but with a short extension of the stalk between each pair of leaflets as in some *Sabal* species.
Crown	The highest part of a layer, the head or group of leaves at the top of the stem.
Crownshaft	The cylinder formed by tubular leaf sheaths at the top of the stem and beneath the crown of a palm.
Cultivar	A variant of horticultural worth; plants selected from a species in the wild or in cultivation and distinguished from the type by one or more characteristics, e.g. the form of *Thunbergia laurifolia* known as 'Augusta's Blue'.
Cyme	A flat-topped or rounded inflorescence with the inner flowers opening first.
Dicotyledon	A class of angiosperms with embryos having two seed leaves (cotyledons) as opposed to one in monocotyledons (q.v.). One of the two great divisions in the flowering plants.
Digitate	Resembling the fingers of a hand.

Dioecious	Having male and female flowers or cones on separate plants (c.f. monoecious).
Diploid	Having two sets of chromosomes, i.e. double the usual haploid number, in its normal vegetative cells.
Endemic	Native to a restricted region only.
Epiphyte	A plant growing upon another plant without deriving any nourishment from it.
Floriferous	Free-flowering.
Genus	A group of species with important characters in common. The first name in a botanical description, e.g. *Caryota* in *Caryota mitis*.
Glaucous	Covered with a blue-grey bloom.
Gymnosperm	A group of higher plants characterised by the production of seeds which are not covered by an enclosed protective structure as in angiosperms; often termed 'naked seed plants'. These include the conifers, cycads and *Gnetum* spp.
Herbaceous	Referring to a non-woody perennial which may or may not die down to a resting rootstock during winter.
Hybrid	The offspring resulting from a cross between two plants with a different genetic composition, e.g. *Hymenocallis* × *macrostephana*, which is the hybrid of *H. speciosa* and *H. narcissiflora*.
Indumentum	A covering of hairs.
Inflorescence	A group or arrangement of flowers.
Infrafoliar	Borne below the leaves.
Infructescence	A cluster of fruits derived from an inflorescence.
Interfoliar	Borne between the leaves.
Lanceolate	Shaped like a lance.
Liane	A woody, tropical climber, usually very vigorous in growth.
Monocarpic	Plants which flower and fruit once and then die, e.g. the talipot palm, *Corypha umbraculifera*.
Monocotyledon	Plants that have a single seed leaf or cotyledon, rather than a pair as in dicotyledons (q.v.). One of the two great divisions in the flowering plants, it includes all the palms.
Monoecious	Having male and female flowers or cones on the same plants (c.f. dioecious).
Monotypic	A genus having only one species.
Mucilage	A gelatinous secretion produced by many plant organs, which swells on contact with water.
Oblanceolate	The reverse of lanceolate, with the broadest part of the leaf towards the tip.
Ovary	The female portion of a flower, which contains the ovules that are fertilised by the pollen.

Ovate	Egg-shaped.
Ovule	The structure from which the seed develops after pollination.
Palmate	Shaped like the palm of the hand or like a fan, with all ribs or leaflets arising from a central point.
Panicle	An inflorescence in which the flowers develop into a complex branched arrangement.
Petiole	The stalk of a leaf.
Pinnate	Feather-like, with leaflets arranged on either side of a central axis or rachis, often terminated by an individual leaflet.
Plumose	Softly feathered.
Raceme	An unbranched inflorescence consisting of individual flowers attached to a central axis by pedicels (stalks), e.g. the flower groups of the jade vine, *Strongylodon macrobotrys*.
Rachis	The central axis of a compound leaf or frond or inflorescence.
Rainforest	Dense forest usually with many layers of vegetation and often under a closed canopy, generally supporting lianes and epiphytes.
Rhizome	A thickened, often elongated, horizontal stem, found underground or on the surface of the soil.
Scandent	With lax climbing stems which may need support.
Sepal	A division of the calyx outside the petals.
Solitary	(Of flowers) occurring singly in each axil.
Spadix	A fleshy, spike-like structure bearing the flowers, often surrounded by a large bract (spathe).
Spathe	A large, often showy bract at the base of a flower or inflorescence.
Species	Composed of similar but distinct individuals that interbreed freely among themselves; a distinct plant within a genus. The second name in a botanical description, e.g. *mitis* in *Caryota mitis*.
Spike	A dense raceme in which the individual flowers have no stalks. This arrangement is common in palms, e.g. in the genus *Arenga*.
Stamen	The male pollen-producing organ of a flower.
Staminode	A vestigial stamen which may be very modified in shape and infertile.
Stigma	The receptive part of the style. Pollen grains adhere to the surface, which is often sticky.
Stilt roots	Oblique, lateral roots above soil-level, also called prop roots.
Style	The piece of connective tissue between the stigma and the ovary.
Suprafoliar	Above the level of the leaves.
Syncarp	A fused carpel.
Tender	Not hardy; subject to damage by frost.
Tetraploid	Having four times the haploid number of chromosomes in its normal vegetative cells.

206

Tomentum	A dense covering, usually of short hairs.
Trifoliate	Composed of three leaflets.
Umbel	A usually flat-topped inflorescence arranged like the spokes of an umbrella, e.g. in *Ixora* species.
Understorey	The vegetation layer between the canopy and the ground in a forest community.
Vivipary	The habit of producing young plants on a parent plant.
Xerophyte	A plant adapted to grow in arid environments.

$\mathcal{S}$elect bibliography
THE HISTORY OF GLASSHOUSES

Hix, John. *The Glasshouse*, London, Phaidon, 1974

Kohlmaier, Georg and Aartory, Barna von. *Houses of Glass: a nineteenth-century building type*, Cambridge, Massachussetts, MIT Press, 1986

Koppelkamm, Stefan. *Glasshouses and Wintergardens of the Nineteenth Century*, St Albans, Granada, 1981

Muijzenberg, Erwin W B van den. *A History of Greenhouses*, Wageningen, privately published, 1980

Woods, May and Warren, Arete. *Glasshouses: a history of greenhouses, orangeries and conservatories*, London, Aurum, 1988

THE HISTORY OF THE PALM HOUSE

Diestelkamp, Edward J. 'The design and building of the Palm House, Royal Botanic Gardens, Kew', *Journal of Garden History*, 2, 3 (1982), 233–72

Diestelkamp, Edward J. 'Fairyland in London. The conservatories of Decimus Burton', *Country Life*, 19 May (1983), 1342–44

Diestelkamp, Edward J and Nelson, F Charles. 'Richard Turner's legacy: the Glasnevin curvilinear glasshouse', *An Taisce Journal*, 3, 1 (1979), 4–5

THE PLANT COLLECTIONS

Blombery, Alec and Rodd, Tony. *Palms: an informative practical guide to the palms of the world; their cultivation, care and landscape use*, Sydney and Melbourne, Angus and Robertson, 1982

Giddy, Cynthia. *Cycads of South Africa*, Capetown, C Struik, 1984

Herklots, Geoffrey. *Flowering Tropical Climbers*, Folkestone, Dawson, 1976

Lötschert, Wilhelm and Beese, Gerhard. *Collins Guide to Tropical Plants*, London, Collins, 1983

Uhl, Natalie W and Dransfield, John. *Genera Palmarum: a classification of palms based on the work of Harold E Moore*, Kansas, L H Bailey Hortorium and the International Palm Society, 1987

RAINFOREST ECOLOGY

Jones, David L. *Ornamental Rainforest Plants in Australia*, Frenchs Forest, New South Wales, Reed, 1986

Richards, P W. *The Tropical Rain Forest: an ecological study*, Cambridge, Cambridge University Press, 1966

Rubeli, Ken, *Tropical Rain Forest in South-East Asia: a pictorial journey*, Kuala Lumpur, Tropical Press, 1986

Index of plants – scientific names

Page numbers in *italics* refer to illustrations; numbers in **bold** refer to plant descriptions

Index of plants – principal common names

Page numbers in *italics* refer to illustrations; numbers in **bold** refer to plant descriptions

Index of people

Page numbers in *italics* refer to illustrations

PICTURE CREDITS

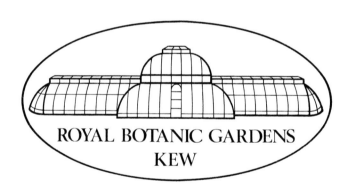

ROYAL BOTANIC GARDENS
KEW